TIGER
BALM
KING

D1673729

SAM KING

TIMES BOOKS INTERNATIONAL
Singapore • Kuala Lumpur

For Cheryl-Ann and Sadie-Jane, once again, with love.

Photographs of Haw Par Villa by kind courtesy
of Ho Kok Hoe.

© **1992 Times Editions Pte Ltd**
Published by Times Books International
an imprint of Times Editions Pte Ltd
Times Centre
1 New Industrial Road
Singapore 1953

Lot 46 Bangunan Times Publishing
Subang Hi-Tech Industrial Park
Batu Tiga, 40000 Shah Alam
Selangor Darul Ehsan
Malaysia

Set in Goudy 11 over 13.5 points

Printed in Singapore

ISBN 981 204 326 8

Acknowledgements

This is a reconstruction of the life of the late Mr Aw Boon Haw, also known as the Tiger Balm King and as one of the greatest philanthropists of his time. Many people, including members of the Aw family, have given generously of their time and knowledge to make this book possible. I owe them a great debt of gratitude:

The late Aw Swan, who devoted many nostalgic hours during the last years of his life to numerous interviews with me. "Many stories have been written about my father," he said, "but none has really revealed the man behind the public image; what he was as a private person and as a family man."

Madam Lim Saw Swee (Mrs Aw Swan), who had so many memories of her own. Except for brief periods, she lived with her famous father-in-law in Singapore and Hongkong until his death.

Madam Ooi Geik Cheah (Mrs Aw Boon Haw III), who was married to the philanthropist for thirty years and remembered life with an often unpredictable husband with wistfulness tinged with occasional regret.

Ms Sally Aw Sian, who seeks no publicity and yet is often in the limelight. I am especially grateful to her for extending to me the privilege of access to her collection of materials relating to her late father.

Mrs Aw Cheng Chye, who so kindly gave me much valuable information particularly concerning the late Aw Boon Par.

The late Soon Sit Aye, a personal assistant to Aw Boon Haw in the early days of Rangoon and Singapore. Aun Ee Han, a former senior manager of the Tiger Balm concern who was closely associated with Aw Boon Haw for most of his working life. The late Saw Teik Leong who was a lifelong employee from Burma. Soon Kim Seng, who was once a member of the Aw Boon Haw household and worked in the business in various capacities.

The many relatives, associates and former employees who each helped to fill in the missing gaps in the Aw Boon Haw story.

One for the family album. Mr and Mrs Aw Boon Haw (Tay Piah Hong) soon after their marriage in 1905. He is in the typical attire of a Baba *gentleman of the period; she is in* nonya *clothes and richly adorned with tiara, thick hair pins, necklace,* kerosang, *bangles, ankle rings and belt, all crafted in solid gold. Diamond ear studs and rings of matching gems on her fingers complete her ensemble.*

Prologue

His unusually large ears turned red, his nostrils flared and he exploded into an uncontrollable rage. The man who had become a millionaire selling little jars of ointment paced the floor and swore. "Damn! And damn again!" he said. "Gone! All that I've worked for. Ruined, finished. Damn the shorties."

His agitation translated into more expletives loaded with venom, he cursed in his native Hakka dialect alternating with gutter Burmese he had learned in his youth roaming the streets of Rangoon. "…! and …!" he ranted, but there was none to witness his despair.

Tirelessly, the Tiger Balm King paced the lushly-carpeted floor amidst the rich surroundings and found cold comfort in the ambience of the room. He was detained in a luxurious room in the Peninsula Hotel, one of Hongkong's finest. His "captors" were no ordinary hunters, they were the Japanese military. It was totally against the man's nature to be under any restraint. A born rebel, he had always done as he liked and never cared about the consequence. He swore again and pounded the table. The teapot jigged and the teaspoon somersaulted when his heavy fist hit the polished wood.

Aw Boon Haw was sixty and the world was at his feet – until now. He was one of the most respected tycoons in Asia, wealthy beyond calculation – he professed no knowledge of his exact worth – and was more admired than any of his contemporaries. He had become a legend in his own lifetime.

His commercial empire boasted a string of pharmaceutical companies and newspapers stretching from Burma, where his very first operation was established in Rangoon, to Siam, Malaya, Singapore, the East Indies, Hongkong and China. Great wealth gave him power and influence. When he roared with displeasure, others took notice. The pens of his numerous editors spoke for him. Honours great and small were bestowed on him for his philanthropy, his considerable contributions to education and for championing the cause of his compatriots. He was an endless source of curiosity to many for his unique and, occasionally, bizarre lifestyle. A frequent target of the envious, he showed his scorn in ignoring their barbs.

Money, power, magnificent mansions and adulation men only dream about were all his to savour. But now, in his darkest hour, not one of his four wives was with him; not even Kyi Kyi, his favourite second wife, always his shadow until now.

The bombing of Pearl Harbor, and the Japanese invasion of Hongkong and Malaya were totally unexpected. Before his departure for Hongkong, his younger brother, Boon Par, had warned him of the impending conflict in Asia. The Japanese had conquered half of China, their forces were massed in Indo-China. The British were rushing troops and materials to make Singapore an impregnable fortress. But Boon Haw had made light of these signs. "The short legs are too deeply bogged down in China to escalate the war," he assured his brother.

Boon Par replied, "They have taken Indo-China, and they won't stop. Malaya will be next, and Hongkong which is even closer."

"You are always looking on the gloomy side," Boon Haw said. "I still say Japan will not be so reckless. If it will make you feel happier, I shall only make a short visit. I must go there for there is much to do."

Boon Par pleaded, "Jee Ko (second elder brother), you must not leave now. There is going to be a war. We must be together when it comes. You must be here as you are the head of our family."

But Boon Haw's mind was made up. "I shall be back before anything happens, if anything happens at all."

"Are you taking the risk of our never seeing each other again?" the younger brother asked. "I feel uneasy about this journey you are going to make. Call it superstition, call it what you like, the fear is deep in my heart. I beg you, forget Hongkong, forget the business there. We have all we could ever want here in Singapore. I cannot carry on alone without you."

"Boon Par, you know I would do anything for you. But we cannot run away from fear. Do not worry, neither of us is about to die. We are destined to lead a long life. So many depend on us for their living, so many benefit from our generosity. There is still much work for us. I'm too young to die; so are you. Do not fear, my brother, heaven will protect us for the good we have done and will continue to do."

Boon Haw flew to Hongkong two days later.

There was not a sadder man than Boon Par.

The bombers flew over the island into the rising sun. Aw Boon Haw watched, seated in the terraced lawn of his hillside mansion overlooking the Fragrant Harbour. "The British are showing off their strength to warn the Japanese," he said happily to himself.

As the dinner gong shattered the morning calm, the Tiger began walking towards the house for breakfast. Suddenly the earth trembled, a series of explosions followed even before the echoes of the gong had faded. The planes that had heartened Boon Haw just moments ago were not British machines. They were Japanese, and they had circled back to rain down death and destruction. The war he did not believe would come had really arrived.

Boon Haw was a very worried man when he learned that

SAM KING

Singapore was also bombed and that Japanese troops had landed in Malaya. He exerted all his influence but failed to secure a passage on a ship or plane to be with his family in Singapore. They must be saved from capture should Singapore fall, if there was a way. He cabled to his brother, "Evacuate with family to Rangoon stop Will try my best to join you later stop"

Boon Par read the cable and cried. "I will never see Jee Ko again," he sobbed out.

The war grew increasingly worse as the bombing intensified and more people were killed. Hongkong found itself completely surrounded. Thousands of British, Canadian and Indian troops were no match for the better-prepared enemy. Its capture was inevitable. The Japanese onslaught battered Hongkong into submission on Christmas Day, seventeen days after the first bombs had fallen. Victorious soldiers rampaged through a shell-shocked, terrified city.

The Tiger was trapped.

Accounts of atrocities committed by the invaders in China were fresh in Chinese minds. The still-unforgiven horror of the Rape of Nanking sent shivers down the spines of parents with daughters. They were further horrified by the terror which struck in their midst when, early on the day of the surrender, Japanese soldiers massacred doctors, nurses and orderlies in an emergency hospital after raping the women. The colony, long under the benign rule of a Western power, was now at the mercy of a rapacious conqueror.

The day after the fall, while the black fumes from burning oil dumps were still darkening the grey skies, a sedan drew up along the entrance to the Tiger's mansion. The gateman trembled with fear when he saw the fiercely-moustached Japanese standing on the other side. He bowed almost to the ground and could find no words in reply when the officer asked if Aw Boon Haw was in the house.

Boon Haw came out when he heard his name mentioned. It was his first encounter with an active Japanese officer. He felt no fear, he was confident no harm would come to a personage such as he. The colonel recognised his quarry instantly; he had been supplied with photographs of those earmarked to receive "invitations." He bowed stiffly and said, "Good morning, honourable Aw Boon Haw. I am Colonel Ito of His Majesty's Imperial Army. Please give me the honour to come into the house. I come as a friend."

The well-built and bow-legged Japanese spoke correct but accented Cantonese. The Tiger was surprised and intrigued. The courteous speech and courtly manner put him at ease. "What is it that you want in the house? It is my private residence," the Tiger replied in Hakka-flavoured Cantonese which did not match up to the colonel's more refined brand.

"I bring greetings from our commander-in-chief, the great General Sakai. I have come with an invitation from our honourable commander."

Curiosity got the better of discretion. Also, the man sounded friendly. Aw Boon Haw told Ah Cheong, the gateman, to let the Japanese in.

"My humble apologies for causing the honourable Aw so much trouble," Colonel Ito bowed again and followed Boon Haw into the house. They sat in the lavish reception hall surrounded by precious objects. A nervous *amah* served tea.

"What can I do for your commander?" Boon Haw asked after both had sipped.

"Ah, yes, the invitation. General Sakai requests to meet all the leading citizens of Hongkong. I have a list and the honourable Aw Boon Haw's name is at the top. The general has great respect for you. I have therefore come to invite you first. I shall be honoured if you will get ready for me to escort you to him."

"Where is the place?"

"It is somewhere suitable for important people."

"How long will the meeting last?"

"Ah, yes, how long? Hard to say. Maybe a few days."

"A few days? Why must a meeting last so long?"

"Hard to say," the colonel repeated, his politeness wearing a little thin. "I think the general has many things to discuss. Maybe you should take some clothes with you. You will be very comfortable, I promise."

"But I prefer to sleep in my own house."

"I understand. But I have my orders. General Sakai is a good man. He can also be very stern if he is disobeyed. Please be gracious and accept the commander's invitation. We will feel sad if unpleasant things should happen to a man of respect like the famous Aw Boon Haw."

Aw Boon Haw realised that the "invitation" was in fact a command couched in polite language. He accepted that he was in no position to bargain. Without another word, he got up and went into the room to change.

His frightened household was in tears when he was driven away. Each member dreaded what could happen to the patriarch who had been so anti-Japanese. Was it going to be the end of the great Tiger Balm empire? A recurring thought that brought a chill that refused to perish: Will they chop off his head as they had done to so many?

Spleen vented and body exhausted, the Tiger stretched out on the quilted bed and reflected. He had scorned his brother's warning; perspiration dampened his brow as he recalled the younger man's words: "... never seeing each other again, a very uneasy feeling ... the fear is deep in my heart."

The fear was contagious. The Tiger sat up abruptly. Boon Par's words became starkly ominous. A tear trickled down his cheek; and then another and another. He was glad there was no one to see this frailness which he had never exposed.

One

L
ike many other rural communities in China, Chung Kan was a poor village. Situated in the remote district of Eng Teng, in western Fukien province, this village had more Hakkas than the native Hokkiens living in it. The Hakkas were the only major dialect group of Chinese without a province of their own. The Hokkien people call them *kheh*, meaning "guests."

The Hakkas were scattered like gypsies throughout the Middle Kingdom. Clannish and shrewd, they were the "wandering Jews" of China. Wherever the Hakkas settled, they did so in groups, as much for protection as to preserve their dialect and customs. Prone to quarrels, they often reacted violently when others jeered at their outsider status. Thus, they preferred isolation rather than be maligned as pariahs of the Chinese race.

Two Hakkas might be most fluent in the dialect of their host province, but they would use no other except their own when conversing with each other. The rapport was instant if both happened to bear the same family name. Claims to kinship, no matter how obscure, followed just as quickly. A Hakka always looked out for another Hakka and seldom married outside his group. Such behaviour fermented suspicion and the more the Hakkas flocked together, the more they created distrust.

In Chung Kan village lived a humble herbalist and his family. Like most of the community, he was a Hakka. The Hokkiens came to him only as a last resort. His fellow Hakkas, though they held the herbalist in high esteem, were either too poor or too frugal to pay for cures. Many possessed some knowledge of herbs and homemade medicines and resorted to self-medication to save what little money they had. It was a constant struggle for the physician to make ends meet. He would gladly toil in the sun but he had no land to till.

One day a letter arrived from a place called Rangoon. The herbalist was amazed that someone had written to him from some foreign land. He read the letter with increasing wonder.

"It's the capital of a strange country," the letter said. "It belongs to a race of brown-skinned people who do not seem to be masters of their own country. Many officials are people with dark skins who come from another land called India. They work under higher officials from still another country, even further away. These people have red hair. Even their white skin is covered with hair. I think they are ashamed of their fair skin because they like to expose their bodies to the sun so that they may become brown like the local people.

"Even the customs are strange. The white people eat with a tiny hoe and knife. They eat plenty of meat, mostly bullock meat cooked in large pieces. One piece is enough to cook four dishes for five people back home.

"The dark people eat with their fingers. Many like to eat off the leaves of the plantain and they eat as much rice as we do. It is very hard to teach these people to use chopsticks. They are so unrefined."

The herbalist read on, fascinated and envious:

"But this is a good country to make a living. Everyone is free to carry on a trade as long as he does not break the many strange laws. It is easy to get along with the petty officials if one is prepared to make little gifts every now and then. I own a little shop which brings me more profit in a month than I could earn in a whole year in our mother country. I employ three servants. One does the housework, two others help in my shop. The natives are quite content to work for three meals a day and some money to spend. Soon I hope to save enough to visit all my relatives and to buy some land in the village.

"I have been away for a long time. It will please me very much to be able to see you and your family again. And to see all our kinsfolk who, I hope, have not forgotten me. Please write and tell me if all of you are in good health. I am very homesick for Chung Kan."

That night the herbalist, whose name was Aw Leng Fan, wrote

to his long-forgotten cousin. There was more sorrow than joy in his reply. Sorrow over the many relatives who had died and the many hungry mouths to feed.

"The village is poorer than ever. I, too, would like to leave the village and to have a better life even though I do not hope to prosper as you have done. But I am getting old and this is where I shall be buried. My son Chu Kin is strong and healthy and he has learned all I know about herbs and curing sickness. Perhaps he can go in my place – please help your nephew to open his own medicine shop. Chung Kan is no place for a young man like him, in a country so poor.

"I pray for your good health. May your fortune grow daily."

For a long time there was no reply. Just as the herbalist was beginning to think his cousin would not assume responsibility for his son and was probably frightened into silence by the suggestion, another letter reached him.

"You have made the right decision. There are many sick people who need attention. There are also many of our countrymen living here. They will want to consult a physician of their own kind and Chu Kin will have many patients.

"Send him to me as soon as you can, and I promise you neither he nor you will regret it."

Chu Kin needed no further urging. He stuffed whatever herbs he could carry in one sack and his meagre belongings in another. With the blessings of his family and the well-wishes of the Hakka community ringing in his ears, he set off for the coastal town of Amoy. He secured passage in a junk and set sail for the southern seas.

The monsoons blew strong and the fragile craft tossed wildly in the turbulent seas. The young fortune-seeker, a landlubber all his life, had his first taste of seasickness. He self-medicated to no avail. His father had no occasion to prescribe for any sickness of the ocean and, therefore, could not provide his son the secret of such a cure. Chu Kin wished he had not left his village, but there was no turning back now.

He survived the journey and finally landed in Singapore.

Standing on the docks, the *tai kong* of the junk, an Amoy Hokkien, directed Chu Kin to look up a fellow Hokkien in a *kongsi* house. The young man staggered on legs rendered wobbly by the wretched voyage. With his sacks suspended from each end of a shoulder stick, he staggered his way to the Chinese quarter in the Telok Ayer area. The British had segregated the various communities, comprising mainly Malays, Indians and Chinese, to avoid friction. The *kongsi*, a rambling timber building roofed with tiles brought over from China, housed some two hundred people. They were all new arrivals.

Some fifty years earlier, the island was no more than a fishing village and a pirate's hideout. An agent for the East India Company, Stamford Raffles, was on the lookout for a new port and trading centre when he came upon the island in 1819. Raffles realised the strategic importance of the island's location. And though the island belonged to the Sultanate of Johore, Raffles persuaded the Sultan and Temenggong to allow the British to set up a trading post for a generous sum of money. Four years later, the British bought the island and Singapore became the property of the East India Company. In time, Singapore prospered and people from all over Asia arrived by junkloads to trade in Indonesian spices, Chinese porcelain and silk, and opium and tea from India.

It was in Singapore that Chu Kin had his first sight of an *ang moh*, the white man with the red hair mentioned by his uncle. Singapore and all the territory north of it were ruled by these *ang mohs*.

There were brown people, smaller than the white men. They were called Malays. Most of them were either farmers or fishermen. There were also the dark-skinned people whom he presumed to be the same kind of people who helped the white men rule the country where his uncle lived. But these were not government men. Many were labourers with a few petty traders among them. These were the Tamils, toilers under the hot sun.

Chu Kin had never seen so many people from so many

countries gathered in one place. Besides the white men, all of whom behaved in an aloof and superior manner, he was particularly curious about some brown-skinned people who went about in flowing robes. They were taller than the rest and their clothes reminded Chu Kin of the mandarins in China. Like them, they appeared prosperous. These, he soon found out, were Arab traders.

He also observed many Chinese among these foreigners. Though they spoke in different dialects, Chu Kin felt less of an outcast around them. Most were labourers who worked on the waterfront carrying prodigious loads on their leathered backs from *tongkangs* to *sampans* to land. Like him, they had left their country to escape from poverty. There was only one aim: to make a fortune. With this in mind, they cheerfully slogged and slaved.

Many among the hard toilers were indentured workers labouring to be free of their bondage and later to earn enough to help the family back home. They scrimped to build up some capital so as to start little businesses of their own. There was no future in toiling for others. Chu Kin was thankful he was not indentured to any man, and was even more thankful he had a profession, however humble it might be. He would escape the daily sweat in the merciless sun. He felt sorry for the men who toiled bareback in the heat to save their clothes at the expense of skins scorched brown like the natives.

Chu Kin started on the next stage of his journey ten days later. He took another junk to Penang in the north. It was much like Singapore, a busy port and home to many migrants, most numerous of whom were fellow Chinese.

A version of local history had it that Penang became a British possession for a mere twelve dollars. In the early 1780s, a Capt. Francis Light of the East India Company Merchant Navy made frequent visits to the island and the mainland opposite. He lived among the Malays, learned their language and customs, helped them in whatever way he could and generally ingratiated himself into their favour with a view to obtaining trading rights on the island. Penang was then a hideout of the notorious Lanau pirates who terrorised shipping in the Malacca Straits or struck at isolated settlements on the Malayan and Sumatran coasts.

Capt. Light soon became liked and trusted by the natives. When the Sultan of Kedah had an insurrection on his hands, the adventurous captain helped to quell the rebellion. A grateful Sultan Abdullah Shah offered the Englishman a princess of his blood in marriage. For good measure the sultan threw in Penang as the princess's dowry. Not wishing to look a gift horse in the mouth, the dashing captain accepted and offered to marry the princess according to Malay custom. He made a present of twelve dollars to the princess's friends. This was Malay custom. These two gestures endeared the foreigner to the people, not least the sultan.

On his wedding day, Francis Light, later to be knighted by his king, took possession of the island in the name of King George III for use by the East India Company. Four years later, on August 11 1786, the island was renamed Prince of Wales Island in honour of His Royal Highness's birthday. Penang became part of the British Empire, the first of the three Straits Settlements, the other two being Singapore and Malacca. Capt. Francis Light became the first governor of what was to be popularly known as "The Pearl of the Orient." On that day, one hundred Bengal sepoys were encamped on the island to establish British supremacy. The township beside the north channel was named Georgetown after the king.

The island prospered as Francis Light had foreseen. By the time Chu Kin set foot on "The Pearl," its volume of trade had grown a hundred-fold and its population had swelled from a few thousand to some one hundred thousand.

Chu Kin spent a shorter time in Penang than he would have liked. Each passing day made him realise more that here indeed was a land of opportunity. Every morning brought him more patients when they learned of his calling. He earned more in one week than his father did in ten. He wished his uncle was in Penang so that he could stay and seek his fortune there, but his father's wish prevailed and Chu Kin sailed for Rangoon in a fishing boat.

Neither the young man nor the uncle had ever met, but identity was soon established and kinship claimed when Chu Kin produced his uncle's letter. The elder man offered food and shelter until the newly-arrived nephew could stand on his own feet.

Mindful of the hard times in China, Chu Kin set about to build a little business of his own. With the help of a small loan from his uncle, he opened his own medicine shop. He was grateful and promised to work long hours to repay it. The loan equalled the bribe to the dark-skinned official for permission to set up shop. The humble shop was named Eng Aun Tong, the Hall of Everlasting Peace.

Chu Kin was a good herbalist. His gentle demeanour and concern for people soon won him a fair number of patients. They were mostly poor people, so many paid in kind. It was not unusual for a patient to offer a chicken or a dozen eggs. Sometimes it was a cut of pork and a basket of vegetables. Though cash was short, Chu Kin seldom found himself with a barren table.

The uncle was pleased with Chu Kin's progress but concerned that the young man remained single. Being a Hakka, he would like to see his nephew marry one of his own kind. But there were few Hakkas in Rangoon and even fewer Hakka maidens of marriageable age. Each time he visited his nephew, he was sad to see him leading such a lonely life. No wife to support him in making a living, no one to cook, clean and to lend a shoulder when problems arose. It was his constant worry that Chu Kin, out of desperation and loneliness, would mistress one of the dusky Burmese maidens who seemed to be always in the vicinity, willing and waiting. His cousin in China would surely be unforgiving should he fail his charge.

The uncle turned matchmaker in earnest. Unfortunately, his Hakka friends could turn out no candidate. So he asked members of the Hokkien, Teochew and Cantonese communities if there were any parents looking for a son-in-law. They, however, were not exactly enthusiastic over a Hakka bridegroom. The uncle refused to be discouraged. He renewed his search with more urgency. Chu Kin eventually had a bride found for him. She was a Teochew named Lee Kim Peck.

Kim Peck assumed the running of their humble home from the day she stepped in as a shy bride. She cooked, sewed, washed, scrubbed and kept the house shipshape. What had taken Chu Kin hours to perform sloppily, she completed in half the time with twice the result. When her household chores were done she helped her husband mind the shop. He was happy to have someone share his life, to have a wife who cared for him as he had never been cared for in his life. Whatever any Hakka woman could do, Chu Kin believed his Teochew wife could do better.

The first months of their married life was blissful. The herbalist's thoughts no longer turned towards the land of his birth as often as when he was a lonely bachelor. The fortune he had come to seek was still nowhere in sight and the dream of returning to his village a wealthy man gradually faded. Chu Kin now had a wife. Home was where he made his living, where he shared his life with Kim Peck. Home was Rangoon, for better or for worse. Perhaps when fortune smiled on him a little, when he had some money to spare, he would take his wife and the children yet to be born to meet the folks in Chung Kan. That would be the day. To show his children their roots. To present his parents their grandchildren. And to bring them gifts which they never had.

Freed of all domestic drudgery and pampered by a devoted wife, Chu Kin could now turn all his attention to building up his business. His gentle nature and genuine concern brought him many more patients, both Chinese and Burmese. The Chinese, some of whom were well-to-do merchants, were frugal in their spending habits. Even though Western medicine was within their means they came to Chu Kin for cheap treatment and asked for cheaper fees into the bargain.

His cup of joy overflowed when his wife bore him a son. The joyous father named the boy Boon Leong, "gentle dragon" in the Hokkien dialect. His life in this foreign land had taken root and borne fruit. Another milestone in his exile. The home village receded further into the distant past. Chung Kan became a memory, no longer a magnet.

The mythological dragon, a symbol of prosperity, did not live up to Chu Kin's expectations. He had named his first-born after a heavenly creature, but it had treated the honour with disdain. Many years soon passed without any progress to family fortunes. There was, therefore, renewed rejoicing in the Aw household when Kim Peck produced a second son. This happy event brought Chu Kin's exile to the year 1882.

Chu Kin now had two sons, yet not even the suspicion of a fortune was realised. So Chu Kin studied his newborn's horoscope to pick an appropriate name. Of one thing he was certain; no longer would he indulge in myths although a phoenix would pair well with a dragon. It must be something strong, wily and courageous. He finally settled for a predator and named the baby Boon Haw, or "gentle tiger." Ruthlessness tempered with compassion.

With a tiger in the family, Chu Kin hoped that his father's dreams and those of his own would start to take more concrete shape. A tiger signified glorious deeds and not idle dreams. A winner and free from want.

Another son joined the dragon and the tiger three years later. Chu Kin chose to remain earthbound and named the boy Boon Par, a "gentle leopard."

In 1884, the British merchants agitated for the total annexation of Burma. The British Foreign Office heeded the pressing calls of its empire builders and, in 1885, sent an ultimatum to Mandalay. Among the demands were the appointment of a British envoy in the Burmese court and the acceptance of his advice on the conduct of the kingdom's foreign affairs. To add insult to injury, the British demanded that no British envoy henceforth be required to remove his shoes according to court etiquette when he approached the king.

The Burmese had no choice but to reject the humiliating ultimatum. The British sent a powerful force up the Irrawaddy River to subdue Mandalay. Their mission was accomplished with the loss of only four men. King Thibaw surrendered on 29 November 1885 and the British shipped him off into exile. On 26 February 1886, Britain annexed Burma and incorporated the country into the British Empire.

With the whole country now under their control, the British set about reorganising the administration. Government was modelled largely on the Indian Civil Service example. English became an increasingly important language in government as well as in commerce. New schools were hastily built to teach the children the new language. Local government servants were organised to attend evening classes to learn the rudiments. Indians versed in English were brought over to teach. The British were never comfortable dealing with others in a language other than their own.

Chu Kin realised that his sons would be handicapped if they grew up without a knowledge of the "white man's" language. So although Boon Leong was sent to a Chinese-medium school, Boon Haw and Boon Par were enrolled in an English school when it was time to begin their education. But Boon Haw was not destined to learn English. He roamed the streets whenever he could sneak away from school and mixed with bad company. He got into fights and came home bruised and battered, yet boasting to his mother that he handed out more than he received. He was his father's despair and teacher's sorrow. The last straw that snapped his father's patience was his expulsion from school for beating up his teacher.

Chu Kin packed his wayward son off to China. The boy arrived in his father's birthplace to find that Grandfather had died. An uncle took him in to be raised with his other sons. He attended the local school but, as usual, was indifferent to his studies. Old habits die hard. As much time was spent out of class as in. The despair of his father, he became the problem of his uncle.

Some years after Boon Haw left Rangoon, his brother Boon Leong fell ill and died. Chu Kin was devastated. Out of three sons he now had only one with him.

The years passed without much improvement to the family fortune. Reluctantly, Chu Kin allowed Boon Par to seek work in a pharmacy to ease his burden. He was a disappointed man, looking older than his age and frail as a physician should not be. When Chu Kin finally died, Boon Par inherited the business as his father had wished, having given up on Boon Haw.

It was a heavy responsibility for Boon Par to shoulder. But somehow, he had to keep the family going. His heart was not in herbs. The pharmacy and all that he could learn from it was his life and his future. He asked his mother for permission to send word for Boon Haw to return. The distraught woman readily agreed. She had cried when her second son was sent away, wept again when her eldest son died and grieved intensely when her husband passed away. With Boon Haw home again perhaps her sorrow would be easier to bear.

Two

The mother could hardly recognise her son when Boon Haw came home. The scrappy urchin had grown into a strapping young man. If appearance was deceptive, his demeanour was certainly familiar. The aggressiveness labelled him her son. Bold and brash as ever, he had now also acquired a matured confidence. Boon Haw was as glad to be home as his mother was to have him back. The past was forgiven if not forgotten. The prodigal son was home at last.

Happier perhaps than the mother to see Boon Haw was Boon Par. Not only could he now hand over his responsibility to his brother, he could also pursue his interest with complete freedom. He had no hesitation in handing over the business. "You are the eldest in the family," he told his brother, "and it is only right that you should run the business."

"And what are you going to do?" Boon Haw asked his brother. The practice was too small to require two physicians.

"I shall learn what I can about Western medicine. In time, we can team up and open a bigger shop. You can prescribe Chinese medicines and I can do the European kind. In this way we won't lose a single patient. He can choose between East and West and the fee will stay with us."

This was the beginning of a brotherly team that was to reap great rewards.

Boon Haw looked on his new responsibility as a challenge, and he thrived on challenges. His aggressive nature set him tasks which others would avoid. Sparse though his knowledge of herbal treatment might be, he dealt with patients with an easy assurance that would have made his late father proud. His industry was a wonder to his long-suffering mother. She had missed this wilful son, and she now heaped the accumulated affection of the absent years on her prodigal offspring.

Where he lacked in expertise, Boon Haw made up with enthusiasm. Those who had no choice but to come to him were at first sceptical of the young physician's ability. But his forceful personality and his gift of persuasion convinced them. His bravado often won over the patients. "If you are not cured the next day, I'll return your money," he would tell the doubters. They were shamed into willing themselves to get well.

The business began to grow, Boon Haw winning new patients with charm and glib talk. The family had their three full meals a day. Boon Haw had more money to continue his new pursuits. He had acquired a roving eye in China and there was no lack of winsome maidens in Rangoon to lead him on a chase. He was in his element when out prowling and, like his namesake, he put his all into every hunt. He was, by all accounts, a successful young prowler.

In the dispensary where Boon Par worked was an elderly pharmacist. The old man liked to work in his tiny laboratory experimenting with various compounds. He pounded, mixed, blended, stirred and boiled what were to Boon Par, mysterious ingredients. When the substance seemed set to his satisfaction he would pour it into jars of all shapes and sizes, label them and put them aside. Boon Par was intrigued. He was awed by the old man's constant experiments and what seemed to him an obsession with medicine.

One day, no longer able to contain his curiosity, Boon Par asked the old man everyone called U Thaw, "Why do you make so much medicine and then put them away to be forgotten?"

His face wrinkled in a toothless smile, U Thaw answered in a voice hardly audible, "Young man, I have not yet discovered what I seek. So I keep on trying."

"What is it that you seek, Uncle? There must be enough

medicines on your shelves to cure every sickness."

"Perhaps. But what I seek is one medicine to cure my sickness. One day, I hope to discover it."

"And it will make you rich?"

"It is not richness I seek. I am old, I have no family and my wants are few. I seek satisfaction in my work. To find a medicine that everybody can afford, that everybody will find useful."

"And that will also make you rich."

"I won't live to enjoy it, even if I know how to enjoy it."

If anyone can impart knowledge, it would be this old man, Boon Par thought to himself. He would learn all he could and do whatever the old man asked him to do. The master was agreeable. The self-appointed pupil was delighted.

Whilst the tiger prowled, the leopard burned the midnight oil. He pored over basic medical books which the pharmacist allowed him to read and watched with fascination everything the old man did. As time went by, a close relationship developed between the two. Boon Par became the old man's assistant and was occasionally allowed into the laboratory to conduct experiments of his own. He was the last to leave and the first to report for work.

Struck by the young man's single-mindedness, the old man asked Boon Par one day, "What makes you work so hard, my young friend?"

"Money," was the quick answer.

"Is money so important to you?"

"With money I can run my own business and be my own master. In this way I can make much money."

"But you already have your own business."

"It is not making money."

Money? U Thaw decided he knew too little about it to pursue the subject further. Yet, U Thaw marvelled at the young man's doggedness. Surely such industry deserves its reward? He had grown quite fond of Boon Par, not having married and therefore having no children of his own. The young man deserved a break, he decided.

One day the pharmacist called Boon Par into his little work-room. On shelves and tables was a confusing array of jars, vials, bottles, tubes and paraphernalia that hallmarks a chemist's trade. It was more like a witch's workshop than a chemist's laboratory, Boon Par thought. But he was impressed nonetheless.

The old man said, "I am too old to have much use for money and have too little energy left to make more money than what I need. But you are young and ambitious, and I have faith in you. I think I have something which will help you to be your own master. But much will depend on you. I can't guarantee richness. But I may possess the means for you to realise your dreams."

The old man picked up a small glass jar from his table and unscrewed the lid. Inside the jar was a thick compound. "This may one day make your fortune," he said simply.

Boon Par peered in the little jar, excitement stirring in his breast. He controlled himself and asked, "What is it?"

"It is an ointment I discovered. I made it out of my own formula. It is my secret."

"What does it do? What can it do?" the young man asked, scepticism creeping into his voice.

"For me, many things. Numerous ailments afflict the old. I am old. I have pains in my joints and I have wind in my belly. I rub my joints or my belly with my balm and soon the pain goes. I have used it for some time now, and I cannot go without it."

"If it is so good why don't you manufacture and sell it?"

"As I have said, my needs are few and I have all I want. I am too old to go into business. But you are young, and from what I can see, you will make good use of it."

"I do not mean to offend you, Uncle. But why do you want to give your secret formula to me? Why not to others?"

"Why not to you?" the old man countered. More in surprise than a rebuff, the old man added, "You are a strange young man. You seek my help but when I offer you my life's work you are reluctant to accept it."

Boon Par couldn't think of a good answer. Even if he could it was unlikely he would tell the old man. Do not show unbecoming eagerness by all means, but at the same time never look a gift horse in the mouth.

"I don't know what to say."

"Then don't say anything. Just accept my gift with grace. And make good use of it. When you have made your fortune, and I'm confident you will, I hope you will use some of it to help the less fortunate."

"I shall not forget your kindness," a grateful Boon Par promised.

"Good. Tomorrow, I shall teach you how to compound the ointment. And you must keep the formula in a safe place. We shall go over the process step by step. The rest is up to you."

Boon Par was too excited to eat his dinner that night. Even his favourite dish, pork stewed in soya sauce, was left untouched. He scalded his lips with steaming chicken soup and left the table with Boon Haw in tow.

"Off again to chase itchy girls," his mother thought. But her sons went into their room where Boon Par told Boon Haw of the old man's gift. The elder brother was quick to recognise the potential. They talked far into the night and arrived at a scheme to exploit the old man's gift. The extrovert Boon Haw was to take charge of the project. Introverted Boon Par would be the backroom support.

"What shall we call it?" Boon Par asked.

Boon Haw thought long and hard. Ten thousand was a magic figure in Chinese calculation. Gold was synonymous with wealth. *Koh*, meaning something pasty, sounded messy. *Ewe*, meaning oil, was more acceptable. Ban Kim Ewe would sound impressive on Chinese ears. Thus, the Ten Thousand Golden Oil was born that night.

Boon Haw, the organiser, set the operation in motion. In a few short weeks the balm that was to win the world was launched.

The Aw household was never the same again. Over the feeble protests of Mother, the budding entrepreneurs took over her kitchen and turned it into a workplace. Containers filled with ingredients for the manufacture of the ointment littered the kitchen floor. The sturdy timber dining table groaned under the weight of packing materials. Pots and pans supplemented the specially fabricated utensils to hold, mix and boil the compound. Where the once sacrosanct kitchen used to be filled with the appetising aroma of fragrant dishes, it now reeked with pungent odour; a mixture of menthol, wax, eucalyptus and all the secret ingredients that went into the making of the salve.

Partly due to limited funds – all of Boon Par's savings from his job in the pharmacy had gone into the venture – and mainly because of their desire to preserve the secret formula, Boon Haw asked his sisters (three girls were born after Boon Par) to join his labour force. Mother volunteered her help even as she complained about being deprived of her kitchen.

"Mother," Boon Haw assured the good woman, "please don't worry about what we eat now. When we are rich, I shall get you the best cook to prepare our meals and you shall have whatever you wish to eat." Boon Haw had no doubts that they would become rich. Even more than his brother, he was determined to make a fortune and enjoy whatever wealth could buy.

The original ointment, though effective in many ways, looked crude and prone to vary in its consistency. Boon Par applied his pharmaceutical knowledge to improve the product. Boon Haw contributed whatever he knew about herbs and herbal lore. Between them, the brothers came up with an ointment that had a more acceptable appearance and a consistent quality.

The main ingredients were wax and petrolatum to give the ointment bulk and body. Camphor, eucalyptus oil, mentholatum and a dash of clove oil gave it a bite and piquancy that distinguished the concoction. The final compound had a creamy colour and a smooth texture. The brothers were satisfied with their final effort.

Each tiny glass jar was painstakingly hand-filled with the molten ointment. They were left to cool and solidify overnight. The job of wrapping each jar with colourful labels and packing them into lots of a dozen bottles commenced the next morning. Every step was done by hand.

The manufacturing process was a jealously guarded secret of the Aws'. They took care to mix the various ingredients in their correct proportions and in the right sequence away from prying eyes. Each step was carefully monitored. For instance, solid wax was melted to a certain temperature before adding petrolatum and these were allowed to blend for a fixed period prior to taking the procedure another stage further. The wrong sequences and intervals between mixes could result in something quite different to that intended. A series of trials and errors had perfected the whole laborious and tricky operation to an art. The original process would remain more or less unchanged throughout the Aw family's control of the business.

Boon Haw's flair for promotion then surfaced. It was likely that the Aw family fortune would have remained a dream if not for his talent. Every customer who came to seek a herbal cure was persuaded to buy a jar of his golden oil. If the customer resisted because of doubt or lack of money, a jar would be pressed on him as a token of goodwill. In return, would the valued customer be kind enough to recommend the ointment to his friends. Boon Haw made up a list of cures his medicine would provide. Rub it on for aches, pains, soreness and insect bites or to prevent bites; inhale the vapour to relieve a cold and even swallow a pinch with warm water to get rid of a stomach ache.

He visited every Chinese shop in the vicinity to sing praises of his product and to persuade the proprietors to stock up on his cure-all. Most politely rejected the unknown product. Their shelves carried an abundance of ointments from England and other countries, which were already well known to most people. Undaunted, Boon Haw persuaded the non-believers to take his ointment on consignment with offers of generous commissions.

Golden Oil sold slowly but steadily. The majority of users found it effective. Of equal merit perhaps was the convenience of carrying a little jar everywhere and to be prepared for any eventuality. And it was cheap, far cheaper than imported ointments. It began to find favour with rural communities, many living far from the medicinal aid available only in larger towns. To the poor, Golden Oil became a sort of first aid. In many cases, the only cure-all.

Meanwhile, Boon Par had not remained idle. While his brother attended to the sales side, Boon Par busied himself in his makeshift laboratory at home. The self-taught pharmacist experimented with formulas of his own to make other medicinal products.

Boon Par eventually succeeded in producing two medicines of his own. "Headache Cure" was a potent analgesic sold in powder form. It was soon to enjoy wide acceptance and second only to the ointment in churning up the profits. "Chinkawhite" was a clear, bitter mixture guaranteed to move the most stubborn bowel within the hour. Those with a weaker constitution would find it hard to keep up with the frequent need to empty. "Chinkawhite" also became a top seller.

The brothers' shop had, for some time, been selling a product called "Jin Tan" which, among other things, claimed to sweeten the breath. The budding entrepreneurs soon produced a rival of their own and called it "Balashin Sai," or "Pat Kwa Tan" in Chinese. It was a square tablet, flat and hard, consisting mainly of liquorice with a trace of menthol. It claimed to sweeten the breath and relieve sore throat, cough and nausea. It became another success.

Boon Haw now had a line of medicines to sell. What was lacking was a trademark that would be striking and hard to forget. The names of his products sounded cumbersome and quite meaningless to a non-Chinese. He aimed for a far wider following. What could be more logical than his namesake for a trademark? Boon Par had no objections. The ointment was re-baptised Tiger Balm and all the other products also adopted the Tiger trademark.

Boon Haw travelled the country extensively to popularise his Tiger brand medicines. His business acumen seldom failed him. A reluctant dealer was soon talked into stocking up. The incentives he offered were irresistible. "Don't pay me now. Sell what you can and keep half of the proceeds," was an inducement that never failed to entice.

Boon Haw provided his own selling aids. He gave free racks and display cases to his dealers to display his wares. These he ordered in bulk as he did with all his other materials and had them attractively finished with a fierce springing tiger. Every product carried a "directions leaflet" indicating its uses. And everywhere that Boon Haw went, he distributed samples of his Tiger Balm.

Within a year, dealers whom Boon Haw had pleaded to accept his medicines were now begging him to supply them with whatever stock he could spare. Gradually, the fifty-fifty arrangement was revised to monthly credit terms and finally to a cash basis except for a few loyal supporters. By coincidence or by design, the main dealers came mainly from the Hakka community.

With money to spend and a compelling inclination towards a pretty face, Boon Haw became more than ever a rogue with the girls. His constant travelling afforded him unencumbered opportunities to indulge in this pursuit. The comforts of home were to be found where he happened to be at any particular time and it was only to be expected that, given the circumstances, he should live up to the tradition of the travelling salesman.

Three

The house Chu Kin rented had outlived its usefulness. The Aw family moved into a larger bungalow. Every member of the family pitched in to help in the manufacture of the medicines. Some staff, including women, were employed to help out in the heavy work.

Mother dreaded the thought of her son falling into the clutches of some calculating woman. Especially one who was not of his own race. She had seen many Chinese marry Burmese wives with indifferent results. Their children were tolerated but never completely accepted by either community. She disapproved of such unions. Her sons were destined for greater things. Boon Haw must find a Chinese wife, soon. If he was not capable of finding one of his own kind for himself, someone must find her for him.

Chinese maidens of marriageable age were scarce. The few who came her way, willingly or otherwise, Mother found unsuitable. Too young at fourteen or too old at twenty-four – Boon Haw was then twenty-three and a bride even one year older would be considered more an elder sister than a wife – too thin to bear strong sons or too fat to avoid laziness: Mother turned down one after another to the despair of matchmakers.

Friends and relatives who visited Penang had come home with glowing reports of the comely, gentle maidens there. From an early age, these girls were trained to be perfect wives and mothers. This training was a heritage handed down from mother to daughter. Few attended schools for a very good reason. The educated girl inhibited the husband-to-be, intimidated him if he was less educated. A man wanted a wife to run his home and warm his bed but not to compete or be superior. A homebody fetched a premium.

This breed of maidens was to be found among the Baba community in Penang. If Chu Kin had been alive he would approve although he had thought their language and their manners somewhat alien. But they did pray to the right gods and pay respects to their ancestors. Didn't they flock to the temples each festival day?

Kim Peck listened with growing favour as her late husband's clansmen extolled the virtues of Nonya maidens. "They don't step out of their house unaccompanied," said one. "Do you know they don't even show their faces to strangers," said another. "When they must look to see who is outside, they do so discreetly by parting the curtains and allowing only one eye to peep out!"

A well-nourished uncle added his enthusiasm to the general acclamation as he drooled, "They cook the most delicious food. Chinese as well as their own special kind. I always ask for their *babi rendang* whenever I go and I always have room for an extra bowl of rice."

Their manners were impeccable and their behaviour beyond reproach, according to a young admirer. And the maidens followed the old Chinese customs of what one might call the mating game. This took place only once a year and commenced after sunset. The night of the unmarried maidens was called Chap Goh Mei, the night of the fifteenth day of the first moon. It was also the beginning of a busy season for matchmakers.

The eager maidens began preparations for the husband hunt long before Chinese New Year. Where others shopped and sewed new clothes only for each of the first three days of the Lunar New Year, they prepared a new wardrobe for the fifteenth day as well. Only the finest would do for the all-important day because if they failed to catch or be caught, there would perhaps be a wait of another three hundred and sixty-four days before the next opportunity came their way.

On the night set aside for these impatient spinsters, the moon shone its brightest and the stars winked indulgingly as if a million gods were looking down from the heavens above and wishing them a fruitful hunt. Dressed in her finery and bubbling with enthusiasm, the most bashful maiden assumed a boldness that would have been unpardonably unbecoming on any other day. Singly or in the company of other like-minded friends, she ventured forth amidst the din of exploding crackers to catch herself a husband. A chaperone remained a discreet distance away to ensure the rules of the game were observed and no untoward hanky-panky occurred.

This was the night of the swains as well. The gentle predators were on the prowl and the tantalising face or half a face fleetingly glimpsed through parted curtains could now be matched up with the rest of her. The waiting game was over.

A shy glance drew a coy look in return. If a bolder glance elicited a smile and a third and longer look inspired a nervous giggle from the delighted maiden, the young man could feel assured that he was regarded with favour. Mindful of the rules and scrupulously avoiding any show of impropriety to the lurking chaperone, the gallant suitor followed his new-found love a respectful distance, striving with increasingly less effort to catch her looks and bask in her smile. After what would be considered a proper interval the now besotted young man worked up enough courage to approach the alert woman-in-attendance to declare his intentions. The invitation, albeit a coy one to pay court, had borne fruit.

The process of matchmaking commenced from here. Girl met boy and boy found girl matching up to his expectations. Equally profiting from the meeting under the benevolent moon and stars was the chaperone who now turned matchmaker and could look forward to a generous *ang pow*. She had no doubt about her ability to convince the respective parents of the suitability of the match. Had she not arranged a hundred matches before now! If some had turned out sour, a matchmaker could not be expected to guarantee marital bliss as well. Her game was matchmaking, her aim was a generous fee. That was all that mattered.

For the maidens whose ventures came to naught, the magic of Chap Goh Mei evaporated with the dawn. Not for them the satisfaction of being envied, for the distinction of finding a man on her own. They could only envy the lucky ones who had a man in their net. It was back to the confines of their home, back to the windows to peer through curtain slits and to fantasise over the young men they did not catch. But bless the matchmakers. They would bring salvation yet. If one wished hard enough, surely one of Cupid's proxies would come knocking before next Chap Goh Mei?

It was one of these matchmakers who eventually found a Penang daughter-in-law for Mrs Aw Chu Kin.

Boon Haw had lived a fuller and wilder life than most men twice his age. He liked his lifestyle and he was busy building up a fortune. Marriage was not yet in his plans. A few wild-sown oats in early life might be worth whatever trouble that might come later on. By his reasoning, a man of twenty-three was still too young to cease philandering, especially when the inclination was strong and the means available. But he was also mindful of Mother's anxiety over his love of the good life. To sacrifice variety for the accustomed, which marriage would entail, was a denial he was not quite prepared to make. But despite his wilfulness, Boon Haw retained a great measure of filial piety towards his mother.

One day, soon after his return from one of his frequent absences, his mother served him a bowl of chicken soup prepared with rare herbs and ginseng. This homemade essence of chicken was one of the secret recipes of the Aw family. Generations of Aws had been fortified with the brew against illness and strain, both physical and mental. In Boon Haw's case, perhaps his mother felt the need to restore her son's manly vigour.

Boon Haw sipped the bowl of soup. His mother sat opposite and silently studied this prodigal son who seemed a little more of a stranger each time he returned from a trip. He looked strong and healthy, and that was important to a mother. He was intelligent and, unlike the boy who used to shirk everything not connected with his pleasure, was now more hardworking than any young man she knew. Anyway, he was far more successful in business than she dared dream of. There was money to spend and good food to eat. What more could one expect of life? Her lot of contentment was apparently not his idea of fulfilment. She sensed this son was headed for far greater achievements than her simple mind could contemplate. The path to the top was bound to be strewn with heartaches. The balm for such aches would be the comfort a good wife could provide.

A wife was what Boon Haw needed, Mother decided. A wife to smooth the difficult path ahead and to prevent him from being entrapped by some scheming woman. A wife would bring Boon Haw home more often and he would therefore spend more time with her.

"Son, you are a grown man now and so you should find a good wife and settle down."

Mother's abruptness did not surprise Boon Haw. He knew his mother was concerned over his numerous liaisons and he often indulged in a secret laugh over his mother's unworldliness. Boon Haw now smiled at his mother and countered, "It is easy to find a wife but what do you think is a good wife, Mother?"

"A woman who can and who is prepared to look after you, my son. One whom you can look up to. Someone who can make you stay at home more than you have."

Boon Haw laughed. To humour her, he said, "Where can I find such a wife? I could marry a Burmese girl but will you approve?" He was aware of his mother's bias and therefore thought that she would not press him further. But he himself goaded her on when he smugly added, "I don't mind marrying if you can find me a wife to meet with your approval."

It was the mother's turn to smile. "You can safely leave that to me. Now drink up your soup and take a rest."

Boon Haw's mother began her search for a matchmaker the very next day.

Sungei Dua, "second river" in Malay, is the name of a village situated some six miles from Georgetown. The *sungei* which gave the village its name was the smaller of two streams in a farming community. The villagers living in the outskirts were mostly Malays. Some owned small holdings of rice fields and coconut groves. The majority were squatters with a half-acre plot and an attap hut built on stilts some three to six feet above ground.

Sungei Dua itself consisted of a cluster of houses in different shapes and sizes. Most were thatched but distinctly unstilted. A few two-storey structures stuck out like sore thumbs among the humbler dwellings. These belonged to better-off families. The roofs were laid with corrugated iron sheets and the floors were made of concrete. Those living in the village were mostly Chinese who preferred resting their homes on solid ground rather than on stilts. They owned all the shops and conducted all the businesses in the area. There was even a pawnshop which accepted farming tools among other things. And if you had no article to pledge, the moneylender would gladly accept the next harvest of coconut or rice for a cash advance.

While many Chinese in the village thrived on commerce, there were others who chose to till the soil. One of them was a young man who had worked very hard and who now owned his house and plot just outside the village. He grew coconuts and fruits and made a good living. He employed new migrants to help in his plantation and, in time, when his crops produced bigger yields, he built himself a bigger house. Tay, the proud landowner, decided that it was time to find a wife. He married a girl from Canton one month later.

Over the years, the Tay family grew to seven children – five girls and two boys. As the girls blossomed, the business of finding suitable husbands for them began. A girl joined the marriage market at the age of fifteen or thereabouts. Every parent with a marriageable daughter grew more anxious with each passing year. By the time a girl turned twenty, she was considered an old maid. That was the age of desperation for the parents and their daughter.

A girl could not be blamed for her spinsterhood if all a hopeful swain could see of her was half a face through parted curtains. Prudes they were not; prisoners of propriety they certainly were.

Piah Hong was the second daughter in the Tay family. She was twenty and unmarried. Her elder sister had been a happy wife well before the age of desperation. Piah Hong, too, should have been a happy wife long before now.

But the matchmakers must have had more pairings than they could cope with during the five years her parents waited for a son-in-law. There was, therefore, some ill-concealed delight when a matchmaker finally came knocking at the door. Decorum forbade a parent showing undue anxiety to marry off a daughter. It frowned on singing her praises. With one daughter overdue and three more to go, Mrs Tay could be forgiven if her welcome somewhat overwhelmed the matchmaker. The visitor was a slight old lady dressed in traditional Chinese garments of black silk trousers and a colourfully embroidered brocade blouse buttoned down the right side. The sheen of her lacquered white hair was matched only by the gleam of a solid gold pin that pierced her little bun. To lend more distinction to her profession, she wore a pair of tiny cloth boots over tinier feet bound at birth. In spite of her wispy appearance, her courtly clothes and refined manners gave her a rather commanding air. This was a quality which had given some matchmakers an added advantage. Where persuasion made little headway, a little intimidation often carried the day.

"So kind of you to honour our humble home with your presence," Mrs Tay greeted her visitor.

"I am the honoured one to be welcomed into your gracious home," the matchmaker replied.

"Please sit. Please sit in this chair," urged Mrs Tay indicating the most comfortable chair in the room.

"Very kind of you," the old lady murmured as she tottered on her dainty hooves to the chair reserved for honoured guests.

The matchmaker was accompanied by a Chinese man. He was neatly dressed in the manner of a Baba – white cotton trousers and white tunic brass-buttoned to the throat and topped off by a cork hat – and obviously a merchant. When he uttered his first words it was equally apparant that he was no pukka Baba. His Hakka-accented Hokkien betrayed his origin. The Baba look-alike was a Rangoon businessman who had interests in Penang. He had come to seek a wife for the son of a clanswoman. As he was not familiar with the matchmaking custom of the Babas, he had sought out Madam Khoo to help him in his search.

A proxy of the prospective groom's mother was how Mrs Tay regarded him. On him might depend the success or failure of the match. It would be wise to give him a welcome equal to that given to the matchmaker. Even a warmer welcome, if possible. And who better to create a favourable impression than her daughter. "Piah Hong, quickly bring another cup of tea for the gentleman," she ordered. Madam Khoo smiled in satisfaction; the matchmaker's *ang pow* was as good as in her pocket.

Formalities observed and niceties exchanged, the old match-maker took over. She had sung the praises of the fair maiden whom she hardly knew to the merchant. She now sang the qualities of the faraway suitor whom she had never met. Then it was the mer-chant's turn to woo the mother for her daughter's hand in marriage to Boon Haw even though he was only second string to Cupid's bow.

The merchant painted a flattering verbal picture of a robust young man, the elder of two sons with a thriving business. He was a highly respected physician with prospects of great wealth to come. The mother was old and wanted a daughter-in-law to take her place in their fine house. She was a kind and gentle woman and would treat Piah Hong like a real daughter. Distance should present no problems. The Aws could afford to travel as often as they wished. They would be glad to pay the parents' passage to Rangoon whenever they wished to visit their daughter.

Madam Tay was glad to make the match. The merchant was gladder still to have succeeded sooner than he hoped. The match-maker received the biggest *ang pow* of her life. Piah Hong was sad to have to leave her family but glad that she no longer had to spend her days in waiting.

With a haste that would appear unseemly, Piah Hong and Boon Haw were married amid much rejoicing in both households. Mrs Tay had one daughter less to marry off. Mrs Aw senior had her much-desired daughter-in-law. Boon Haw had a wife whom he hoped would make his mother happy.

Boon Haw spent more time at home in the first few months of his marriage than at any time since the launch of Tiger Balm. As far as his nature allowed, he strove to settle down to a life of domesticity. He got along very well with Piah Hong, and their relationship was a constant source of joy to his mother. But wealth could not be created if he were tied to apron strings. His desire to become very rich and famous had become almost an obsession. He was confident his medicines would all turn out to be outstanding. Before long, he decided to hit the road again.

Piah Hong was all her mother-in-law expected of her. She performed her household chores with good humour and accepted with equal grace the occasional criticism her mother-in-law made on any job not done to expectation. "There are many things I do not know and many things I have to learn. Will mother-in-law who is older and wiser teach me?" she beseeched the older woman. Such humility could not help but melt the mother's heart.

Piah Hong, however, was unhappy. Boon Haw resumed his travels and came home less and less often. After one long absence, Piah Hong asked him why he could not employ others to visit the dealers so that he could be with his family. Boon Haw had an answer to which she had no reply. "I am doing it for all of us. We work so hard and we deserve every cent we make. If you expect other people to look after your business, you can be sure they will cheat you whenever they can. I am not satisfied to be just rich. I want to be the richest. And I am the only man who can make me that rich. Which woman wouldn't like to be the wife of the richest man?"

Boon Haw was a kind husband in other respects. He brought home presents from his trips and he delighted the oft-neglected wife with pieces of jewellery. He had yet to learn to trust the banks. His safes were always stocked with cash. There was therefore a plentiful supply of ready money whenever someone in need of cash had to pawn some jewellery. Boon Haw would offer a little more than the pawnshop rate for an outright purchase.

Piah Hong bore in mind her husband's ambition to be the richest man in the community. Each day, after her household chores were done, she joined the others in the family factory. She did more than her fair share of filling countless little jars of ointment or hundreds of packets of headache powder. Tiny jars and little packets all went to make a great fortune in time to come. The helpful young wife no longer complained as frequently of her husband's absences.

She was a wife who must stand by her man, working so hard for all of them to become as rich as her simple heart could imagine. It was enough for her that he came home to her after each trip. Women were seldom equal partners in marriage, Piah Hong ruminated. All men were alike. They wanted to be more equal than their wives. A woman completely dependent on her husband had little choice but to swallow her pride. She would be wise to think twice before rocking the boat that provided her with all the comforts. Jealousy was a luxury reserved for the very foolish or the lunatic. Piah Hong soldiered on in the kitchen and in the home factory consoling herself with the thought that she was a special partner in her husband's quest for richness. After all, he did trust her with the key to his safe so filled with money.

The day would come when Boon Haw would have acquired such wealth that he would be content to stay home and enjoy the fruits of his labour and hers. That would be the day.

Nobody knew the cause of the fire which broke out in a section of the house set aside for compounding medicines. It was likely that a piece of burning wood had fallen off one of the stoves used to melt the ointment ingredients. As a result, the packing materials and discarded wrappings strewn all over the floor caught fire.

Panic ensued. Some ran out to escape the suffocating smoke. Others dashed for buckets of water to douse the flames. Neighbours, attracted by the screams of the women and the shouting of the men, came running to add their cries of, "Fire! Fire!" to the din. Many helping hands soon put out the flames. The damage was slight. Some drums of raw materials were ruined by water and a few cases of cardboard boxes were charred beyond salvage.

In the heat of the battle to overcome the fire, nobody had thought of saving valued belongings from the house. Except the safe! It was sitting by the roadside outside the house. Piah Hong was sitting on a stool guarding it. As she should. Who else? After all, wasn't she the keeper of the keys?

How the safe was found sitting by the roadside appeared to be an incredible feat brought about by desperation. As soon as the alarm for the fire was given, both Boon Haw and Piah Hong must have visualised a heap of charred bank notes. Both rushed to the rescue. Perhaps panic addled their brains, neither thought of using the key to open the safe and remove its contents. To their dying day they could not account for the superhuman effort of removing the safe outside. It took four hefty men to restore it to its place.

The years that followed the fire episode were good years. Business flourished. Boon Haw, the born entrepreneur, was in his element when he was on the road drumming up even more business and setting up still more dealerships. Tiger Balm began to appear in the most unlikely places. The village grocer stocked it. So did the cigarette vendor, the coffee stall owner as well as the bicycle repairman. The fisherman in his rocking sampan rubbed it on his forehead to steady his stance. The fishmonger rubbed a little on his nostrils to neutralise the fishy odour. The rickshaw puller massaged his weary limbs with it to give him strength to run another mile. The business tycoon used it to suppress his sneezing and forestall a cold. Tiger Balm came to the rescue of rich and poor alike. It was to be found in almost every pocket and in every purse.

The Aw brothers grew richer by the day.

Four

Boon Haw was not unlike other Chinese merchants in his attitude towards staffing his business. Wherever possible a member of the family was put to work when a vacancy occurred. Next came relatives, clansmen and relatives of relatives and clansmen in that order. He had few relatives on his father's side in Rangoon. That left only his mother's relations, most of whom Boon Haw found unsuitable or who did not wish to work for him. Perhaps his being a Hakka was the cause of their reluctance and vice versa; therefore clansmen filled the more senior posts.

Eng Aun Tong moved from the family kitchen to a new address. The site of the factory was not in the best area in Rangoon. Its environment left much to be desired. The neighbouring houses were old, the streets narrow and the people tough in behaviour and rough in appearance. But labour was plentiful and cheap.

The building was large enough for a section to be used for storing materials. Boon Haw saw to it that no supplier was in a position to extort him into paying excessive prices should there be any shortages. The floor above the godown was reserved for the exclusive use of the brothers. Boon Haw converted it into living quarters. It was not always convenient to travel the short distance home to relax whenever pressure of work fazed the spirit. It was also a retreat where they could entertain or be entertained in privacy. The servant who looked after the place lasted only as long as he could maintain his discretion.

Below the brothers' office, work proceeded at a feverish pace. A lot of manpower was needed to keep the factory going at full capacity. Every stage of manufacture was done by hand. A jar of ointment, for instance, was required to go through a dozen stages before it was ready for the salesroom.

When the jars were filled and the contents allowed to cool and solidify overnight, they were taken to a huge table around which sat some ten to twenty women. These women's job was to cap the jars after which they were taken to another table manned by a similar group of women. A label identifying the product and distinguished by a springing tiger was pasted around each jar. The next stage involved rolling the jar into a folded "direction" leaflet and then wrapping it in a colourful piece of Tiger Balm wrapper. The wrapper displayed pictures of the Aw brothers and carried a design finished in multi-colours. A circular seal placed on the top and bottom of each jar completed the packing process of each unit.

Tiger Balm as well as all its sister products were sold to dealers in packs of a dozen each. This required the attention of a different group of women. It was their job to count out the dozens and wrap the lot.

Women were employed exclusively for this operation. Their dexterous fingers could outwrap any man's and they worked for less than their male colleagues. In all the future Tiger Balm factories throughout the Orient, women workers outnumbered the men ten to one.

Since its location did little to enhance the company's profile, Boon Haw, the image builder and publicist extraordinaire, began to look for yet another property to display his products to best advantage. Several possibilities fell through because owners were only prepared to lease but Boon Haw would consider nothing except outright ownership. It was demeaning to pay rent when he could afford to buy. One particular shop in a busy street frequented by the more affluent took Boon Haw's fancy. The owner would not part with it. Boon Haw made an offer which the owner could not refuse. It was enough to buy him three other shops. The deal was speedily concluded and the new owner spent another princely sum turning it into his principal sales outlet. A huge sign over the shop-front proclaimed in Chinese and English: Eng Aun Tong – The Tiger Medical Hall. The Tiger Balm enterprise was poised to conquer the Orient and amass a fabulous fortune.

At the time Boon Haw and Boon Par decided to adopt the Tiger trademark, the most popular among the many tested on the open market, it was also agreed that Boon Par would leave the pharmacy and devote all his time to their business. Boon Haw could not manage alone; production slacked every time he went on a trip.

It was vital that he had the goods to deliver as promised to the dealers. In time, as short a time as possible, they would have a proper factory. For the present, they would make full use of whatever facilities were available; including all of Boon Par's time.

Even with the home front more or less secured, Boon Haw did not spare himself. Every forage into the country brought more orders to supply old as well as new dealers. Every hour at home was spent in his makeshift factory cajoling others to work faster and longer in order to produce more. He was in the thick of activity at every stage of production. Every pressure was a challenge. Every challenge was met and overcome. He worked with a single-mindedness that caused his mother unending worry and his rivals grudging admiration.

Piah Hong was the only one who thought she understood her husband's obsession. He was driving himself in order to make the family the richest of the lot, then he would cease to work so hard. He would travel less and there would be fewer excuses for him to seek the company of women. His philandering had hurt her more than she would admit. But for the present, she had to bear the burden and help him until he was rich enough to relax and enjoy his wealth at home.

Success came their way after years of labour. The trappings of wealth were soon apparent. A fine house to live in with servants at their beck and call, good clothes and jewellery to adorn the family members and ready cash to spend whenever the urge arose.

Piah Hong would have been well contented. But not Boon Haw: "One can remain prosperous only as long as one keeps on working at it," he had told his wife. "The biggest fortune would soon disappear if we keep on spending and not adding. Besides, I am only thirty years old. I want to become somebody everybody will respect. I want everybody to pay attention when I speak."

It was not enough for Boon Haw to hold on to his success or to acquire even greater wealth. He aimed for glory. His ambitions knew no bounds and his energy was bursting its harness. A fortune-teller had said that he was born to do great things. Admirers had sought his wisdom. He determined to prove the fortune-teller right, the flattery well-placed and the admiration well-judged.

Boon Par's role in the business was less visible but not less effective. Since the day his brother had persuaded him to throw his all into the partnership, Boon Par had given his unstinting support. If Boon Haw appeared rash, the younger man was there to sound a note of caution. Boon Haw valued his brother's opinions. Boon Par admired his brother's courage. The brothers made a well-balanced team.

Like Boon Haw did before he was married, Boon Par too caused his mother many sleepless nights. He liked female company and they liked the money he had to spend on them. Mother decided to find her younger son a wife to make him settle down.

Piah Hong's younger sister, the third girl in the family, was still conveniently a maid-in-waiting. Boon Par was reluctant; his mother persistent. To get her off his back, he finally consented.

Boon Par married Piah Lan, or Ah Lan as she came to be called, shortly after. The mother-in-law again rejoiced; but Boon Par's heart was not completely in tune with his mother's happiness.

Five

On 28 June 1914 a nineteen-year-old Serbian student shot and killed the Archduke Francis Ferdinand of Austria-Hungary. One month later Austria-Hungary declared war on Serbia.

Germany, an ally of Austria-Hungary, declared war on Russia on 1 August and on France two days later. When the Germans invaded Belgium on 4 August, Britain promptly declared war on Germany and Austria-Hungary. Japan, for reasons of her own, came to the support of Britain on 23 August.

One nation after another was drawn into the conflict. What had started as a little war in the Balkans developed into what is now known in history as the First World War.

"We must buy up all the materials we can as soon as we can," Boon Haw told Boon Par when news reached Rangoon of the war in Europe.

He was convinced, and he was to be proved right, that supplies would grow scarce as war progressed and prices would escalate. He bought up all he could lay his hands on and felt secure in the knowledge that he was set to face wartime shortages.

The war was to last four years but Eng Aun Tong kept on production. The factory churned out Tiger Balm in even greater quantities. No one complained when prices were increased to justify higher costs and to add a little more to profit. Tiger Balm was indispensable to many.

The Tiger's foresight paid off handsomely, the brothers became millionaires when peace returned. They could now be truly labelled *tua tow ka*y, or big boss, as they liked to be addressed.

Over the years, since a daughter-in-law came into the family, Mother had longed for a grandchild. A mite to fuss over and to pamper would further fill her cup of contentment. Bringing up her own children had been a cross she was happy to bear. Life was hard and money was scarce at the time. But circumstances had changed. She longed to be the doting grandmother and make up for the time she did not have with her children. But the matriarch yearned in vain. There was no little blessing to fill the house with childish prattle or the patter of little feet.

All her friends were proud grandparents. But Mother, at fifty-seven, was as far away from being one as she ever was. It had been a long time since she had rocked a child on her knees or made baby talk that nobody understood.

There were many servants in the Aw family performing a variety of tasks useful or superfluous. Some were young women from poor or broken homes. Mother was a kindly soul who found it hard to turn away these hapless girls seeking succour. She gave them whatever chores there were to do in return for shelter, food and some pocket money. Many hands make little work and, as a consequence, the house was always tidy and the girls were left with much idle time of their own.

Boon Haw did not interfere with the way his mother ran the house. In fact, he was pleased to have so many hands doing the chores as this was a reflection of his social status. He also liked to have women around the house. "Women make a home; men make a mess," he used to say.

Ah Moi was seventeen when she came to work for the family three years earlier. She possessed a happy disposition and was ever ready to do anything asked of her. Mother took a liking to her and within a short time she became a sort of personal maid. Ah Moi served her diligently. To have someone to fetch and carry for her was a luxury long overdue to the eldest member of the family. Mother was a convert to the virtues of her son's balm and was never without it. She rubbed it on her body at the slightest excuse, and sang its praises to whoever cared to listen.

Rather than sit idly watching her mistress administer the balm to various parts of her body, Ah Moi sought to relieve her of both the effort and the complaints. She was a gentle girl with comforting fingers, and her soothing touch gave one a feeling of well-being no balm could match. When her daughters-in-law suffered small discomforts of their own, Mother recommended Ah Moi's soothing touch. It did not take long for the girl to become a favourite with the family. She enjoyed certain prerogatives denied to others. For instance, she had a place at first sitting during meals when the masters were absent and she was not required to help with the washing up. Her clothes were of better quality and she was always asked to accompany the ladies whenever they went shopping or to see an occasional show.

Being so visible about the house, it was inevitable that she caught Boon Haw's eye. Her rosy cheeks and rounded figure were a testimony to the family's indulgence towards her at the dining table. Ah Moi was a very fetching girl indeed.

Ah Moi did not admit to being pregnant until her condition became too obvious to hide. Her increasingly bountiful figure during the early months was attributed to her indulgence at the dining table and to her addiction to snacks. When the cause of her bulging form could no longer be explained away, she cheerfully admitted that she was five months in the family way.

The servants were scandalised. An unmarried woman with child was a social pariah to be pitied; a fallen woman whom no man would marry. It would be far more honourable to be a concubine. A man recognised his concubine's offspring as his own and gave the baby his name. Now poor Ah Moi would have to leave the house and return in disgrace to her family.

Ah Moi remained unconcerned with all the speculations over her future. She behaved like it was the most natural thing in the world for a girl to be pregnant out of wedlock.

Mother had her suspicions. Her sons, pillars of the community though they might be, were no saints where women were concerned. But which of the two, if indeed her suspicion was well-founded, was the father of the unborn child? Both lived at home, and the wretched girl was not one who cringed at the sight of her masters. Brazen though her attitude undoubtedly was, surely she could not be so bold as to flaunt her condition before them if the father of her baby was an outsider. If she asked the girl to leave, might it not be a mistake she would regret all her life? A grandchild by a surrogate mother was infinitely more desirable than none at all. She told Ah Moi to stay for as long as she liked. She could have her baby in the house and they would decide on the next step after the baby arrived.

It was Mother's turn to be solicitous towards the girl. Ah Moi must look after her health to ensure an easy birth and take the proper food so that the baby would be born big, strong and healthy. The servants were baffled. They did not know what to make of it. Had age made her senile, they wondered.

The baby was a bouncing boy, with a lusty lung. He resembled neither the mother nor either of the suspected fathers. Nonetheless, Mother was delighted and fussed over Ah Moi as though she were a daughter-in-law. She wished the child were really her own flesh and blood, and she cuddled it tenderly.

Her love for the child grew with each waking day. She was determined to keep the baby in the family. With more trepidation than she had ever felt, she broached the subject of the baby's adoption to the mother. Ah Moi was willing but did not ask for whom the baby was intended. As Piah Hong was the elder daughter-in-law, Ah Moi was quite certain that she would be the adoptive mother.

Nobody quite knew who started the tradition. But it had been a long established custom for the family to eat their evening meal at half past five. Whatever other business there might be, this family gathering at sundown took precedence. Often, elder members of the clan joined in the family meal.

On this particular day there were only family members partaking of a spread prepared by a hired cook. Mother was glad there were no others sharing this meal. She wanted none but her family to hear what she had to say. It concerned only them and no one else – except Ah Moi and her baby.

As though she was making small talk, Mother said, "Ah Moi's baby is such a beautiful boy, don't you all think so?"

Her daughters agreed but Boon Par remained silent. Boon Haw showed the trace of a smile.

"It is such a shame if he has to go to another home where he is not well cared for," the matriarch continued.

Again the women agreed. Boon Par maintained his silence. Boon Haw showed the beginnings of a frown.

"I have asked Ah Moi if she will consider allowing the baby to be adopted."

Boon Par showed no curiosity.

Boon Haw showed impatience when he asked, "And what did Ah Moi say?"

"She said she would consider it very carefully. It would depend on who would want to adopt her baby."

Boon Haw looked at his wife, "I think a baby would keep you busy and make you happy."

Piah Hong agreed for reasons she alone knew.

"Tell Ah Moi that Piah Hong wants the baby, Mother," he said.

Mother smiled in satisfaction. Her son's acceptance of the baby she construed as owning up. Boon Haw was never to confirm or deny what others thought.

Ah Moi had no hesitation in parting with her baby. "I know Aunty Piah Hong will love him as her own," she said. "He could not hope for a better home. I could not wish for better parents for him."

Ah Moi did not choose to stay. She was a simple girl who would have no part in any complications that might arise. The grateful "grandmother" showed her appreciation in the form of a generous settlement which even Boon Haw would object to if he had known.

The baby, born in 1915, was named Aw Swan.

Six

Tiger Balm soon travelled and became famous abroad. Indian civil servants brought the ointment home for their own use as well as for profit. Siamese merchants imported quantities of the balm to sell to farmers suffering from the effects of prolonged toil in rice fields. It found its way south to Malaya, easing the aches and pains of coolies working in the tin mines and rubber plantations. Villagers in Sumatra, Java and the more remote islands of the Dutch East Indies began to accept the ointment in its quaint glass containers as a poor man's panacea. Production could hardly keep up with demand. It was a period of accelerated growth.

To counter imitations, the Aw brothers introduced Deer Balm. It matched imitations in price but surpassed them in quality. In fact it was Tiger Balm by another name. But the original product was too well entrenched. Users were not prepared to risk a cheaper brand. Tiger Balm remained the bestselling by far. Deer Balm was eventually withdrawn. No imitations or substitutes could dent the popularity of the original balm.

In time, users came to expect more out of their jar than bargained for. If the ointment was made in a stronger form, they argued, then surely its effectiveness would increase. And, as a result, less of the ointment would be required on each application. It would be more economical to use and each jar would last even longer.

The brothers thought long and hard on this. It would mean devising a new formula which might not match the efficacy of the original. A product that failed to live up to expectations would not only be rejected but would likely drag down the good name of Tiger Balm with it.

Boon Par, the would-be pharmacist, was well aware of the difficulties involved in compounding a new ointment. It was out of the question to juggle the compounding process and expect the result to be anywhere near what was required. Any research on a more scientific basis was beyond him as he lacked the tools and the expertise for the job. Their benefactor, the old pharmacist, had died and whatever new formulae he may have discovered had been buried with him. Inventing another balm was too tall an order for the brothers to carry out, or so it seemed.

Until Boon Haw hit on a brilliant idea – colour the ointment and allow human gullibility to do the rest.

From the Indian sub-continent to the remote islands in the East Indies there were countless men and women addicted to the habit of chewing a mix of betel nut, betel leaf, lime and an extract of the gambier plant. No one can say with any certainty how or why the habit originated. Or when. There is one theory which sounds plausible. Long ago some pestilence visited an area in southern India and destroyed the crops. Among the vegetation surviving were the betel leaf creepers and the areca nut. The betel leaf survived because of its bitter taste and acidic content; the areca nut because it was even more unpalatable. But both leaf and nut were just about edible. To assuage the pangs of hunger, the natives were driven to chewing them. A smear of moist white lime on the leaf was added to counter the bitterness. A pinch of gambier, an astringent extract obtained from the leaves of a tropical shrub, was also used in the belief that it would neutralise any harmful effects of the mix, which indeed was mildly toxic. Gambier, among other uses, was also an agent employed in dyeing and tanning. It turned the betel chew a murky red.

In time the habit became socially accepted. It became an adjunct to other social customs such as smoking and drinking. A courteous host always offered his guest the makings of a chew. The poor man kept the ingredients tied up in a piece of cloth. The rich host boasted a brass or silver receptacle with appropriate compartments for each ingredient. There was even a special tool to cut the rock-hard betel nut into more easily masticated pieces. Thus, the humble life-saving chew developed into a social custom.

The habit spread eastwards. The areca nut and the betel leaf thrived in the warm and moist climate of Southeast Asia. Different people in different lands mixed their chew in different ways. The basic process is to smear a little white lime on the betel leaf, add a few pieces of sliced areca nut, sprinkle a pinch of gambier extract. Fold the leaf over the other ingredients into a small lump and the chew is ready. Some favour a bit of clove, others add sugar.

When Boon Haw first thought of the idea of colouring his ointment he asked Boon Par to experiment with chemical agents. The result proved unsatisfactory. Colours assumed peculiar hues. Pungency gave way to offensive smells. It was impossible to reproduce the original in colour with matching consistency. Tiger Balm seemed fated to be compounded only in a very pale yellow.

Piah Hong was no stranger to the chewing habit. Many Nonyas in her native Penang were inveterate chewers, having picked up the habit from their Malay friends who, in turn, had learned to enjoy the chew from the Tamils.

Not wishing to be thought lacking in courtesy, Piah Hong decided on acquiring her own box of chewing substances. No guest of hers would yearn in vain for a chew in her house. No one could say she was behind in social etiquette. They were the leading family in the community. Piah Hong's chewing box was the finest money could buy.

Whenever a visitor chewed, Piah Hong chewed with her. Her chewing was confined to social occasions as Boon Haw detested the habit. But it was this very habit which lent itself to the successful coloration of his balm.

One hot and dusty afternoon, Boon Haw complained of a head

cold and asked his wife for her jar of balm to rub on his forehead. Her personal jar was kept in her chewing box. She took it out and volunteered to rub her husband's head; a chore usually performed by one of the favoured housemaids. Boon Haw declined his wife's offer and chose to self-medicate.

He uncapped the jar, took a look inside and exclaimed, "What is this you have given me! It looks like chicken dirt!"

"What are you saying, you silly man!" Piah Hong retorted. "It is your ointment and we have always used it."

"I never made such rubbish. My ointment is white, not brown like this."

Piah Hong thought for a moment. Then she smiled and finally burst into laughter.

Boon Haw was perplexed. He became angry. "Have you gone senile before your time, woman!" he demanded. "Are you using our imitators' medicine in my house?"

"Never!"

"Then what is this evil-looking thing in my hand?" Boon Haw thundered.

"Don't shout at me," Piah Hong shouted in return. "I think I know what caused the change in colour, if you will allow me to tell you."

"Now you will be telling me you make your own ointment."

Piah Hong ignored the sarcasm. "It must be the gambier I use for the betel nut mixture."

Which was what in fact happened. Piah Hong used thumb and index finger to sprinkle a pinch of gambier extract over her chewing mix. Often, using the same finger with some of the powdery substance still clinging to it, she would dip into the jar of ointment when an itch or a headache demanded attention. The result after a few dips was a brown-coloured Tiger Balm. The beauty of it all was that the additional ingredient affected neither the efficacy, smell nor consistency in any way.

Boon Haw was intrigued. He experimented on the substance

with Boon Par. After some trial and error, they came up with a product that was the original in every way except in colour. It was marketed as a stronger balm and accepted as such because many believed that darker was stronger. To justify the claim, the quantity of one or two ingredients such as mentholatum was increased by minute amounts to give the ointment a more pungent odour.

The quantity of gambier required was negligible in cost. So both the "white" and "red" Tiger Balm were sold at the same price. The goodwill earned was incalculable. From that day on, Boon Haw viewed the chewing habit with more tolerance.

The new balm was actually dark brown rather than red. As brown among some Chinese evoked a derogatory connotation, it was conveniently labelled "Red Tiger Balm." Red is also an auspicious colour among Chinese.

The new balm was an instant success. But it also stained clothes. Gradually, it found more favour with those engaged in heavy occupations such as labourers, field workers, rickshaw pullers and those who favoured darker shades of clothing. The ladies in fine clothes and the gentlemen in sedentary occupations preferred the white variety. To some extent, the class to which one belonged could be distinguished by the type of balm one used.

Seven

By 1919 Boon Haw was one of the richest, if not the richest, Chinese in Rangoon. He was certainly the best known, not only to the Chinese community or to the people of Rangoon, but beyond to every town, village and farm where Tiger Balm found its way. He enjoyed the admiration of his compatriots, friends and foes alike. The Burmese who knew him gave due recognition, but their esteem was tinged with envy and suspicion. The British authorities accorded him the respect due to any successful merchant, for commerce was a language they understood. The British mercantile community regarded him with a certain wariness for they viewed trade as their special province. Boon Haw had as little as possible to do with them and they with him, as long as he kept to what they scathingly called his "quackery."

A flamboyant lifestyle and flair for projecting his image kept Boon Haw constantly in the public eye. No event in which he was involved went unreported in the vernacular press. But his other pursuits went mostly unrecorded. Perhaps this was due to fear of reprisals or because the editors exercised restraint in deference to his position. Whatever the reason, scandal-mongering in print was kept to a minimum.

Despite the meagre publicity attending his romantic liaisons, there grew around him the image of a playboy. Speculation added colour to his exploits. Boon Haw could not be less concerned. "Everyone is given a tongue to talk with," he would say when a well-meaning clansman cautioned discretion. "Whichever way that tongue wags is the reflection of what that person is."

The public looked upon his escapades as the prerogative of the rich. And, as he was richer than most, his claim to such prerogatives was unquestioned. "If one had the urge, why suppress it? If one had the means to indulge, why deny oneself? You would die very much the poorer for not having led a richer life."

But to his credit, Boon Haw was generous. He gave large sums to charity and thereby earned himself more goodwill and gratitude. He seldom turned a deaf ear to pleas for a deserving cause. Even the not-so-deserving received consideration if he thought they would further his personal cause. The *tongs*, or Chinese secret societies, kept in constant touch through intermediaries. He never dealt directly with them. He never regarded his contributions as payment for protection. They served him well and often emerged as his trump card whenever things didn't go quite right. The *tongs* were always in need of funds for reasons Boon Haw chose not to question.

Boon Haw in his more expansive moods would lecture his well-to-do contemporaries. "What one takes from society one must also give back to society," he said on one occasion when complimented on an especially large donation he made to a home for aged people.

An elderly gentleman poor in material things but rich in wisdom asked, "If one takes ten sacks of rice from society does one also give back ten sacks? Or five sacks or just one?"

"That is up to one's conscience and to one's judgement. But I would be foolish to give back all. It takes money to make more money. And the more I make the more I shall be able to give. What will there be left to give if I should give away even the seeds to multiply?"

No one could argue with Boon Haw's logic. Only the naive would give up his all and join the ranks of the dispossessed. Just as important, a millionaire could not be expected to simply give up a lifestyle to which he had grown accustomed.

Schools, temples, orphanages and homes for the aged benefited without any strings attached – except for one. Boon Haw made it known that a plaque bearing his name and that of his brother be displayed in a prominent spot as would befit his generosity. His benefactors were only too happy to indulge him. Donations were invariably made in the joint names of the brothers or that of the firm, but because of the force of his personality, most of the credit went to him.

Since he was so well known, any occasion graced by his presence enjoyed added distinction. Wealth, influence, fame and even adulation of a sort attended him at the age of thirty-seven. He basked in the recognition accorded to his achievements. But one thing still eluded him. That was power. The power to make people sit up and listen to what he had to say. Power to sway public opinion. Time enough for that, he told himself.

Meanwhile, there was the more immediate task of building the biggest fortune any overseas Chinese had ever achieved. To become the richest man in the region, irrespective of race, was no longer an unattainable dream. He had made his first million, other millions would follow. Of this, Boon Haw was supremely confident.

He discovered that his personal prestige sold Tiger Balm. The public reasoned that his product must be very good indeed to have made him such a vast fortune. Believing that he was a walking advertisement for his medicines, Boon Haw determined that he should receive maximum exposure. One way to do this was to attend even more public functions. It was in one of such events that he first set eyes on the girl who was to become his second wife; the woman who would be the greatest influence in his life; the power behind the throne.

The reflection of the sun on golden domes turned into glowing balls of fire. Below the flaming pagodas, scores of saffron-robed priests, both ordained and youthful novices, mingled with the crowds. From a distance they resembled torches fallen from the blazing dome above. Heads shaved and fingers agitating prayer beads, these holy men moved about greeting the faithful and dispensing blessings.

A pretty girl stood spellbound in the blazing sun as she took in the riot of colours and activities before her. There was a profusion of buntings, flags and banners in as many hues and shades as there are in a rainbow. Adding gaiety to the occasion were the throngs of men, women and children who came arrayed in their colourful best. It was the dedication of a new temple.

Tan Kim Kee had come with friends to offer prayers for her mother who was ill. The family was poor, and perhaps like many girls of her position, she had also come to the temple to pray for a good provider when she was old enough to marry. But today was also a special occasion for her and her friends who called her Kyi Kyi. They had been allowed to go out unaccompanied. There were few places young girls were permitted to visit unescorted, but a temple was considered safe. People who went to temples were not supposed to harbour evil in their hearts.

Kyi Kyi's eyes strayed over the vast panorama of people gathered to celebrate and pay homage to the Lord Buddha. She was thirteen and comely. Fair of face and sturdy of build, her comeliness seldom failed to draw a second look. Mindful of her mother's oft-repeated caution to avoid getting baked in the sun, she unfurled her paper umbrella to shield herself from the stinging rays.

Her eyes came to rest on a huge marquee. Beneath its shade sat the important guests, among whom were contributors to the temple. The front row was reserved for the most generous benefactors and their ladies. Kyi Kyi moved closer to admire the wealthy ladies bedecked with jewels and clothed in finest raiments. It must be wonderful to be rich and important, she thought. Perhaps if she remained a good girl and prayed often in the temple, she might one day find a rich husband and take her place among the special people who lived in grand houses with servants to do their bidding.

Seated among the VIPs was a prosperous-looking gentleman in

white. The highly polished gold buttons on his buttoned-to-the-neck tunic glinted in the ray of sunshine that penetrated a gap in the marquee. He shifted his chair in annoyance, and in doing so, he turned his face towards the direction where Kyi Kyi stood. His eyes instantly focussed on the girl and held.

Boon Haw had been bored for the past many minutes. Expecting to hog the limelight, he was annoyed to find other patrons sharing what he thought was to be his special preserve. The chief monk had been effusive in his expression of appreciation for the man's generous donation. He had devoted more time than he should to this guest and then excused himself to attend to the others. A junior monk ushered Boon Haw to a comfortable chair in the front row and introduced him to the other VIPs who were already seated. He measured their importance according to their wealth and judged none to be his equal. He found their conversation dull, their praises hollow and their company dreary. As he strove to think up a suitable excuse to make an exit, the sun had shone through and the vision appeared in the crowd to arrest his attention.

Boon Haw's boredom dissipated. There was now something to interest him. He looked long and hard at the girl who was totally unaware of his stares. There was something about her which stirred his blood. His thoughts flashed back to his youth in China and to the concubines no older than the girl before him. They were sold for no more than the price of a buffalo, sometimes even less, by impoverished parents. But this was Rangoon and not China. This was a country ruled by a Western power which frowned on human slavery.

Boon Haw trained his eyes on the girl and the longer he observed her, the more appealing she became. She looked so pure and innocent. Like a flower waiting to be picked. So unlike the many women he had fancied and rejected. He resented being regarded as an inexhaustible gold mine. He had his fun and rewarded them according to what he thought they were worth. But he was an unusually lavish patron whose generosity was a way of ensuring that he obtained the best available.

Kyi Kyi was lost in her private thoughts as she watched the chattering crowds bustle before her. She was totally unaware that she was the centre of attraction for one of the wealthiest men in Rangoon.

Boon Haw could not resist the urge to find out more about the girl. He beckoned to one of two flunkeys hovering a few feet away. Pointing to Kyi Kyi, who was struggling to keep her position in the pressing crowd, he said, "That fair girl with the umbrella. Go and find out what you can about her. Invite her to refreshments without alarming her. Find out where she lives. Better still, ask her to come up and join me. I want to get to know her."

To have the opportunity to do a favour for the big boss was an honour that could lead to better things. The flunkey, a young Burmese in native garb of sarong, blouse and a piece of cloth tied round his head, made haste to comply. He launched himself into the crowd and elbowed his way in the direction where he reckoned his quarry to be.

Meanwhile, Kyi Kyi's friends had joined her. They were looking for her as it was time to go home. They did not want to worry their parents as it would only result in fewer outings on their own. The girls started off with laughter trailing their departure. By the time the flunkey reached the spot where the girl had stood a few moments ago, she had disappeared into the crowd.

The flunkey trembled as Boon Haw hissed, "You good for nothing person, you can't do the simplest thing." He had visions of being exiled to the packing section of the factory where workers slaved over heavy crates. Gone with the banishment would be the many perks he enjoyed as attendant to the now furious boss. Many had been sacked for smaller failures.

Boon Haw rose abruptly and left. He was too angry to bother with excuses for his unexpected departure.

Boon Par's wife, Ah Lan, had always been in delicate health since her youth. Where her sister Piah Hong had always been robust and had become stout after fourteen years of married life, the last five of which had been a life of plenty, Ah Lan was still as slim as a pole. Her husband's promiscuous behaviour was a constant source of gall. There was nothing she could do about it except berate him for his shabby treatment. This led to endless quarrels to the chagrin of her mother-in-law. Unlike her sister who kept her feelings to herself, Ah Lan chose to air her anger at every opportunity.

When Ah Lan fell ill, Boon Par put her in a hospital. In spite of the family tradition of herbal cures, Boon Par placed greater faith in Western medicine. Or perhaps he wished to get her out of his system for a while.

Ah Lan had to share a humble room with other patients. First-class wards were meant for Europeans. No persuasion could sway the hospital staff to bend the rules for even the wife of the richest *towkay* in Burma.

Piah Hong visited her sister every day, sometimes twice a day. She cooked Ah Lan's favourite dishes and patiently spoon-fed her ailing sister. It was not that the hospital did not provide food or that it was inadequate. The diet was Western and the food was considered "windy" or "cooling" and therefore not compatible with a sick person's constitution. She would have supplemented the hospital's medicine with her own herbal brews if the nursing sister had not caught her in the act one morning and threatened to bar her from visiting Ah Lan.

Boon Haw was persuaded by Piah Hong to show some brotherly concern and made his way to the hospital after work. He grunted his disapproval as he walked into a room full of chattering relatives and visitors of other patients. His mood was foul. His mind had continued to dwell on the girl whose face had been haunting him since he first set eyes on her three months ago.

The sight of his sister-in-law confined in such wretched

surroundings did not improve matters. He felt slighted that a member of his family was denied better treatment. He declined a chair when it was offered, preferring to stand and survey the deplorable conditions before him. He decided to get over the niceties as soon as possible and be on his way.

Boon Haw exchanged some pleasantries with Ah Lan, but just as he was about to take his leave, some disturbance three beds across the room drew his attention. Some men and women surrounded the bedraggled cot of a woman. She was entreating her relatives to take her home. If she must die, the patient moaned, she would rather die at home. A girl started sobbing. Boon Haw shifted his gaze to meet the voice and froze. It was the girl in the crowd. She had gone to visit her sick mother and the talk of dying was too much for her to bear. The thought of being left alone had set her crying.

To approach her here was out of the question. It would only make him a fool to all these people. With haste that piqued Piah Hong, he excused himself and walked out of the ward. Summoning a flunkey waiting beside his carriage, he instructed the man to follow the girl when she left the hospital.

"Make sure you find out where she lives," Boon Haw told the man. "You will be well rewarded. But don't come back if you fail."

The flunkey stationed himself outside the main entrance. When visiting hours ended at six in the evening, a stream of people began to leave. Kyi Kyi came out weeping. She was led away by a middle-aged woman who was trying to console her. They walked along the dusty streets in the gathering dusk and came to a house in the poorer part of town. It was the house of the Ong family. Mrs Ong, the woman who had brought Kyi Kyi home with her, was an aunt who had promised the sick woman to look after her daughter. Mrs Ong was a kindly old soul, but had not much to offer Kyi Kyi as she was poor and had numerous children of her own.

The flunkey lingered outside to make certain that the house

was indeed Kyi Kyi's home. He was assured of this when, peering in through a half-shuttered window, he saw the family partaking of their evening meal. With a smile of satisfaction, and in anticipation of the promised reward, he ran off to give his boss the good news.

Boon Haw paid another visit to the hospital the next day. And the next. His wife was delighted. His sister-in-law showed no emotion. Whatever his motives might be, she was certain that it was not on her account that he had suffered the inconvenience of making daily visits to the hospital. On the third day, Boon Haw's visits terminated as soon as he noticed that the bed which had been occupied by Kyi Kyi's mother was empty. The woman had been taken home to die according to her wish.

Boon Haw sulked. For the first time since the launch of Tiger Balm his heart was not in his business. His magic balm was no cure for his aching heart. He was obsessed with desire for this girl whom he had not even spoken to. He became short-tempered. Life became quite unbearable for those around him. He must scheme a way to win the girl.

Short of abducting her, there seemed no way of having the girl except to marry her. But the obstacles ahead were daunting even to Aw Boon Haw. He had learned through discreet enquiries that the girl was only thirteen years old, fourteen by Chinese reckoning. Such a match would only expose him to mockery. A man of his position would find ridicule a bitter pill to swallow.

Moreover, there were family members to contend with. His mother would object most vigorously. Of that he was certain. She was a woman of principle, imbued with a sense of propriety. Then there was Piah Hong who had stood by him these past fourteen years. She had helped him in their kitchen factory in those early days and their struggle had now produced abundant rewards. Even though his affection for her was as deep as ever, he knew she would feel scorned and bitter if he were to take another.

But Boon Haw was besotted. He was prepared to face ridicule

if this was the price he had to pay for this one indulgence. He sent an emissary to the girl's home. His brief was clear: obtain the mother's consent for him to marry her daughter.

The emissary was dumbfounded to find people weeping on reaching the house. Kyi Kyi's mother had died. The funeral was to take place that day. The emissary remained only long enough to learn that the girl would now be under the care of the aunt. He would return on another more appropriate day to speak to the aunt.

"Kyi Kyi is only a child," the aunt said when the emissary returned.

The emissary was not to be put off. He knew how much the boss depended on him and how extravagantly generous the boss would be if he succeeded. He talked himself breathless. But the girl's foster mother could not or would not be swayed. "Come back in two years," the aunt said. "If Aw Boon Haw is still keen to marry my niece then, we can begin to discuss the match."

Boon Haw was thwarted yet again. This only served to strengthen his resolve. He waited ten days and then despatched yet another emissary. This man, an elderly Hakka noted for his gift of persuasion, came bearing expensive gifts for every member of the family. The aunt's gift of a heavy twenty-four carat gold ornament was overwhelming. She had never owned anything remotely resembling it and was speechless with wonder. The emissary had a captive listener. He spoke with such fervour and with an eloquence to which the unlearned Ongs could find no words for a fitting reply. What appeared to be the greatest barrier, that of age, he brushed off as of little consequence. As though every wife was preoccupied with matters of sex, he discoursed, "A man of seventy can be as virile as a woman half his age. And if the man is very rich, he could easily live to be a hundred. Aw Boon Haw is still a young man."

"But Master Aw already has a wife. How can we be sure that my niece will not be ill-treated?"

"A rich man like Aw Boon Haw can easily afford to set up a second household. I am sure your niece will be very happy. She will have servants and all the money she could ever spend. And fine clothes and jewels and gold to adorn her person."

The Ongs realised that there could not be a better match in terms of material considerations. Kyi Kyi's future would be assured. The girl would, in time, get used to a husband so very much her senior. Right now she needed a father as much as a husband.

For appearance's sake, Mrs Ong withheld consent for the time being. "Please tell Master Aw how gratified and honoured we are for his desire to marry our niece," she said. "I will talk to the girl and you shall have our answer by the next moon."

But Boon Haw had his answer well before the next moon was up. He continued to press his suit with increasing urgency and lavished more gifts on the Ongs each time his proxy called. The final visit was to deliver a red packet containing one thousand rupees. This was the payment to seal the troth. Boon Haw also made it known that any member or relative of the Ong family would be welcome as an employee of Eng Aun Tong.

A senior official of the Hakka Clan Association solemnised the marriage in the home of a friend. No fanfare; no publicity. Totally out of character. But publicity was the last thing Boon Haw sought. He would gladly have dispensed with the formalities if not for the Ongs' insistence. They wanted respectability for the union. More important perhaps were the high stakes that might be involved. Rich men had been known to discard their secondary wives without a penny to their name for reasons which they were not obliged to offer.

Like any four-year-old, Aw Swan was excited over the prospect of taking a long train ride. His mother had difficulty restraining him from running up to the locomotive and staring in awe at the steaming monster. His grandmother took his other hand and together the two women guided him into the second-class carriage.

First-class was reserved for Europeans. Third-class was for the common people and second for the more affluent non-Europeans who could afford first but were compelled to travel second. This three-generation family was on a journey to visit relatives in Mandalay some four hundred miles up the Irrawaddy River. Years later, the little boy having grown into a young man would recall with many a chuckle that episode of his life,

"Our relatives were not expecting us, actually. We ourselves had no idea of going on a trip. It was so sudden. My old man told grandmother during dinner the previous day to pack some clothes and take my mother and me to Mandalay. A distant uncle lived there and my father thought it would be a good idea to pay him a visit. That uncle was never close and we seldom exchanged visits but everybody thought a trip would do us all a lot of good. So we went, none of us suspecting the reason.

"My father was about to marry a young girl. He did not want my grandmother and mother to know as he was afraid they would raise the strongest objections. Especially my grandmother who was always trying to do the right things and to avoid gossip. Everything my father or my uncle did seemed to raise a hullabaloo, and they all came back to grandmother sooner or later. So far, my father had kept the knowledge of this impending marriage from my grandmother and mother, and he was not going to let any last-minute hitches spoil his day. So he packed us off to Mandalay.

"The train journey through some of the loveliest country in Burma was most enjoyable. The visit was not. The uncle I had never seen expected us to bring expensive gifts. When we explained that the visit was a hastily arranged one and left us with no time to buy presents for everybody, his attitude changed from that of a welcoming clansman to an indifferent relative. Grandmother cut short the visit and we returned to Rangoon much sooner than planned.

"My father was not at home when we got back. He was trying to avoid a confrontation with my mother. Anyway, how long can you keep such things secret? My mother soon got to know about the marriage. She had never been more angry in her life. My grandmother supported her completely. 'I have only one daughter-in-law, and she is Piah Hong,' she declared.

"My mother threatened to beat up the new wife if she so much as show her face in the vicinity. She would be quite capable of beating up my father too if he had been around at the time her wrath was fiercest. To add insult to injury was the fact that the new wife was a mere girl, young enough to be her daughter, to be my sister. My mother called my father *gong kia sai* (a knave of a bridegroom) which was quite an insult to a man of my father's worldliness."

And how did the object of all this fuss feel about the whole affair? She was bewildered, to say the least. One day a happy and carefree child looking forward to the occasional outing with her friends, and almost the next moment an orphan and then the child-bride of a man so much older. No one had ever told her what was expected of a bride. Her foster parents had convinced her of the desirability of having a rich husband and protector who would look after her all her life and give her anything her simple heart could ever desire.

Boon Haw installed his girl-wife in the tiny apartment above the store. He was as kind and attentive as his gruff demeanour would allow. He showered her with gifts the likes of which she had not even dreamt about. He would probably promise her the moon if she had mentioned it, so besotted was he with her. That little apartment above the store on 21st Street would occupy a special place in their hearts long after the completion of their many luxury mansions to come.

Boon Haw's contemporaries were flabbergasted. To pay five hundred rupees for a virgin's favour was one thing. It was strictly a business transaction giving one the hope of restoring one's youthful vigour. But to marry a girl of such tender age was carrying the restoration process too far, they mused.

His rivals sneered as was to be expected. But on the whole, he was quite immune to social disgrace thanks to his wealth which placed him above the usual convention. He spent so much time in the little apartment that his family gave up hope of ever seeing him home again. But to sever family ties even for the great love of his life never entered his head. Gradually, when the first flush of passion was contained, Boon Haw returned to the house for the evening meal and then to sleep alternate nights.

Boon Haw's mother made no more references to her son's behaviour. She cautioned Piah Hong against making any of her own. She was determined not to exacerbate the situation. "He has done what he has done," she said. "No good will come out of scolding or doing anything that might cause more bitterness for you. Let us things be."

So Piah Hong resigned herself to Boon Haw's double life. But she made it quite clear that she had no wish to meet Kyi Kyi or to acknowledge her existence.

Eight

By 1921, Tiger Balm and its sister products were penetrating ever deeper into the markets of the Orient. The factory was hard put to meet orders. A shipping department was set up to attend to buyers from as far off as the East Indies who, on not obtaining their full supplies, came to the factory to ensure they got what they ordered.

Dealing in Tiger Balm was certain profit. Demand grew daily. To stock up on Tiger medicines was the aim of every dealer. They fetched a premium in the more remote areas. Where cash was short, barter was acceptable. A jar of Tiger Balm was fair exchange for a chicken or duck and a packet of Headache Cure was good for ten eggs. Turnover was astronomical. For every tin of Western ointment bought, as many as a hundred jars of Tiger Balm were sold.

The Aw brothers never had it so good. Theirs was a sellers' market; demand outstripped supplies and, because of this, dealers scrambled to build up stocks, thus creating even better demand. The goods tumbled out of the factory into eager hands even before the paste on the wrappers could dry. The money rolled in as fast as it could be counted. Sales were mostly on a cash basis. The safes in Eng Aun Tong and in the Aw residence were stuffed with banknotes. Boon Par was quite happy to relax and maintain the status quo so that he could enjoy his wealth more fully. But Boon Haw denied himself the pause he so richly deserved.

After six enchanted months with Kyi Kyi, Boon Haw decided that he had neglected his business long enough. The drive to accumulate even greater wealth could not be suppressed any longer. He must make ready to travel again.

Kyi Kyi had by now settled into a routine of her own. She seldom ventured outside the apartment. Boon Haw would not permit her to be out on her own and he seldom took her anywhere. About the only visitors allowed into the apartment were her aunt or her children. But Boon Haw saw to it that she lacked nothing. He engaged a woman, after careful screening, to attend to Kyi Kyi and to keep her company. This woman had strict instructions to bar all, except those few approved by Boon Haw, from the apartment. Having assured himself that the passion of his life would be well looked after in his absence, Boon Haw resumed his neglected business trips.

Although Siam was Burma's next-door neighbour, Boon Haw had always favoured Malaya. He had become quite familiar with the country and its multi-racial people, having made several visits there to assess its business potential. He told Boon Par, "I think Malaya is an even better country than Burma to do business. It is very rich. The people grow rich on rubber and tin and the British who govern the country welcome anyone who can contribute towards the country's development.

"There are more of our countrymen there than in Burma. They live mostly in the towns, they own their own businesses and many work in tin mines and rubber estates. They own land and become very rich through mining, growing rubber and trading.

"Why, the Chinese there even own their own banks," Boon Haw enthused. "There is the Overseas Chinese Banking Corporation, a very large bank which is wholly owned by Chinese and there is also the Ho Hong Bank, to name only two. I met many Hakka people there the last time I went; many with our family name. And they have the biggest and busiest port in the Far East. From Singapore one could trade with any country in the world. We should set up dealerships throughout Malaya, with a main agent in Penang in the north and Singapore in the south.

"There are ships sailing daily from Rangoon to both Penang

and Singapore and we can distribute our medicines to the East Asian markets more efficiently from these two ports," Boon Haw concluded.

As usual, Boon Haw's enthusiasm overcame whatever reservations Boon Par might have in making such heavy commitments so far away from home. He knew there was none as astute a marketer as his brother, or whose judgement was half as sound. Boon Par did, however, make known his preference for Rangoon as their home base. "Rangoon has been very good to us. We have prospered in Rangoon beyond expectations and our luck may desert us if we desert Rangoon," the younger man cautioned.

"Nobody is deserting Rangoon. We are only expanding into other territories. Malaya is a start. We could aim to eventually expand into our mother country. That would please our father as nothing else could, I am sure. The market in Burma is limited. In a few years we should sell ten times as much outside Burma as in. Mark my words. But we are not leaving Rangoon. We shall keep our homes here and leave our families here."

Boon Haw was off within a week. He was glad to be on the road again, despite regrets at having to leave Kyi Kyi behind. But she was his for better or for worse, and she would be there to comfort him again when he returned. His heart was light and his step was lively as he tripped down the gangway leading to the pier in Penang. Of all the places he had been, Penang was his favourite. It was like a homecoming, with old friends and clansmen gathered to welcome him back to this "Pearl of the Orient." Penang had many delights to offer. Boon Haw reverted to type with little arguing. He was as popular with the ladies as ever.

In spite of the island's many lures, Boon Haw spent only a few days there. He left the matter of establishing an agency undecided. Clansmen exercising the prerogative of family ties clamoured for the business. But they were either lacking in experience or in capital. Boon Haw was not about to set them up in business for free. Of those friends who had capital and experience, Boon Haw deferred making a decision to avoid offending his fellow Hakkas whose support he valued.

Boon Haw crossed over to the mainland and came to the house of a clansman in Bukit Mertajam. The Chinese called it *Tua Suah Kah* which meant "foot of the big mountain." The clansman was known to his friends as Ah Tee (little brother). Ah Tee owned a small medicine shop, the only one in the little town at the time. Like Boon Haw's father, Ah Tee was a herbalist. His business was slow and, had it not been for the popularity of Tiger Brand medicines, which he stocked in fair quantities, he would have found it hard to make a living. There was to be a closer link between the two Aws in later years.

Boon Haw travelled down south to Ipoh, the largest town in the state of Perak. Ipoh was the tin capital of the world. It sat in the centre of the Kinta Valley, a rich tin-bearing district. Tin mines were everywhere. European miners employed huge dredges to extract the ore. Massive metal buckets scooped up huge chunks of earth to be conveyed to a plant for processing. This was a capital intensive, but highly productive, method which only the European combines and companies with ready backing could afford. Their investment could yield overnight returns a hundredfold once the mine struck a tin lode.

The lure of tin rivalled the lust for gold in other El Dorados. The white man came to the tropics to make his fortune. In the process he underwent the rigours of an unaccustomed climate and often picked up the malaria bug. He soaked himself in whisky to combat the fever. A struggle with the fever followed by a bout with the bottle left many a dream shattered and many a body wrecked.

The Chinese did "open cast" mining. This required a fraction of the capital needed to buy a tin dredge. Open cast mining employed pumps to direct high pressured jets of water into the earth to loosen it. The resulting mixture of water and earth was then sucked up by other pumps to flow down a long wooden trough twenty feet wide and two hundred feet long. The heavy tin deposits remained on the bottom while gravel and sand were washed away.

Coolies shovelled up the ore at regular intervals. The ore was then taken to a shed for further processing into pure tin, or as pure as a manual operation would make it. Middlemen collected the ore for shipment to Penang to be smelted and the ingots were then exported throughout the world, but mainly to London which was then the tin trading capital.

Whether through dredging or open cast mining, the land was rendered barren after the ore had been extracted. The holes gorged out of the earth were soon filled with water and all around it lay a thick layer of sand covering the fertile earth beneath. Nothing could grow in such soil and no attempts were made to fill the holes or rejuvenate the land.

Boon Haw lingered in Ipoh and noted how so many of his countrymen had become rich in this land of opportunity. He learned that the Chinese were the only community operating tin mines besides the Europeans. And Chinese mines were mostly owned by a single person. The Chinese miners did not like partnerships or corporations. They swam or sank on their own. Boon Haw deduced from the many fine mansions owned by the Chinese that few of them ever drowned in their mines.

A Chinese mine employed only Chinese coolies. Mining was backbreaking work and the hours were long. From dawn to dusk the labourers wielded a heavy *changkol*, a broad blade cudgel with a six-foot handle, digging into the muck to separate the rocks and rotting wood and keep them from being sucked into the pump. The muck reached up to their calves, their trousers were soaked to the knees and their sweat flowed down their backs in spite of the shade of a two-foot diameter straw hat.

The *kongsi* provided bed and board, and the *kepala* was the undisputed boss of the outfit. No women were allowed in the *kongsi* house. This house was usually a rectangular structure some eighty feet long by thirty feet wide and sleeping up to sixty people.

The timber floor was raised a few feet above ground to keep out the damp. Everybody slept on the floor, each with his own straw mat, pillow and blanket.

The majority of mine workers were Hakka. Working alongside the Hakkas were Hokkiens, Teochews and Cantonese. The Hakkas, as was their habit, kept to themselves as much as they could without arousing resentment in others. They were fond of dog meat, convinced that it contained health giving and recuperative properties which other meats lacked. Violent quarrels often flared up when someone accused a Hakka of turning a pet dog into stew. But they were also among the hardest workers. This quality made them much sought after as mine workers and to some extent mitigated their unusual eating-habits.

While their menfolk mined tin for others, the Hakka women engaged in mining for themselves. These were the *dulang-washers*, so-called because of the way they mined for tin. Their one and only tool was a pan shaped like a *wok* some eighteen to twenty-four inches in diameter. It was made of cork and light to work.

The *dulang-washers* were mostly girls and young women who could be spared from household chores. They panned for tin in streams and rivers in the vicinity of mines. A pound of ore would fetch many times what a rubber tapper would be paid for a day's work.

They were a distinctive group even among their own. Their clothes and behaviour set them apart. They were dressed all in black except for a red scarf tied over the head and knotted under the chin. Over this was a straw hat of the kind favoured by their men. The sleeves of their cotton blouse were inches longer than their arms and the trousers dragged the ground. Black canvas shoes protected their feet. The idea of all this coverage was to keep out the sun as completely as possible in order to preserve the fairness of their skin. In spite of the long hours spent under the sun, the *dulang-washers* were among the fairest of Chinese women.

These female miners travelled from one site to another on

bicycles. They went two to a bike, each taking turns pedalling; the passenger sat on a large carrier mounted behind. It was a sight to see these women in black cycling in groups of up to fifty. Numbers encouraged boldness. The usually inhibited Chinese maiden became a tease who delighted in making caustic remarks at any boy she happened to encounter. She might break out into song, usually ribald in flavour and never failing to raise a lot of unladylike laughter.

Kuala Lumpur was very much a replica of Ipoh on a larger scale. Like the tin capital, the population was overwhelmingly Chinese engaged in shopkeeping and other forms of commerce. The Klang Valley was second only to the Kinta Valley in tin deposits. Again, like Ipoh, Kuala Lumpur was a rubber collecting centre. Rubber from estates throughout the state was sent to this capital town to be graded and exported. Here also was the seat of the British High Commissioner of the Federated Malay States, Sir Laurence Guillemard. Sir Laurence was concurrently governor of the Straits Settlements and maintained two official residences in the Government Houses of Singapore and Kuala Lumpur.

The train journey to Singapore was a slow, dusty and tiring ride. But once he alighted from the train in Tanjong Pagar and stepped out into the bustling streets of this port city, Boon Haw's pulse raced with the pace of commerce evident everywhere. He checked into a hotel frequented by Chinese merchants and which had served him well in past visits.

Later that day, Boon Haw made his way to a Western clinic instead of the Chinese pharmacies. A young man greeted Boon Haw with easy familiarity. He was quite a few years younger. Slim and pleasant looking, his black hair was centre-parted and smoothed down with brilliantine. He wore a Western-style suit in white cotton drill and sported a tie, so unlike other Chinese who wore a tunic buttoned to the throat such as Boon Haw did.

He was Dr Hu Tsai Kuen, one of the earliest Chinese in Singapore to obtain a medical degree.

Dr Hu was distant kin to Boon Haw. Although younger in years, he was senior antecedently. An ancestor had married very late in life and much to everyone's surprise, his young wife had borne him children who became uncles and aunts to nephews and nieces old enough to be their elders. In the proper order of lineage, Tsai Kuen the younger man was uncle to Boon Haw. But in the interest of an easier relationship both decided to dispense with familial formalities and address each other by name.

"Boon Haw, when did you arrive?"

"Yesterday. Are you making a lot of money as a Western doctor?"

"I am only a new doctor. But I can't complain."

"How is the family?"

"Everyone is in good health, thank you. Are you staying in the same hotel?"

"Yes, I like it there," Boon Haw answered defensively. "You must have dinner with me tonight. And any entertainment you like after."

Tsai Kuen did not rise to the bait. He was a serious young man dedicated to his profession. Having had the advantage of observing the worst and best of both East and West, he often found himself caught between two sets of values of different cultures. What seemed right to one was taboo to the other. What was tolerated as a harmless diversion in the East was condemned as philandering in the West.

"How long will you remain in Singapore this time?"

"Long enough to see if I can set up an agency. Do you know of any able person who can be trusted?"

"I know of many who seem able but I cannot vouch for their honesty."

Boon Haw did not pursue the subject any further. He spent the next few days visiting the many medicine shops in town renewing friendships and lining up more business. Every one clamoured for bigger supplies. They wanted Boon Haw to set up production in

Singapore. They would be more than prepared to advance any capital he might need.

Boon Haw had no intention of allowing anyone, even kinsmen bearing the family name to participate in the business. He turned down every offer of equity participation with all the grace he could muster whilst inwardly annoyed that they should think he did not have the money to set up a factory of his own if he really wanted to. He did not want to manufacture here. Not as far as he could see. And he did not find anyone he considered sufficiently able, honest and financially sound to run an agency without compromising the reputation of Tiger Balm.

But Boon Haw did commit himself to buying a house in Singapore.

"You must bring Piah Hong with you the next time you come," Tsai Kuen said over dinner in his modest home a few days after Boon Haw's arrival. "And bring your boy, what's his name, Aw Swan?"

"If I bring one wife and leave the other behind there is bound to be trouble for me," Boon Haw said with a sly smile. He had not yet told the younger man of Kyi Kyi, not really knowing how to come to it.

Tsai Kuen thought Boon Haw was referring to Boon Par's wife, Ah Lan. He said, "I don't see why you should be in trouble if you left your brother's wife behind. You are under no obligation to take her anywhere even though she is your wife's sister."

Boon Haw's reply was blunt. "It has nothing to do with Ah Lan, though God knows she is trouble enough. The problem is, I've married another woman. Piah Hong is furious. So is Mother. My new wife is staying in another house. I am in enough trouble as it is. There will be other times for visits – when tempers cool down and people accept what has been done."

Tsai Kuen's years of study in the West had acquired him some Western values and moral. He therefore viewed polygamy with disfavour. But he was gracious enough to offer Boon Haw his wishes for a long, happy and productive life with his new wife.

Boon Haw came to like and respect Tsai Kuen from their very first meeting. He found this young kinsman quite different from the others who were always expecting favours. He had a good, if not yet a lucrative, practice. Boon Haw did not have much of an education, but he had a high regard for those who were well educated. Tsai Kuen was bilingual. He spoke, read and wrote Chinese and English with equal facility. He was also proficient in Chinese dialects. Altogether a man of many talents and qualities which Boon Haw admired.

The club was very exclusive, for Chinese only. Members were mostly business tycoons. Women were welcome only as paid companions for an hour or a night. The club was situated in Keong Saik Road, later to be notorious as one of the higher class red light districts. It occupied the two upper floors of a three-storey house. A coffee shop did round-the-clock business on the ground floor.

Boon Haw was an indifferent gambler. He liked an occasional flutter, but his impatient nature made him avoid games that demanded long sittings. He didn't have time to pass. "Better to do it on your back in bed with one than on your backside at a gambling table with many," he would crudely reply whenever asked if he would like to while away some time gambling.

Many members had little or no education, but were endowed with a business acumen which no amount of learning could impart. And because of their background and upbringing, these wealthy club men were elegant neither in their speech nor in their manners. They were blunt and pragmatic, but courteous to one another in their own way; and scrupulously honest in their business dealings. They had little use for lawyers and trusted them even less. There was little need for written agreements. A trader's word was his bond. Transactions involving vast sums were concluded with a nod of the head and a sip of tea. A man who broke his word became a social pariah and shunned by his peers for the rest of his life.

Three men were engaged in a game of cards. One man said,

"Whoever wins the next hand will go upstairs. The other two will pay. Agreed?" A second man asked, "How much?" The third man answered with a question of his own, "How much does the best cost?" "Twenty dollars," said the first man. These three club members were gambling for a lady companion that night.

The first floor of the club boasted a spacious and comfortable lounge with gaming and dining tables, a small kitchen, bar and rattan reclining chairs. Three *amahs* served members on this floor. *Amahs* were spinsters dedicated to a life of domestic service. They came from Kwantung Province and wore black trousers and a white blouse to identify their calling. Their hair was braided into a queue to denote spinsterhood.

The floor above contained three small, but comfortable, bedrooms. Each bedroom had a four-poster bed covered with a mosquito curtain – the buzzing of a mosquito could dampen the ardour of the most passionate lover. This was the "upstairs" referred to by one of the three gamblers.

The man who had asked how much the bet would cost emerged the winner in a game of "twenty-one." He called one of the *amahs* over. The other partners each handed ten dollars to her. The winner of a night of joy gave the *amah* one dollar as her tip and said, "Send the best girl."

Boon Haw was an interested observer to what had transpired among the trio of gamblers. He had been invited to the club by a merchant named Lim Ah Seng. Lim made his fortune speculating in commodities from the East Indies.

Lim offered Boon Haw some brandy which the latter declined. "I'd prefer some tea," he said.

"Anything else with it?" Lim asked in a manner which left Boon Haw in no doubt what he meant.

"We'll see about that later."

As the two new friends sipped their tea, a stout man approached. He sat with them uninvited when he learned who Lim's guest was and began to engage Boon Haw in conversation. The genial man was a member of the Lee clan, reputed to be one of the biggest landowners in Singapore. Like other members of the club he was a very wealthy man. He also liked to gamble. It was not long before he asked Boon Haw if he would like to join in a game of cards or whatever form of gambling he preferred.

Boon Haw demurred but Lim was for it. Not wishing to disappoint his host he agreed to play a few hands.

"What shall we play?" Lee asked.

"Something that does not take up much time," Boon Haw said.

"What about *pah kau*?" Lim suggested.

It was agreeable. *Pah kau* was a game in which each player was dealt three cards with an aggregate of ten as the highest score.

Boon Haw lost steadily. He was not used to losing.

"I'm tired of this game," Boon Haw said after losing another five hundred dollars. "Let us draw cards, highest card shall be the winner," he proposed.

No one responded for no one regarded drawing cards as a proper game. Lee stepped in to save Boon Haw from embarrassment and to uphold the club's reputation. No challenge from a guest had so far gone unanswered. "What shall we bet?" he asked.

"What I have lost," Boon Haw said.

"And how much would that be?"

"Five thousand dollars."

"Fine," Lee said. "We will cut a deck for five thousand dollars. Who else would like to join in?"

Lim said he would but Boon Haw thought it would be better for just him and Lee to challenge each other. Lim asked the *amah* to bring a new deck. Acting as referee he unwrapped the deck and shuffled it long and expertly. He smacked the deck down on the table and said, "Who will cut first?"

"Our guest shall have the honour," Lee said graciously.

Boon Haw cut the deck to reveal a four of clubs. The many onlookers now gathered around sighed in sympathy. Lee stretched out a hand with a confident smile. He turned over a card with a flourish and this time a groan came from the members. He had cut a three of diamonds.

"What luck!" exclaimed Lim.

"No, it's not over yet," said Lee. "It's my turn to cut the deck first for the next round."

The cards were ceremoniously shuffled by referee Lim and then thumped on the table. "Are you two set?" he asked.

"Shall we double the stake to ten thousand dollars?" Lee asked Boon Haw. Never one to back down, Boon Haw was more than willing. He went one better. "I'll double it again to twenty thousand. Win or lose, this will be the final draw. Are you agreeable, my friend?"

Lee was just as game. With a smile and a bow he answered, "Very agreeable, my honourable friend."

Every member present suspended whatever he was doing to gather closer to the table where a fortune was to be won or lost on the flick of a card.

Lee turned over the king of hearts. There was loud applause.

Boon Haw cut and held up the ace of spade. No cheer this time, only groans.

The session ended with Lee giving Boon Haw a ride in his Model T-Ford; one was going home, the other to his hotel. The room upstairs could wait another day.

"What are you going to do with the money you won last night?" Tsai Kuen asked Boon Haw the next day.

"Put it in Ho Hong Bank for later use."

"Have you thought of putting it into a house instead?"

"Why would I want a house in Singapore? I like living in hotels."

"A house is always a good investment. It is better to live in your own house than in a hotel. You will want to bring your family for visits and they will be far more comfortable in their own house where they can do their own cooking."

"Do you know of any house?"

"There's one in Tanglin. But I don't know if it is still available.

The owner is a friend who is building a bigger mansion. He is the son of a millionaire who made his fortune in sugar."

"Where exactly is this house? Can I have a look?"

"It is a little out of town. In the countryside, in fact. At the end of Orchard Road. Mostly fruit orchards and vegetable plots. But the area is bound to develop soon. Many wealthy people are buying land there. I'll get in touch with the owner and let you know."

"Hurry. I'm returning to Rangoon soon."

Boon Haw saw the house. It was a large, two-storey mansion of concrete, brick and timber. Gracious and spacious. There were five bedrooms in the main house and five more in the outhouse behind. A house for a large family and its entourage of servants.

Boon Haw liked the location. The house was situated at the confluence of three roads: Orchard Road, Tanglin Road and Nassim Road. It is a house where luck flows in from all directions, he told himself. He decided to buy it without bothering to consult a geomancer to determine its *feng shui*. The house, known as No. 2 Tanglin Road, became the first property of the Aw family in Singapore.

Boon Haw now had a stake in Singapore with the purchase of the house. It would provide a base for any expansion of the business into Singapore should he ever decide on it. He leaned back in his chair in the hotel room and idly examined a hundred dollar bill, one of ten which he had drawn from Ho Hong Bank that morning. He held it up against the ceiling light and noticed the watermark on it. Was it the head of a dog or a cat? It was neither. It was, in fact, the head of a snarling tiger. Boon Haw's interest was aroused.

He dug into his pocket and brought out more bills of other denominations. A tiger snarled at him from every note he held up against the light. Was it an omen? Was Singapore beckoning to him? He suddenly felt a close affinity with the island whose currency notes bore an image of his namesake.

Nine

Great sorrow came into Boon Haw's life when his mother died. He loved her dearly. He was wilful when young, he felt remorse when his father passed away. As if to make recompense for the love he denied his father, Boon Haw gave his mother all the affection that was within his person to give.

When Mother became ill, he cancelled his trips and even left Kyi Kyi on her own to be by her side. As herbal medicines did little good for her, she reluctantly consented to undergo Western treatment. But only in her home. The matriarch had no trust in hospitals.

The best doctors were placed on constant call; no cure was too expensive. But all of Boon Haw's money could not save his mother. She died at home as she had wished.

He grieved. It gave him little consolation that he had kept his promise to give his mother a life of ease and luxury. No longer could she enjoy what she deserved. His thoughts were taken back to the time when their good life had really begun ...

It began with a rickshaw for his personal use. It was special, with brass trimmings and leather seats. His puller was a Hokkien immigrant whom Boon Haw had freed from bondage and who now recognized Boon Haw as his employer. With his increasing prosperity, Boon Haw decided he now deserved a gharry to be driven about in greater style. The coach, though second-hand, was sound. It used to be owned by a British merchant who had to return to England in a hurry.

Boon Haw, having decided to step up into the world of the elite, was annoyed that a new coach to his specifications would take a year to build. So he bought the merchant's coach which was delivered without the pony. The animal did not go with it. It would cost twice as much again. What good was a coach without a horse? Though incensed at what he thought was dishonesty, impatience overcame his anger and a horse was soon harnessed to his new status symbol.

But this was not the end to Boon Haw's woes. To add insult to injury, the Burmese coachman refused to work for him. He felt that it would lower his standing among his fellow drivers to have a Chinese boss after years of service to a white master. What good was a coach and a horse without a coachman? Boon Haw was in a dilemma. There weren't many coachmen around. Boon Haw had always admired the way these well-trained breed of drivers went about their business. Swallowing his ire, he offered the Burmese twice what his former master paid. The Burmese overcame his prejudice.

The coach was in perfectly good order. Unfortunately, it carried the stigma of being used and therefore a taint to the image he strove to build. The nearest thing to a coach builder in Rangoon was the rickshaw builder. The haughty carriage found itself in a factory among dozens of carriages drawn by manpower. Boon Haw's instructions: "Make it into a new carriage." The proprietor was only too happy to oblige when the question of costs was not discussed at all; he was not about to look a gift horse in the mouth.

Boon Haw was delighted with the transformation. The conservative black on the carriage was replaced with brown. New leather upholstery covered the padded seats. Brass lanterns and trimmings were polished to a mirror-like gloss. The rickshaw maker had lavished all his skills to turn out this sparkling coach fit for a king. Boon Haw would have been even more pleased if he had not been talked out of painting the carriage yellow with black stripes to proclaim his namesake. As it was, a tiger painted on each side of the coach served to boost his ego. He would wait another day to ride a tiger, he promised himself.

A man of means should own the house in which he lived. It was demeaning to rent. Boon Haw decided to be a house owner.

The house he found was in disrepair. Its occupant had fallen on bad times and was unable to sell it as it was a big house of three storeys. Repairs would cost as much again as what the owner was prepared to accept for the house as it stood. Boon Haw recognised the possibilities. He thought of his coach, and he was certain he could do an even more spectacular job on the house. Money was no object. Money could do wonders.

He would buy the house, but to be certain that its ownership would not cast misfortune on his business, he decided to consult a geomancer. In his heart, Boon Haw harboured some cynicism, but his associates, especially the failed tycoons, were always cursing the wrong *feng shui* as the cause of their ruin. He had a lot to lose. More important, he believed that he was fated to have a lot more to gain. Gains beyond reckoning. So why take a chance?

On the appointed day, the geomancer turned up suitably robed and carrying the paraphernalia of his calling. With tinkling bells and guttural chants he poked a wand into the ground and looked heavenwards. Then he lowered his gaze towards the east. The process was repeated in the other three directions of the compass. Finally, he turned towards the house and gazed long at it. Suddenly, the little bell in his hand began to tinkle urgently. It stopped as suddenly. The man pronounced, "This house has auspicious *feng shui*."

The owner who had been driven to selling his house could now afford a smile. A cynical smile followed by one of gratitude. If the *feng shui* was good, why had he been left in such dire straits. *Feng shui*, indeed!

Boon Haw spent a sum equal to what he paid for the house in renovations. He took time off to supervise the work. He cancelled his business trips. Even his love life was largely neglected. Each morning found him at the site to harass and harangue the contractor into speeding up the project. He was impatient to move into his new residence.

Boon Haw was fastidious. Everything must be done right and every fixture must be of the best. He didn't want a broken down house made habitable again. It must be a house with a new identity. Every vestige of the original must be obliterated so that none could recognise it as the house which belonged to the past owner. It would house a new master. It would be known as Aw Boon Haw's residence, the abode of the Aw family.

The contractor, Mr Lim, was a patient man. He listened and nodded and kept his counsel. He was also a wise man and refused to be antagonised. Why cause hostility when there were future profits to be made? He was determined to retain Boon Haw's goodwill. Forbearance was a virtue he had long cultivated in the conduct of his trade.

The contractor knew his job and took pride in his work. The craftsmen he employed were among the best; he brooked no shoddy work. When he spotted a carpenter driving a nail into a window, he made the wretched man take it out and replace it with proper joinery. As work progressed and the high standard of his work became apparent, Boon Haw began to have more respect for the contractor's expertise. He backed off from interfering and, as a consequence, renovation of the building was completed ahead of schedule. The house was handsomer than its new owner had visualised.

Having moved the family into a new residence, Boon Haw felt that it would be appropriate to move his factory as well. Considerations of prestige demanded more fitting premises for the manufacture of his now-established products. His competitors would not have the opportunity to label his medicines as "kitchen products." His reputation and that of Tiger Balm must be upheld. Another building was bought and Mr Lim again commissioned to do what was necessary to turn it into a proper factory.

Whilst the contractor and his men worked round the clock to meet Boon Haw's deadline, the boss himself and his brother were busy planning the layout of the factory. Boon Par was responsible for this department. His knowledge of English and experience in pharmacy served him well. Guided by an old volume of illustrations on laboratory equipment, he paid local artisans to fabricate stoves, smelters, mixers, pans and other necessary equipment so that his medicines could be compounded in a more professional manner. Operations were streamlined as much as present constraints would allow. A tap was installed to fill the countless jars of ointment where previously a ladle was used. This saved so much of the hot molten balm from spilling. Other labour-saving devices were used to measure out the powders or shape the breath-fresheners into more uniform sizes.

The new factory opened on a day chosen as auspicious by a soothsayer. Ceremonies invoking the goodwill of the gods and to bring luck and prosperity were acted out with great fanfare. A clan association provided the customary lion dance to make the occasion even more memorable. The heart-throbbing beat of the drums and gongs and the unending ear-splitting bursts of fire-crackers drowned the greetings of well-wishers, and brought many from around to join the noisy throng. Boon Haw surveyed all the good-natured hubbub on the steps of his factory entrance with obvious satisfaction. Such publicity could do his business nothing but good.

Boon Haw soon employed more workers. Though his family members had long since relinquished their duties in the home factory and were still finding it difficult to adjust to a life of leisure, Boon Haw considered it beneath their position to work side by side with his employees. The days of struggling to build up a business were over. A new chapter had dawned on them. From now on his womenfolk would lead the life of the idle rich.

The prosperity of the brothers was the envy of less successful relatives. Appeals for favours in one form or another had become a regular feature in their dealings with those who claimed family ties. Many had been given employment in Eng Aun Tong doing work which was non-existent and drawing pay for showing their faces for an hour or two a day. The bolder among the relatives gave the impression that Boon Haw owed them a living just because they bore the family name. They wanted to be agents for Tiger Balm or in some capacity which would ensure them an easy income without sweat. Owning a Tiger Balm agency would be like watching money falling into one's lap. Boon Haw appointed none but those who merited it.

One relative offered Boon Haw a son for adoption. Boon Haw was reluctant, the relative was insistent and impudent. Normally Boon Haw would dismiss such a person with scant ceremony. But this was a cousin whose father had taken him into his home when his juvenile delinquency had caused his own father to banish him to their village in Eng Teng. He had spent time with this cousin who later migrated to Burma on hearing of Boon Haw's increasing prosperity. Now this cousin reckoned Boon Haw owed him a favour.

"You are near middle age and you still don't have a son of your own," the cousin said. "I have many and I believe in sharing."

"But I do have a son," Boon Haw protested. "Aw Swan is five years old and we are all so fond of him."

"Aw Swan is only an adopted son," the cousin persisted. "Not of our own blood. My son is six. His great-grandfather is our common grandfather. Blood is thicker than water. You want your own blood to inherit when you go. Not an outsider."

If Boon Haw had felt insulted he did not show it, which was remarkable for a man with a volatile temper. He must indeed feel greatly indebted to the father of this impudent cousin to bear such talk.

Boon Haw had never owned up to siring Aw Swan. His mother's suspicion had never been corroborated. The boy's natural mother had disappeared from the scene without divulging the name of her child's father. But if Boon Haw was indeed the father, to be told that Aw Swan was an outsider was a great insult to both. Boon Haw let it pass and said, "I am not concerned who will inherit my fortune. I assure you I intend to live for many more years. So let us not talk or think about who will be my heir. I thank you for offering your son to me. But I must say no."

The cousin was not one to be put off so easily. "I have brought my son with me. Why don't you let him stay here. Get to know him better and you will get to like him, I am sure. You can make up your mind later."

Boon Haw agreed. Others with no ties at all had lived in his house.

The cousin smiled in satisfaction. The first move in his scheme had taken root. He was determined that one of his sons should benefit from the still greater wealth that Boon Haw was to amass.

Aw Swan was happy to have a playmate so near his age. Piah Hong in time took a liking to the boy and was pleased to see the two youngsters getting along so well. When the subject of the boy's adoption was raised again, Piah Hong was in favour. Boon Haw did not raise any objections this time. It was one of the concessions he was prepared to make in the hope that Piah Hong would desist from further confrontations over Kyi Kyi.

The boy was renamed Aw Kow. As he was older than Aw Swan by a year he was regarded as the elder son. Aw Swan was relegated to the No. 2 position. Whatever birthright was his was therefore inadvertently forfeited.

With two boys to occupy her, Piah Hong now had much less time to brood in bitterness. However, she did not feel less betrayed. In the seclusion of her bedroom after her bedtime snack, she sat by the open window and thought back to the early days when she and Boon Haw had been so close and shared so much of their time and expectations. She was glad to have shared with him the task of laying the foundation for the business which had now made them so rich. No one could take that satisfaction from her. Not even Kyi Kyi who lived in luxury and who never had to scald a finger with molten ointment filling up countless little jars. No, Kyi Kyi could never be part of that life.

Boon Haw wasted little time getting down to the task of expanding production. He had promised his Malayan and Singaporean dealers increased supplies and he meant to keep his promise. More staff were engaged and more equipment was fabricated and installed. He spent all the time he could spare supervising the expansion. He drove one and all concerned to near nervous wrecks in his determination to get everything in place and working in half the time his foreman said it would take.

Boon Par had urged a slower pace of expansion. His philosophy was different to that of Boon Haw. Where Boon Haw believed in playing hard and working harder, Boon Par was for consolidating their gains and allowing more time for leisure. As usual, Boon Haw's viewpoint prevailed. Boon Par could not help being carried along by his brother's drive to get things done in the shortest possible time. Although lukewarm at the beginning, once his brother completed the factory expansion, Boon Par pitched in with enthusiasm to ensure that the old and the new blended for a smooth operation.

Since his last visit to Singapore, Boon Haw had wanted to buy a motor car. He had been impressed by its style and convenience when Lee, the landowner, had given him a ride back to his hotel in the Ford. So much more prestigious and faster than a horse-drawn carriage. The carriage was of a bygone era. It was now the age of the motor car. Everybody who was anybody was driving or being driven about in one. As he was more of a somebody than most anybody around, Boon Haw decided that acquiring a motor car was top priority. But his time had been fully occupied by other matters.

Kyi Kyi began to demand more attention and therefore more of his time. The factory expansion project had also taken up energy and precious hours. To cap it all, his mother's failing health had caused him considerable concern.

Boon Haw pacified Kyi Kyi by allowing her more freedom to go out and visit her aunt. The only condition he placed on her movements was that she must at all times be accompanied by her housekeeper. He was also generous with spending money. The teenage wife was never more happy than during her visits to her aunt, and even more delighted on seeing the children's smiling faces when she showered them with gifts. Her every visit was an occasion eagerly looked forward to by every member of her aunt's family. She always came laden with food and presents.

Meanwhile, Mother's health had improved, or so she insisted. She was looking as poorly as ever and her appetite was that of a grasshopper. But she did not take to her bed as often as before and all her loved ones presumed that she was indeed better. The pressures having eased somewhat, Boon Haw decided to acquire his car before he was required to travel again.

He knew next to nothing about motor cars. He asked his brother for advice. Boon Par was forever reading all sorts of books and magazines in English and in some of them were pictures and write-ups of automobiles from Europe and America. Like most men of his period, he was intensely interested in the shining vehicles that had become the latest status symbol of the rich. He gave instructions to an assistant to gather all the information available pertaining to motor cars sold in Rangoon. The next morning, he placed a stack of brochures before his brother and said, "Here are your cars. Choose the one you like. I think they are all beautiful. But since you are buying it, it will be up to you to make the choice."

Boon Haw did not read English and he could hardly tell the difference from one car to another. He pushed the brochures back to Boon Par and said, "You choose one for me. I just want the best."

Boon Par picked three likely models and showed the illustrations to his brother.

"Which is the dearest?"

"This one."

"Buy it," Boon Haw decided with no further question.

"*Tow kay*," the maid called softly. Boon Haw came out of his reverie with a start. "*Tow kay neo*" (boss lady) asked if *tow kay* would like some tea."

"I'll join her in a while." He looked around. The room was empty, the house silent. The clock struck three. His remembrances had taken up an hour. None had dared intrude into his grief. Boon Haw sighed over the passing of an era. Goodbye, Mother. He composed himself and left to join his wife.

Ten

U Song was born in Rangoon of Chinese immigrant parents. When he left school at age eighteen, he was one of the best educated Chinese youths in Rangoon. He turned down a position in the Civil Service, a distinct honour for a Chinese in Burma. U Song's father decided that he needed his son more than the government did. He was a trader doing business with his native China. Joo Kim, the boy's Chinese name given to him at birth, was his eldest son and would one day inherit the business.

In time the bright Joo Kim was elected to membership of clubs, guilds and associations which he served in various capacities with distinction. Eventually he became a leading member of his community. It was inevitable that his many qualities did not go unnoticed by the authorities.

The Chinese community, although a minority group, had grown into a significant constituent of the population. By and large, they were law-abiding and desired nothing more than to be left in peace to earn a living and lead the kind of life they chose. But this desire for peaceful existence was often disrupted by the more unruly elements among themselves, the chief of which were the secret societies. It was a scourge that nobody seemed able to contain.

Due to the peculiarity of the Chinese situation, the British created a department known as the Chinese Protectorate. Its function was to deal exclusively with matters involving Chinese and pertaining to the Chinese community.

The head of this department, a senior British civil servant, bore the title of "Protector of Chinese," which was somewhat misleading as his function was not so much to protect but to see to it that the Chinese toe the official line. The British were firm but fair. As long as you kept your noses clean, you were allowed all the freedom to prosper. The whip and carrot approach served well to govern His Majesty's subjects in this corner of the far-flung empire. But not well enough to control the activities of the secret societies or *tongs*.

The British therefore recruited the Chinese to keep an eye on other Chinese. Some were attached to the staff of the Protectorate. Others were people of standing appointed on an honorary basis and given titles such as Justice of the Peace. Song Joo Kim was appointed a JP because the administration considered him well qualified.

He became known as U Song, a Burmese courtesy accorded to men commanding respect. He was forty years old and the youngest JP appointed. Others were venerable members of society in their sixties and seventies.

The *tongs* observed a code of conduct peculiar to their illegal activities. Members who flouted the rules were punished according to the severity of their misdeed; from demotion to execution in extreme cases. But even among the most disciplined groups there were members who capitalised on their connections to enrich themselves on the sly. These were mostly the smaller fry.

These destroyers, as they were sometimes called, would not dare extort from those already protected by the higher ups. Their prey were the roadside hawkers and petty traders striving to earn a living. They were beaten up if they did not pay "protection money."

Their plight was brought to the attention of the young JP.

U Song listened to the daily litany of outrages suffered by the hawkers. He decided to act with evidence gathered. The Chinese Protectorate was brought in. The Protectorate, in turn, sought the help of the police who had been unable to take action because no victim was willing to report to them for fear of revenge.

The police mounted an operation which severely curtailed the activities of the *tongs*. It was unfortunate that many of the *tongs'* victims were also prosecuted in the drive to clean up the city of crime. To set an example, the police charged shopkeepers with withholding information. Many were taken to court and stiff fines imposed. This gave the *tongs* the excuse to get back at the man who instigated the operation. A meeting of the bosses elected the leaders of the Ho Seng and Kian Teck gangs to take their cause to the Tiger.

From earlier days when he travelled the countryside in search of outlets for his medicines, Boon Haw had enjoyed the protection of minor members of the *tongs*. As he prospered, the higher hierarchy of the *tongs* sought his patronage. He neither condoned nor discouraged their strongarm tactics. Neither did they attempt to extort or intimidate him, being aware that he was a man of consequence and therefore one to befriend rather than to antagonise. Boon Haw was often ready to part with his money when a member of his staff conveyed a *tong's* request for donations to a "charity." His payments were for charity; never for services rendered, he made it understood.

There were two *tongs* which were particularly ready to serve the Tiger and keep an eye on his interests. The Ho Seng and the Kian Teck *tongs* were among the first to hitch their wagons to the Tiger's star. Over the years, they had looked upon Aw Boon Haw as their patron even though the man had never recognised them as his personal minions. It would look bad in the eyes of the authorities should he be linked to secret society activities. But everyone knew the *tongs* in Rangoon held him in high esteem. He became known as *Lau fu* ("Tiger" in Hakka dialect).

Boon Haw heard accusations of the mistreatment of Chinese – shopkeepers were brought to court for no better reason than the fact that they did not want to have anything to do with the police; the poor street vendors were rounded up and carted off to jail because they did not have a licence to hawk, and the authorities refused to give them licences. Accounts of atrocities were highly exaggerated and designed to enlist Boon Haw's sympathy.

The target of the *tongs* was U Song. The two underworld bosses called him a spy and a traitor to his own people. They branded U Song a "running dog" of the British.

Boon Haw listened to one side and was incensed. He judged U Song guilty. He knew U Song well. They had moved in the same circles and belonged to the same clubs. In fact he had liked the man for his courteous and refined ways; an elegance which Boon Haw had not quite fully cultivated in spite of the august company he kept.

In Boon Haw's mind, U Song had now become an outcast among his own kind. He would put this troublemaker in his place when he saw him again, Boon Haw promised.

His opportunity came not long after.

One of the highlights in the calendar of social events of the Chinese Merchant's Club was the Lunar New Year dinner. It was a gathering of the elite. Membership did not guarantee an invitation. The privilege to dine with members of the uppermost crust depended on whether one belonged to the right layer. It was not only an occasion to feast, but also an affirmation of who the current top people were.

The dinner was held in the club's premises, and the food prepared by the best Chinese restaurant in town. The cuisine varied each year. There were four choices reflecting the four main dialects in the community – Hokkien, Teochew, Cantonese and Hakka. This year's menu was Hakka, which pleased Boon Haw because he thought they were doing him an honour, being Hakka himself.

The first three days of the New Year were considered the most auspicious in a celebration lasting fifteen days. Everyone made their traditional round of visits to elders to pay respects and wish them health and longevity for the coming year. The club held its dinner on the fourth day of the first moon so as not to interfere with members' obligations to kith and kin during these three days. It was also near enough to the first day of the year to ensure that the season's spirit was still at its zenith.

The president of the club, an old gentleman still thick of mane but sparse of beard, gave a speech. He urged financial support for the Chinese Nationalist Government and proposed a toast to Dr Sun Yat Sen, founder of the Chinese republic. Everybody drank to that. More Hennessy tippled into tumblers. Ice cubes and water followed. What would have been a sacrilege to the Frenchman, this mix was the stuff that made for hearty *yam sengs*.

"And now," the president said, "I am very happy to call upon a very distinguished member to address us. You know him, his generosity, his kindness and his readiness to help one and all. He is truly a leader we can look up to. Gentlemen, I give you Master Aw Boon Haw."

Boon Haw was taken by surprise. He did not expect to be accorded this honour. But it would be an unpardonable lack of courtesy to excuse himself. He stood up and bowed. He looked his audience over and suddenly his smile vanished, his expression hardened. His ears turned red and nostrils flared. A sure sign of anger. He had spotted U Song who was seated some distance away from him. Now he had a subject to speak on.

Never in the history of the club had there been such insults hurled at a fellow member. Boon Haw repeated the accusations made by the secret society bosses but took care not to divulge his sources. He sincerely believed he was championing the cause of the downtrodden and berated U Song for his alleged mistreatment of Chinese.

The gathering was dumbfounded. What had started off as an amiable get-together of friends had degenerated into a bitter confrontation between two of the club's most respected members.

Boon Haw delivered the ultimate insult in the hearing of all present by calling U Song a "running dog."

In any other setting, it would not have been unexpected for the JP to defend his honour in ways equally foul. But U Song chose to depart with dignity. He stood up after Boon Haw's tirade and in a voice loud enough for all to hear, he said, "My misguided friend, you have done me a grave injustice in front of all our friends. I promise you, you have not heard the last of this. The day of reckoning will come." With that, he left the club vowing never to set foot in it again as long as Aw Boon Haw remained a member.

The family was at their morning meal when the servant came into the dining room. He looked frightened. "There are many policemen at the door," he said in a trembling voice. "They asked to see the big boss."

"Get Tian Kew to see what they want," Boon Haw said without a pause in his eating. Tian Kew was a sort of major-domo of the household whom everybody sought to get things done.

Tian Kew came into the dining room a few minutes later. He looked even more frightened than the servant. "They want to search the house," he said in a barely audible voice.

"What did you say?" Boon Haw barked.

"The policemen want to search the house," Tian Kew repeated.

Boon Haw did not believe what he heard. "What did you say they wanted?" he demanded in a tone harsh with anger.

"They want to search the house," Tian Kew intoned yet again.

"Search my house?" Boon Haw thundered. He stood up abruptly and, in doing so, tilted the table. There was a crashing of crockery. He swore in Burmese.

"Don't they know whose house this is? Don't they know who Aw Boon Haw is? Where are these fools, I'll deal with them."

The police party was led by a chief inspector, an Englishman. The officer recognised Boon Haw from photographs supplied. Nonetheless, he stepped forward, gave a smart salute and asked formally, "Are you Mr Aw Boon Haw?"

The Tiger stared at the man and remained silent. He was

seething.

The Inspector repeated, "Are you Mr Aw Boon Haw?" and after a pause added, "Sir."

That much English Boon Haw understood. "Yes," he growled.

The chief turned to a subordinate. "Please read out the warrant to Mr Aw."

Boon Haw asked Tian Kew to interpret. As faithfully as he could, Tian Kew said, "The authorities are in possession of information which alleges that you, Aw Boon Haw, and your brother, Aw Boon Par, are involved in the illegal trafficking of opium. It is furthermore alleged that you are involved in the printing and circulating of counterfeit currency notes. We are duly authorised to conduct a search of your premises and to remove any evidence found therein. Furthermore, I, Cyril Taylor, a Chief Inspector of Police, am empowered to take any action deemed necessary, which action includes the arrest of you and your brother where warranted."

Boon Haw listened in disbelief. There must be a mistake. The warrant must have been meant for another house. But the names on it were his and his brother's. There was no mistake. But what a preposterous allegation by whoever it was who had set out to do him harm. Didn't they know that he did not need to stoop to such despicable acts to make money. No mint could produce more wealth than his Eng Aun Tong.

The shock benumbed. He recovered and exploded in anger. He raved and ranted to no avail. He would have turned violent if not for the restraining hand of Boon Par who asked to see the warrant. As far as the younger man could tell, it was a genuine document properly issued by a magistrate.

Boon Haw never felt more humiliated in his life. He glared at the police officer, muttered an obscenity and stalked into the house. Boon Par turned to the Chief Inspector and said, "You may search my house. But I shall hold you responsible for anything missing or any damages done to my property."

The police searched all day. They turned up neither opium nor counterfeit money. Or any other contraband.

The Chief Inspector apologised for the inconvenience caused. But his apology did not constitute an absolution. He posted a police constable to stand guard outside the house when the search ended. "I have to obtain further instructions from my superiors," he told Boon Par. "We may be required to return for another search."

Return he did, two days later. Again the search uncovered no evidence of any wrongdoing by the brothers. But the guard outside the house caused much shame to the occupants. "We are like prisoners in our own home," Piah Hong complained. "May lightning strike dead whoever he is who puts us to this undeserving shame."

Before the day of the first search was half over, the city was rife with rumours and speculation on the crimes the Tiger Balm King and his brother had committed. Curiosity brought many to stare and to trade gossip.

Boon Haw was devastated. His pride was shattered. Not even Kyi Kyi could offer solace. "My reputation is in the mud," he told her. "How can I face the world again?" What hurt more was the fact that he had no idea who was behind this disgrace.

Although the case against the Aw brothers was never established, the stigma remained. Loyal friends and associates dismissed the incident as not worthy of further comment. But there were many jealous competitors who hoped to benefit through Boon Haw's fall. And there were those who hated his guts and arrogance, for he had indeed become arrogant at times with the weight of great wealth behind him.

Surprisingly, sales of Tiger brand medicines did not suffer. In fact, they actually increased. The publicity attending the raid generated an intense interest in the man and his medicines. Those who had never used Tiger Balm were persuaded to sample it. Many became hooked.

If Eng Aun Tong emerged from the scandal with its colours

flying higher than ever, the glory did not reflect on Aw Boon Haw. Although absolved, rancour remained. People continued to come and gaze at the house, to point to the man when he emerged. It was too much for a man long used to admiration and respect.

Boon Haw made a decision that was to have far-reaching effects on the family and on his business in the years to come. He decided to leave Rangoon. He had a ready-made refuge in Singapore. The hand of providence must have been guiding his hand that night in the club when the flick of a card had won him twenty thousand dollars and, indirectly, a house. And it could not be anything but a good omen for him that every Singapore currency note bore an image of his namesake. He would start another Tiger Balm operation in Singapore. It would far surpass Rangoon in time. Boon Par was against the idea. He protested, "Why should we go to another country? Our roots are here. Our home is here and we have done very well for ourselves in Burma. I know you are still suffering the disgrace done to us. I, too, have suffered. But we will live it down. It will soon be forgotten."

Boon Haw was not persuaded.

Piah Hong refused to accompany her husband. She would rather return to her beloved Penang. At the back of her mind was also the fear that she would have to meet Kyi Kyi who was bound to go with Boon Haw. Worse still, she might even have to live with her.

"I shall remain in Rangoon with the boys if you will not allow me to go to Penang," Piah Hong told her husband.

Boon Haw did not insist. He would be very happy if the two women could be friends. But he would not lose any sleep over Piah Hong's intransigence. She would have to come around sooner or later. There was no way he would give up the girl who had become such an important part of his life.

Boon Haw installed Kyi Kyi in the house in Tanglin Road. It seemed so huge after the modest flat above the shop. She was overawed. "The house is so big it frightens me," she said.

Boon Haw gave her an indulgent smile. "You are the mistress and there will be as many servants as you like to do the work."

It did not take Kyi Kyi long to settle in. The doting husband engaged two maids to be at her beck and call and one more to cook the meals. She missed Rangoon and her relatives, but her new life with all its freedom more than made up for it. The other wife was a thousand miles away. Piah Hong was no longer a constraint.

The new household established, Boon Haw was impatient to set up a shop. It was his wish to use Singapore as a base for Malaya and the East Indies. Until he built a new factory all his supplies would come from Rangoon.

He found a two-storey shophouse in Amoy Street, in the heart of the Chinese business district. Two employees from Rangoon were put in charge of the shop and some local workers. One week after taking possession, Boon Haw opened his shop for business. Eng Aun Tong now had a home in Singapore.

Eleven

Ships of every description, from sleek liners carrying dreamers to the fabled East to grimy coastal tramps and unwieldy junks that plied the humid Malay archipelago, called at Singapore at one time or another. The swampy fishing village that Stamford Raffles had acquired from the Sultan of Johore one hundred years earlier for less than the cost of a tramp, had developed into the busiest entrepot in the region, a mecca for ships from the four corners of the earth.

The Western industrialised countries, particularly Britain and Holland, shipped their finished products to Singapore to be distributed to one of the many thousands of islands that made up the East Indies. Produce such as spices and raw materials such as rubber and tin were brought to this great port to be processed, repacked and shipped with its value increased a hundredfold.

Seamen had found Tiger brand medicines a useful and in many ways an effective stand-by on the high seas. They were seldom without a supply when they sailed. Inevitably, they introduced the virtues of the medicines to the natives of whichever island they happened to trade with. In time the natives became dependent on Tiger Balm and its stablemates. The more astute among the seaman turned this dependency into a lucrative sideline. Not only did they sell Tiger Balm to natives for cash, many conducted barter trade with the medicine as the medium.

Until Eng Aun Tong established itself in Singapore, these seamen had obtained their supplies from Chinese medicine shops. Stocks were limited then and the seamen could never get enough.

Now they no longer needed to ingratiate themselves to gain the favour of the medicine shop proprietors, but they could obtain much larger quantities at a lower cost. Boon Haw's prices to the trade or to individuals who bought in quantities were the same. "Why not?" he countered when asked to account for this. "Their money is of the same colour, isn't it?" As far as Boon Haw was concerned, whoever bought his medicines was a favoured customer; the more he bought the more favoured be became.

Merchants who used to travel all the way to Rangoon now came to Singapore for Tiger Balm. Javanese merchants and assorted seamen vied to obtain supplies from Singapore. It was little wonder that the branch was constantly running out of stock. Whenever possible, and he often made it possible at the expense of the local shops, Boon Haw favoured the enterprising sailors and the traders from the Indies.

Without the traders from Java, Chinese and Javanese alike, Tiger Balm could not have established such widespread use on the island. In that one island alone, there were an estimated forty million potential users. If the whole archipelago was considered, a grouping which included Sumatra, Borneo, the Moluccas, Celebes and Java, there would be over one hundred million people who might conceivably be customers. If these traders and sailors were helping to spread the popularity of his medicines, often at great risk to themselves from encounters with pirates, Boon Haw reasoned that they deserved more consideration. Much more. After all, they were staking their lives to enrich him.

Within a few months of his opening the Singapore branch, Boon Haw had accumulated fat accounts with the Oversea Chinese Banking Corporation and the Ho Hong Bank. With this initial success grew a resolve to develop the Singapore end of the business to surpass the operation in Rangoon. It was as good a way as any to tell those concerned that Aw Boon Haw could do very well without Rangoon. The bitterness lingered.

On one of his trips to Rangoon, Boon Haw told his brother, "As

I am spending most of my time in Singapore I think it would be best for all concerned if I took Piah Hong and the boys with me." Boon Haw had, in fact, decided to pull up roots and make his new home in Singapore. A permanent home, with or without his brother. But it was not time to tell his less adventurous brother.

"But Piah Hong does not like Singapore," Boon Par reminded his brother. His sister-in-law was the last good reason for Boon Haw not to forsake Rangoon. "And there is bound to be trouble between her and Kyi Kyi," he added.

"No one can really say he does not like a place until he has seen it," Boon Haw replied. "Where Kyi Kyi is concerned, I think Piah Hong will have to face the fact that she is not going out of my life. The sooner she realises this the better it will be for her. I am taking her to Singapore when I return there next week."

Piah Hong allowed herself to be persuaded. She came to live in Singapore towards the end of 1923, one year after Kyi Kyi. It was to be her home for the rest of her life. She was thirty-eight years old, more than a little overweight, but still youthful in appearance. Life had been kind to her where her material needs were concerned. Kyi Kyi had been a bitter pill to swallow and four years was a long time to nurse a hatred.

Boon Haw had prepared Kyi Kyi well for her first meeting with Piah Hong. "You must try to show some humility and defer to her as much as you can," he told her. "Remember, she is so much older than you and you must therefore show her all the respect that is her due. Treat her like your older sister," Boon Haw told the seventeen-year-old mistress of the house.

"What shall I do if she assaults me?"

After eighteen years of marriage, Boon Haw knew of Piah Hong's temper and her strength. He had not forgotten her extraordinary feat in helping him move their safe during the fire of so many years ago. He had seen Piah Hong slap a maid for misbehaving and send the girl reeling across the room. But he was confident she would be sufficiently gracious to receive the young

Kyi Kyi in a more friendly manner. "I don't think she will," he assured her. "I shall be with you when she arrives and I shall see to it that nothing happens."

The time for the long-overdue confrontation was here. Piah Hong had taken her sons, Aw Kow and Aw Swan, now nine and eight respectively, to Penang for a visit on her way to Singapore.

The sea voyage from Rangoon was a joy to the boys but an ordeal to the mother. Seasickness confined her to her cabin. The two maids who accompanied the family took turns comforting her. Compared to the sea trip, the tedious train journey to Singapore was a blessing in spite of the monotony, heat, dust and specks of coal in the eye.

Two employees of Eng Aun Tong met the train when it pulled in at Tanjong Pagar. A convoy of rickshaws then conveyed Piah Hong's entourage and a mountain of luggage to the house in Tanglin Road.

The boys ran into the house to explore their new home. Piah Hong mounted the three marble steps leading to the main doorway with reluctant steps.

Boon Haw helped her up the last step and led her into the hall. He seated his wife in one of two beautifully carved rosewood chairs separated by a tall table of similar design. The chairs were works of art, but were also hard and uncomfortable.

A maid servant appeared with a lacquered tray holding a pot of tea and two porcelain cups without handles. She set this down on the table between the chairs. Piah Hong wondered where her young rival could be. She had expected Kyi Kyi to offer her a welcoming cup of tea as soon as she arrived. But now it seemed a mere servant was to do her the honours.

"This is Eldest Boss Lady," Boon Haw told the servant. She was a woman in her forties and dressed in the manner of her profession; spotless white blouse starched stiff and loose black trousers. Her still jet black hair was braided into a thick queue which hung down her back to her waist. "This is Ah Woon, the chief housemaid,"

Boon Haw told his wife. "Ah Woon, go upstairs and ask Second Boss Lady to join us."

The servant took it as a matter of course that the woman she had all along addressed as "Boss Lady" was now to be demoted to Second Boss Lady. She had previously worked in a household where there were six boss ladies. But no matter how many women the boss married, a servant would address each as "Boss Lady" without appending whichever position she held in the matrimonial hierarchy. It would be grave discourtesy otherwise.

"Boss Lady, the boss invites you to join him and the other Boss Lady downstairs," Ah Woon said to Kyi Kyi who had gone upstairs when the first rickshaw puller had deposited his burden under the house porch. She was all nerves as she awaited the summons to appear before the woman who had so long intimidated her. Steeling herself and determined to face whatever was in store for her, she followed Ah Woon downstairs.

The good servant had been briefed on what was required though it was nothing new for her. She had witnessed confrontations between an old and a new wife and was quite prepared for this. But there was a difference in this particular meeting. Whereas it had always been the new wife coming to pay obeisance to the elder wife in the latter's home, the present called for an elder wife coming into the house of the junior missus to lord it over her. Ah Woon braced herself for whatever the outcome.

The servant poured some tea into the dainty little cup and handed it to Kyi Kyi who stood some distance away, making every effort to avoid the older woman's eye. Boon Haw sat in the other chair and watched without a word. He was confident that Kyi Kyi would acquit herself satisfactorily after his coaching. Kyi Kyi held the cup with both hands and approached Piah Hong as one would approach an ogre. She glanced quickly over the cup half hiding her face and found Piah Hong's eyes staring at her.

Kyi Kyi would have fled upstairs had she not heard Boon Haw's voice gently urging her to do her duty. Piah Hong said not a word nor did she give any sign that Kyi Kyi's presence before her was unwelcome. The younger woman, in order to get over the ordeal as quickly as possible shuffled the few remaining steps towards Piah Hong. Still holding the cup of tea before her and striving not to spill the contents, the seventeen-year-old second wife knelt before her thirty-eight-year-old senior and said in a trembling voice, "Elder sister, please drink a cup of tea."

Boon Haw looked on with approval. He shifted his gaze to his elder wife and waited in apprehension for her response. It was a crucial moment for all three. For Boon Haw, it might mean an irreconcilable difference with an unbending wife. For Piah Hong, it could possibly result in alienating the affection of her husband of eighteen years. As for Kyi Kyi, her status in the family would be assured if Piah Hong accepted the tea; if she did not, she supposed they would live in enmity the rest of their lives. Boon Haw had seldom wanted anybody to do anything more. He wanted Piah Hong to accept Kyi Kyi's offering with all his heart.

Through the centuries, Chinese men have taken secondary wives with consequences mostly amiable rather that hateful. Piah Hong suddenly realised that her husband was only following tradition. He was no better nor worse than those who had preceded him. She was tired of nursing a hostility which seemed to affect no one but herself. Piah Hong had two choices – reject Kyi Kyi's gesture and risk her husband's anger, or be gracious and accept the offering for her own peace of mind.

She looked at her husband as if to say "you fickle man, I'm doing this for you who do not deserve it" and, stretching out a chubby hand encrusted with diamond rings, lifted the cup and drank.

Kyi Kyi accepted the empty cup with a grateful nod for she was too overcome for speech. She stood up and handed the cup to Ah Woon who was witness to this conciliation between the wives. Kyi Kyi fled upstairs to her room to cry for joy and relief. Boon Haw uttered an appreciation which was lost on Piah Hong. She was trying to reconcile the fact that she had swallowed her pride and acknowledged a mere girl as her peer. The husband made a silent promise to buy Piah Hong the biggest diamond he could find in Singapore as much for Piah Hong's magnanimity as in his relief of avoiding a very traumatic confrontation. His relief was perhaps greater than Kyi Kyi's.

With his wives and children together again, family life resumed. To give greater effect to his new domicile, Boon Haw enrolled his sons in a Chinese school. A rickshaw puller was hired to take his boys to school each morning and to wait there until classes finished in the afternoon. He was to pull no one else until the boys were seen safely home each day.

He bought a motor car, a big thirty-horsepower Dodge from a British firm called Guthrie's. All the automobile agencies were owned by Europeans. He engaged an Indian driver because many Chinese did not take to the job. He would have engaged a Malay, who more or less monopolised the profession, but Boon Haw could not speak the language. His Indian driver, or *syce* as they were called, could understand the brand of Hindi he had picked up on the streets of Rangoon.

He joined clubs but picked only those which he considered would further his ends, both personal and business. In clubbing he favoured those with limited membership which assured exclusivity. He wooed publicity at every turn but was always on guard against intrusion into his private life. This contradictory attitude only served to fan the slightest gossip surrounding his behaviour. This in turn made him become even more jealous of his privacy. It was not always possible to find a private club which could treat a member's activities within its walls with any degree of privacy.

With social position – Boon Haw was a celebrity thanks to the fame of his Tiger Balm – came social obligations. In this respect he was less discriminating than in his choice of clubs. He continued to build up a reputation for philanthropy. He contributed to school building funds; but only to Chinese schools. "We must do what we can to perpetuate our language and culture in foreign lands" was a theme he often espoused to his less concerned compatriots. "The government builds schools to teach a language to serve its own ends. We are Chinese, not English. We should first learn our own language properly and then learn a foreign tongue if necessary. We must contribute towards building as many Chinese schools as we need and to their upkeep for as long as it is needed."

Chinese education had been a pet interest since the time when prosperity had begun to smile upon him in ever greater measure. In Singapore, he had been a benefactor since 1920, the year he had acquired his Tanglin Road residence. Promoters of the Singapore Chinese High School, destined to be one of the finest Chinese schools in the region, had approached him for a donation. He was told that one of the supporters was the Sugar King of the East, Oei Tiong Ham. Oei was even richer and with far wider business interests than the Tiger Balm King. Feeling that he was in good company, Boon Haw contributed four thousand dollars.

Tiger Balm outgrew its premises in Amoy Street within a year of its occupancy. Its staff had grown to ten. A few more expatriates from Rangoon had been added; Harban Singh, the *jaga*, had sent for his wife and son from the Punjab. The business needed to move into more commodious quarters.

When Boon Haw decided to make Singapore his main base, he had set out to find a manufacturing facility to lease. Rangoon just could not match the increasing demand for medicines any longer. To manufacture locally meant not only ready and abundant supplies, but also a great saving in transport and handling charges. The search proved fruitless. What was available was either too small to suit his requirements or too far from labour-abundant areas. Workers were not prepared to travel long distances to work. There was no public transportation. The most common form of transport for workers was the bicycle. But even bicycles were beyond the means of workers labouring in the low-paying factory that Boon Haw envisaged.

Boon Haw decided to build his own factory-cum-headquarters. That would take time. There was the matter of acquiring a site near to where potential workers lived. An architect had to be found, and a contractor who would not cheat. Red tape had also to be overcome, but Boon Haw was prepared to pay the bribes expected. The whole project would take at least a year, probably longer.

Meanwhile, the shop in Amoy Street was cramped each time a cargo arrived. There were now six expatriates living in the shop. Four of them slept on camp beds placed along the passageway. Boon Haw had not learned to trust his local employees. Until the new factory came into being, there was urgent need to find bigger accommodation for merchandise and manpower.

Boon Haw found his new shop not far from his Amoy Street premises. He paid a substantial sum in "tea money" to induce the sitting tenant to vacate in his favour. It was a much bigger and newer building situated on a street fringing the Chinese merchants' enclave.

This new business address in Cecil Street served him well until his own modern building was completed two years later.

The year Boon Haw moved into his second shop in 1924 was also the year he acquired another wife – a third wife nineteen years after Piah Hong and only five after Kyi Kyi. He was then forty-two years old.

Twelve

E ach time Boon Haw visited Rangoon, and each time he
returned to Singapore, he would stop over in Penang for
some rest and recreation. The island saw so much of him,
or vice versa, for a variety of reasons. The only safe and reliable
route between Rangoon and Malaya was by sea, and Penang was
the nearest Malayan port to the Burmese city. His very first
Malayan visit when he was a bachelor had begun in Georgetown
and memories of the good times he enjoyed had lingered. The
scenery was beyond compare, the food as good as any gourmet
could expect and the people most hospitable.

In no other place which he had visited could Boon Haw find
diversions as varied and satisfying as in Penang. It was indeed a
paradise for the jaded businessman. If one needed opium to buck
up one's spirit, one could ask for the smoking paraphernalia to be
brought into one's room, or else an opium den was always a short
rickshaw ride away. So was a gambling den, for whatever stakes
one chose to play. You named your game and it would be waiting.
Almost anything could be arranged for some money.

Nowhere else in Malaya was Boon Haw's favourite diversion
more palatable than that to be found in this "Pearl of the Orient."
It was indeed his favourite playground. There was never any lack
of partners to participate in the games he liked to play.

The two women with him were sisters nicknamed "Black
Snake" and "White Snake," after two famous female characters in
Chinese mythology. Black Snake, the elder, was twenty and dusky

for a Chinese. White Snake's complexion was the colour of polished rice. She was eighteen. Seen together, their nicknames were appropriate. Dusky or fair, they were uncommon tarts. Boon Haw favoured the fair and well endowed. But White Snake the desirable was not available without Black Snake. So Boon Haw broke his own rule, and he did not regret it. Black Snake proved to be a charmer with few equals.

"I feel very relaxed whenever I am in Penang," he said as one sister massaged his legs while the other rubbed his forehead with Tiger Balm.

"Then why don't you stay here longer. You come for a few days and then you are gone again," Black Snake said.

"Why don't you make a second home here?" White Snake added. "You can easily afford it and you will not have to live in a hotel where there are so many other people that you cannot have the privacy you desire."

"A home is not complete without a wife," Boon Haw replied. "Besides, I already have two wives in Singapore."

"Our father had four wives. And he was not a rich man," Black Snake said. "We would not be sharing this bed with you if he had not left us destitute. You are rich enough to have as many wives as you wish. Men are lucky."

"You should marry a wife in Penang," White Snake added. "Then you can make another home here. No more hotels. No more avoiding people you do not want to meet."

Improbable as it seemed, were they suggesting that he give them up in favour of a wife? Or were they hinting that he should marry one of them? He was not prepared to take the first course. The second was unthinkable.

"Are you tired of me already?" he asked in jest. "Or do I have to marry one of you to keep you both?"

"Oh, no!" Black Snake said. "It is always the man who tires of the woman. As for marrying one of us, you know that you will be the laughing stock of all your friends if you marry a woman who sleeps with a man for money."

"Then who do you suggest I should marry?" Boon Haw asked.

"With your money there should be no difficulty. Not even if you are an old man. And you are not old."

"Or sickly or ugly," White Snake added.

"But do you realise that if I have a wife here I shall have to tell you both to go away? You will not get any more money from me. You are only doing yourselves harm talking in this way. I do pay you very well, don't I?"

"More than we could ever expect," Black Snake said. "And you have also been very kind to us, bringing us presents and those special foods from Burma. My mother said the salted fish you brought from Rangoon was the best she had ever eaten."

"Then why do you want to marry me off?"

"You have become like an uncle to us. Someone we are very fond of. And we would like you to enjoy the comforts of a home, with a wife to attend to your needs. We are not trying to get rid of you. It is more like trying to make an uncle happy. People would think what we are saying is stupid. It is like robbing ourselves."

To humour them Boon Haw said, "All right, I'll try to find a wife."

"We can help you find one," White Snake said. "Our mother has some matchmaker friends. What kind of girl do you like? Black or white like us?"

Black Snake laughed at her sister's joke. Boon Haw also laughed. To humour her further, he said, "Go ahead. Ask your mother to find a wife for me. I shall give her a big *ang pow*."

"Yes, I'll ask mother tonight. But what must the girl be like?"

"As long as she is an *anak darah* (virgin) I don't mind."

"And do we also get an *ang pow* when you find your virgin wife?"

Did they indeed. It turned out that Boon Haw was so pleased with this third wife that he set up the sisters in a little shop of their own.

Madam Ooi was a third generation Nonya. Her knowledge of the customs and traditions of the Babas and Nonyas was well known. She was an acknowledged authority on Nonya weddings and for this reason was often pressed by friends and relatives to be the mistress of ceremonies at weddings.

Mistressing and matching were allied functions and it was therefore not surprising that Bibi Ooi also earned an income matching up people.

Her husband was a local-born who preferred to be identified as a true-blue Chinese speaking the Hokkien dialect rather than a Baba mouthing a bastardised version of the language. He cultivated a speech that was as pure Amoy Hokkien as he could make. He looked and behaved more like a *sinkeh* from China than a Peranakan, to the embarrassment of his family. He carried his chauvinism to the extent of keeping a queue, which grew thinner as he grew older and which eventually resembled a pig's tail. Where others strove to shed the ways of the old country and become localised, he was proud to look and behave like a Chinaman.

The apple of the couple's eye was their younger daughter, a gentle sixteen-year-old named Geik Cheah. Like most Nonya maidens, Geik Cheah never went to school, but was taught what was regarded as more vital to a girl than reading and writing. She learned to cook the dishes for which the Nonyas were famous. She learned to sew and to keep a scrupulously tidy house. She was taught the art of attending to a husband's comfort and well-being.

Bibi Ooi was determined to equip this daughter, like she had done for her elder girl, with all the womanly virtues that made a man feel most appreciative. She loved her child deeply and like all fond mothers she would do everything possible to ensure her Geik Cheah got a good match. Now, the time had come.

Black Snake and her sister gave most of their earnings to their mother. Their last visit with Boon Haw had been especially rewarding.

He had been amused by their offer to find him a wife. Amused and touched. He had given them a bonus for offering a service beyond what was expected of them. Now, as they handed the money over to their mother, Black Snake said, "He has been very kind and generous to us. We like him. And we would like to do him a favour."

"What more could you do for him? What more could a woman give a man than her body?" The mother was indignant.

"He is looking for another wife. To live in Penang and to look after him whenever he comes."

"Do you girls realise that once he has found a wife here, he will not want to see either of you again? You may not find another patron who is so generous," the mother said.

White Snake, only eighteen but already worldly-wise, said, "I don't think so, Mama. Men, especially the rich ones, will fool with women no matter how many wives they have. They will be faithful for a while. And then they will want other women. They cannot be expected to eat the same food every day. I'm sure he will be even more generous if we find him a wife."

If anything could make the mother share her daughter's viewpoint, it was the thought of a fat matchmaker's fee from the millionaire. "Does he have a matchmaker?" she asked.

"That's where you come in, Mama," Black Snake said. "We told the man that our mother had many friends who were matchmakers. You will help to find him a girl through your friends, won't you, Mama?"

"As long as I get a big *ang pow*, I'll be happy to do it. I'll start looking today." The mother smiled and added, "He'll be good for at least one hundred dollars."

The mother of the "snakes" set out to look up a matchmaker friend that same afternoon. It began to rain before she was half-way there. The rain came down in torrents and her waxed paper umbrella was no match for the deluge. A rickshaw ride would cost at least twenty cents and that would be a waste. She therefore sought shelter in a coffee shop where twenty cents would buy her ten cups of *kopi O*. Being a coffee addict, she soaked her system with caffeine at every excuse. There could be no better excuse than being caught in the rain and waiting for it to stop.

She met an acquaintance who was also sheltering from the rain. Over several cups of *kopi O* with each successive cup coming blacker and stronger, the women gossiped. The acquaintance happened to be a part-time matchmaker known as Bibi Neo. She offered to help when she learned that the famous Tiger Balm millionaire was looking for a *seh ee* or junior wife. "I am on my way to deliver some *batik sarongs* to Bibi Ooi," she said. "She's a well-known matchmaker and should have a list of *anak darahs* seeking husbands."

"Bibi" was a refined form of address for older Nonyas. Bibi Ooi not only knew of several mothers-in-law-to-be, but she herself was one. She had set her sights higher than most mothers for her daughter Geik Cheah. She could afford to pick and choose. Geik Cheah was only sixteen and even ugly ducklings had found handsome husbands by way of a handsomer dowry. Even husbands could be bought if one was desperate enough and the parents had the means.

But Geik Cheah was different. She was pretty. More than that, she had a very fair skin, the hallmark of true beauty, an asset which would stand a girl in good stead if all else failed. Where Geik Cheah was concerned, Bibi Ooi could well afford to be complacent.

Bibi Neo arrived at Bibi Ooi's house from the coffee shop half an hour early. The *sarongs* were delivered with much appreciation. They were specially imported from Batavia which produced the best *batik* cloth. Her original mission accomplished, Bibi Neo lingered over more *kopi O* to talk shop. She gradually coursed her conversation to the subject of a millionaire on the lookout for a wife. "He is looking for a third wife," she said. "He comes to Penang on business very often and would like to have a wife living in

Penang. I am sure you have heard of him. This man's name is Aw Boon Haw."

Who had not heard of him? Every one of her friends used Tiger Balm. She herself used Tiger Balm. Every Tiger Balm wrapper carried a picture of the man and his brother. But just to be sure she heard right, Bibi Ooi asked, "Did you say Aw Boon Haw?"

"Yes."

"The Tiger Balm *towkay*?"

"The same."

"Why does he want another wife?"

"They say he wants many heirs of his own blood. His two sons are adopted." This could all be true. It was also as good a reason as any.

Bibi Ooi thought for a moment and asked, "How old is the man?"

"About forty. But I was told he looks like a man of thirty. Rich men always look younger than they are. Good food and plenty of it, an easy life and ginseng tonic keep them young and vigorous."

Bibi Ooi did some quick calculation. If the man was forty, he would be twenty-four years older than Geik Cheah. Her elder daughter Geik Heoh had married a man who was older by twenty-four years and they now had four children. Geik Heoh was coincidentally a third wife although her husband had been a widower when he married her. If one marriage to a man so much older had turned out to be a happy one, there was no reason why her second daughter's marriage could not be as successful. It was certainly a better match than Geik Heoh's as far as wealth was concerned. Everybody knew that Aw Boon Haw was one of the richest men in Malaya. Bibi Ooi decided that this man was an opportunity which came along once in a lifetime.

"I think I would like to match him with my daughter Geik Cheah," Bibi Ooi told Bibi Neo without preamble. "I've taught her all I know and she will make any man a good wife."

Bibi Neo was delighted. She had thought of her friend's daughter as a possible candidate. In fact, she did not know of any girl with better credentials. Any man would be proud to marry her once he had seen how fair her skin was and how healthy she looked. But she had been hesitant, afraid that her friend would take umbrage over the idea of her young daughter becoming somebody's secondary wife. But now Bibi Ooi herself had actually suggested it, her job was going to be far easier than she had thought.

Boon Haw himself did not consider a sixteen-year-old too young for him at all. Hadn't he married one three years younger? But that was neither the matchmaker's nor anybody else's business. He had been surprised when Bibi Neo appeared at his door two days after he had offhandedly agreed to the sisters' suggestion that he marry a Penang girl and set up a home in the island. The millionaire studied the photograph Bibi Neo showed him and liked what he saw. A young and pretty girl in typical Nonya garments and with elaborate Nonya hair arrangement to make her look older than she was.

"A picture tells me little," Boon Haw said. "She looks very pretty here but she may be deaf or dumb or even lame for all I know. Can I see her in person?"

It was not the proper thing for a strictly brought up maiden to face a suitor, even in the presence of a chaperone. With Geik Cheah, one had to contend with not only propriety but her intense shyness. The mere mention of a boy's name coupled with hers would make her blush to the roots of her hair. No, Bibi Ooi thought, it would send her child into a panic if she was told that she was to be presented to a prospective groom for his approval. Quite undignified, to say the least. But somehow she had to be shown to Boon Haw or the wretched man would lose interest and Geik Cheah would lose a rich husband. On top of that, she would lose a rich son-in-law. The mother decided on a ruse to show her child to the suitor.

One of the most famous places of worship in Penang was the Ayer Itam Temple. Actually, it was a collection of buildings on a hillside some five miles from Georgetown. Each building housed a different deity. Each day hundreds from near and far came to worship one god or another depending on what favours these mortals sought.

A great attraction to locals and tourists alike was the tortoise pond. It was about half-way up the steep climb to the uppermost level of the temple domain. Boon Haw had his first look at his future third wife on the terrace overlooking the pond.

Bibi Ooi had requested the matchmaker to inform Boon Haw that it would be breaking all the rules of propriety for her to bring Geik Cheah to meet him in his hotel. It would be equally unbecoming for him to present himself at the maiden's house. Since he found the normal exchange of photographs not to his approval, she would depart from normal custom and take her daughter to a neutral, but respectable, ground for him to observe her. But he was not to approach her or attempt to engage her in conversation. Would Mr Aw Boon Haw be kind enough to go to the Ayer Itam Temple the next day and make himself comfortable in the coffee bar by the tortoise pool? Mr Aw would and did.

On the day appointed for the viewing of the prospective bride, Bibi Ooi told her daughter to put on her best clothes as they were going to the temple to make some offerings. Geik Cheah was delighted when she learned they were going to Ayer Itam. It was one of her favourite places and she could never tire of watching the tortoises in the polluted pond as they clambered over one another in their clumsy attempts to get to the vegetables strewn by passers-by. There were so many of them, from tiny ones no bigger than a fist to ponderous creatures which must weigh more than she did.

Geik Cheah was eager to see the tortoises again. Her mother had bought a small tortoise from the market that morning and she was to set it free among the others as an offering to the gods. She would buy vegetables from the stall nearby to feed the reptiles and laugh at their silly antics as they tumble over one another in the rush. It was going to be a very happy day for her.

Geik Cheah chose a pink *samfoo* outfit trimmed with maroon-coloured lace on the edges. It was an appropriate colour for pink was auspicious for betrothals, but she was not told of the true reason for the outing. She braided her long tresses with special care as her mother had told her. She tied a pink ribbon to the end of her braid and made it into a little bow, and hummed a happy tune.

Bibi Neo was waiting near the bridge leading to the temple when Geik Cheah and her mother arrived in a rickshaw. It was a hot day. She had an umbrella over her head. As soon as she saw Geik Cheah she rushed forward and held the umbrella over the girl. "You must not expose yourself to the sun," she said. "It will burn you black like a coolie woman and no man will give you a second look." Turning to the mother she asked, "Have you eaten, Bibi? If you have not I would like to treat you and your daughter to some *laksa* after Mr Aw Boon Haw has left us."

"We all love *laksa*. That would be very nice, thank you. Is Mr Aw Boon Haw here yet?"

"He arrived even before me. I shall go ahead and tell him you are here."

Mother and daughter began the fateful walk to the pond. Vendors lined the route. They sold the usual items that visitors bought as souvenirs and promptly discarded when they reached home. A kiosk half-way up the path offered the specialities for which Penang was noted: shrimp paste, salted fish and a smelly concoction called *blachan*. A few feet away was a pile of durians, a spiky fruit with an awful smell but whose taste addicted those who dared to sample it. An old man selling the fruit split a durian and invited Geik Cheah to help herself. But the smell of durians mixed with that of *blachan* was too much for them and they hurried past the stall.

Bibi Neo met them again at the foot of the steps leading up to the pond. "Mr Aw Boon Haw will be looking out for you and your daughter. As you have requested, he will not approach you. Just behave naturally and stay near the pond for as long as possible, or until I come and tell you that Mr Aw has left." Bibi Ooi climbed the last few steps as casually as she knew how with her daughter in tow. Geik Cheah headed straight for the pond. It was dirty. The water was a slimy green caused by rotting vegetation and tortoise waste. Huge boulders protruding out of the water served as platforms for the reptiles to sun themselves. Tortoises big and small churned the water to fight for the vegetables thrown to them. Nearby was a man selling *kangkong*, a vegetable favoured by the reptiles. One catty costs one cent. Geik Cheah bought five cents worth and was set for half an hour of delight.

A short distance away, a prosperous-looking gentleman took equal pleasure in observing innocence at play. Boon Haw watched while Geik Cheah frolicked, oblivious of the stares and smiles of approval directed at her. After a while Bibi Ooi came up to her and said, "Geik Cheah, why don't you release the tortoise now? It must be hungry."

She handed the girl a paper bag containing the reptile. "Don't forget to make a wish before you let it go. I have asked the temple keeper to write your name on its shell." Geik Cheah peered into the bag and saw her name written in red paint which had not quite dried.

The little tortoise scrambled into the dirty water and was immediately lost to view. Where other girls would wish for a rich and handsome husband, it would be safe to assume that Geik Cheah wished for another early opportunity to come and play with the tortoises.

The Tiger had spotted the girl immediately as she emerged from the lower yard. It was easy to tell she was the one, even among so many other girls who were in the vicinity. She was indeed the fairest-skinned girl he had seen. Pretty as most girls in their first bloom are, but not beautiful. A well-fed figure which he appreciated in a woman. Most of all, this fair maiden was the most refreshing thing he had seen in a long time; since Kyi Kyi five years ago. She was younger than Kyi Kyi by two years. But Kyi Kyi had been three years younger when she became his wife. Now he was about to marry another girl who was not much older. Boon Haw had decided that Geik Cheah was to become his third wife.

The matchmaker hovering nearby hastened towards Boon Haw when the latter waved to her. "I have seen enough of the girl and I think she will make a good wife," he said.

"Now I want you to tell Bibi Ooi that I will marry her daughter. Please give her this *ang pow* as a token of my intention." The token turned out to be four hundred dollars, but the curious Bibi Neo was not to know it as Bibi Ooi did not open the unusually large red packet until she had reached home.

The millionaire reached into his pocket and brought out another *ang pow*. "This is for you," he said to the matchmaker who eagerly accepted it. "It is for the part you played today. There will be a proper one for the marriage later." This was the carrot to make the matchmaker outmatch all her past efforts. "I want you to come to my hotel this evening to discuss the plans."

Boon Haw left the temple without asking to meet his intended mother-in-law or his wife-to-be. He was confident Bibi Neo would do what was necessary.

Three happy women adjourned to a nearby coffee shop for refreshments. Bibi Ooi was happy because she was about to become the mother-in-law of a millionaire. Bibi Neo was happy because she had just received a generous *ang pow* with the promise of a far larger one to come. Geik Cheah was happy to have seen her tortoises and to be now enjoying her second bowl of *laksa*.

"Tell me what you know about the Ooi family," Boon Haw asked the matchmaker when she visited his hotel that evening.

Her clients had been mostly working-class people whose fees were modest but who made heavy demands on matchmakers. She had never in her wildest dreams expected to be in such close proximity to a millionaire, much less to be making a match for him. She had been in a state of awe since their first meeting. It was only the constant thought of earning the biggest fee of her career that made her gather her wits about and behave like a matchmaker should.

"The Ooi family is very honoured that you have asked to marry their daughter Geik Cheah. Bibi Ooi told me just now that she would like her daughter to be married in the proper Chinese manner. Do you have any objections?"

"I have no objections as long as it is reasonable. But you have not told me what I want to know."

The matchmaker told Boon Haw as much as she knew about the Ooi family. She gave a brief description of all that she knew for each member of the household, omitting only the opium habit of an errant son called Ah Bah. She added that they were very genteel and respectable people and, as their daughter was to be only a secondary wife, Bibi Ooi was very anxious that she should be properly married so that people would not say that she was nothing more than a rich man's mistress.

Boon Haw replied that he appreciated that. He, too, would like a proper marriage so that any child of theirs would be duly recognised as his legitimate heirs. Bibi Neo indulged in a private smile when she heard this. She had let Bibi Ooi believe that the Tiger Balm boss was marrying again because he wanted his own children. He was now confirming her guess.

"Are they well off?"

"They are not rich. But they are not poor either. Just ordinary people but highly respected. The father is a physician. He is quite old. They are now living with relatives as they had to sell their house recently."

Boon Haw deduced that the family must be in humble

circumstances if they were required to live with relatives. That did not suit him at all. He would prefer them to be living in a house of their own. His private life was his own and he abhorred inquisitive relatives prying into his affairs. He made one of his instant decisions.

"Listen carefully to me," he said. "I want you to tell Bibi Ooi to move into another house as soon as possible. No one is to live with her except her husband and her daughter. And a servant. If there is no servant, ask her to get one. I shall pay her wages ..."

Bibi Neo interrupted to say she did not think Bibi Ooi could afford to rent a house.

"Please don't interrupt until I have finished. It is important that the Ooi family move into another house as soon as possible. I know it is sudden and they may not be able to afford it. I am going to give you some money to take to her. It is for the house. If it is not enough please ask Bibi Ooi to see a good friend of mine." Boon Haw handed the matchmaker a business card of one of his Penang dealers. He then gave her four hundred dollars to be delivered to Bibi Ooi. The woman's eyes popped at the sight of so much money. It was not only sufficient to pay a whole year's rent on a bungalow but there would be enough left to furnish it.

"I have to return to Singapore in a day or two."

Rebuked but uncowed, for she was determined to earn the matchmaker's fee, Bibi Neo interrupted once again, "So soon? What about your marriage to Bibi Ooi's daughter?"

"Please hear me out. As I said, I am returning to Singapore soon. I have some very important matters to attend to. But I shall be back in two weeks. When I come back, I expect to visit them in their new house without relatives around."

"Would you like me to proceed with arrangements for your marriage when you return? Would you like me to go to the temple and ask for an auspicious day?"

"That won't be necessary. Just go and do as I have told you.

Convey my regards to Bibi Ooi and her daughter. I shall get in touch with you again when I return. Go now and thank you for all your trouble. I am expecting visitors."

Bibi Neo passed Black Snake and White Snake on her way out. She knew they were on their way to see the millionaire, but she had not expected them to be the visitors he mentioned. "I must not gossip about this until he is safely married to Bibi Ooi's daughter," she made a silent resolution. Well she should, for the marriage could well be cancelled if news of the millionaire's indiscretion reached Bibi Ooi's ears. She would take it as an unmitigated affront to her and to her daughter's dignity. The matchmaker would be left with no *ang pow*.

Boon Haw returned to Penang exactly two weeks later. In that time he had accomplished more than he thought possible. He had acquired a site for the construction of his new factory and headquarters. Mr Lee, the landowner he had met in the club in Keong Saik Road, had recommended an architect who was now busy drawing up plans of the building.

He had much to be happy for, besides the anticipation of acquiring another wife so young and innocent, business was better than even he could wish. When the new factory was completed, profits could be expected to sky-rocket. It would be capable of producing ten times Rangoon's capacity; that was one of the vital considerations the architect must take into account.

Kyi Kyi had not raised too much of a fuss when he told her he was returning to Penang so soon after the last visit. She was unhappy but not insistent when Boon Haw told her she could not accompany him. She had not suspected anything. Neither had Piah Hong, who, since the day she arrived had not felt comfortable living in the same house with Kyi Kyi. She had come to regard Boon Haw's comings and goings as a matter of course. It was therefore a very happy millionaire who stepped off the ferry and climbed into a gharry for the ride to the hotel.

He was about to marry another young wife. The thought of enjoying her favours was enough to make him go limp with desire. As a result he allowed himself to be subjected to what he called silly rites when he and Geik Cheah were married a few days later.

He moved into the house with his new in-laws. Bibi Ooi had succeeded in renting a modest but gracious house in the heart of Georgetown. It was one of the few detached houses remaining in busy Penang Road. The structure was a two-storey affair of brick and timber. It sat some distance away from the road and was surrounded by a high brick wall. Boon Haw approved the choice for two reasons: it was well situated and the high walls ensured privacy.

His honeymoon lasted two weeks. He would have prolonged this new-found bliss but was too impatient to find out what progress the architect had made. Now that he had committed himself to the building, he was anxious to hasten its completion.

Boon Haw returned to Singapore to be confronted by a sullen and silent Kyi Kyi. As she refused to speak, he thought her bad mood was due to a tiff she must have had with Piah Hong. But during dinner she and the elder wife talked with no apparent signs of rancour on either side. Kyi Kyi was as respectful as she could be towards her senior who, despite the resentment she harboured towards the younger woman, had condescended to be more agreeable. Boon Haw was puzzled. He tried to draw out the reason from Kyi Kyi by making small talk but the woman remained tightlipped.

Still the doting husband, he bought Kyi Kyi a three-carat diamond the next day as a peace offering. Kyi Kyi accepted the sparkling stone with an expression totally opposite to the lustre of the diamond. Her attitude was beginning to annoy him, and it was only his great affection for her that prevented his temper from flaring. Nothing he said or did seemed able to dissipate the sullenness in her. "What have I done or said to make you put on a face you see only in funerals?" he demanded.

"You should know," she finally snapped at him.

"I don't know. Tell me."

"You should know. You old philanderer!"

For Boon Haw, it was the last straw. He thundered, "What do you mean, calling me such a shameful name?" It was the first time in their married life Boon Haw had raised his voice at her. But his quick mind grasped the situation the next instant.

Kyi Kyi continued before he could say another word, "You told me you were going to Penang on some important business. Two trips in one month. Two weeks away each time. And you wouldn't take me. All because you wanted to take another woman to bed. You are a lusty old man!" She spoke with a venom Boon Haw had never heard before.

For the first time ever, the thrice-married millionaire was uncomfortable, a feeling he had never had before with any of his wives. But he was far from admitting guilt. After all, was it not a man's prerogative to have as many wives or concubines as he wished, especially one as wealthy as he. It was an honourable thing he had done, to marry Kyi Kyi and Geik Cheah instead of making them his concubines. Kyi Kyi was becoming hysterical as she continued to attack Boon Haw.

"Do you remember how old I am? Eighteen. Only eighteen. Other girls of my age were still playing with dolls when you married me. Many girls of eighteen are still virgins and spinsters. But I, at eighteen, am too old for you and no longer fit to share your bed. You are a rotten egg," she spat the words at him furiously and paused to catch her breath.

Though Kyi Kyi's fury surprised Boon Haw, he was by no means chastised. "Who told you I got married in Penang?" he shouted back.

"Everybody knows. People are laughing at you for marrying girls young enough to be your daughters. Are you not ashamed of yourself?"

"Why should I be ashamed? I married Geik Cheah honourably, which is more than I can say for others who buy young girls for their bodies. She is seventeen years old (according to Chinese custom) and no longer a child. Her parents are very respectable people. Her father is a physician," Boon Haw lowered his voice, hoping Kyi Kyi would do the same.

Piah Hong, now somewhat portly after nineteen years of marriage, half of which had been in leisure and plenty, ambled into the room. She had heard the quarrel and was incensed by her husband's self-indulgence. She glared at Boon Haw and, pointing an accusing finger at him, added her rebukes to those of Kyi Kyi.

"Jee Ko, you are not a good man. You already have two wives. If you think I am old and no longer give you pleasure, Kyi Kyi is young enough to be your daughter. Do you find her no longer desirable? How can you make us lose so much face? I am very angry with you. You have no shame!"

Piah Hong had her own reasons for backing Kyi Kyi. It was humiliating enough to share her husband with another woman, namely Kyi Kyi. But to share him with two was an even more bitter pill to swallow.

Though more chauvinistic than any man could be, Boon Haw rejected the idea of telling these two angry women where their proper places were. A wife should never criticise her man but accept whatever he did in the best interests of all. He was less than remorseful. After all, like countless others before him and no doubt many more after him, he was only exercising his prerogative in taking a third wife. It was no big deal. It happened every day.

The women remained silent. Another person would have left it at that. But Boon Haw felt the need to justify himself further. "I expect Geik Cheah to bear me many sons." Immediately, he regretted his words. For the first time in his life he was really ashamed of himself.

The women retired quietly to their rooms, each to suffer her hurt alone and in tears. Boon Haw was left to squirm by himself.

If time does not always heal wounds, it does ease the pain to a bearable degree. Piah Hong had lived with her husband long enough to be philosophical about his involvement with women. First, he had allowed himself to be captivated by a mere slip of a girl and then made her intrude into their happy union. Then he had taken another young girl into his life even before Kyi Kyi had reached maturity. She prayed there would not be others to push her still further into the background.

Kyi Kyi regarded Boon Haw's insensitivity to her feelings as a personal affront. She was quite certain that he had not tired of her. But why did he do what he did? Was she to be replaced as favourite by a new wife? Not if she could help it. Although consumed with jealousy, Kyi Kyi gradually learned to live with a situation she was powerless to change. She consoled herself with the fact that she was still so young, almost as young as that wretched Geik Cheah. If she played her cards right, she would retain her premier position. She vowed to do everything within her power to remain queen of the roost.

Thirteen

B oon Haw stayed away from his beloved Penang partly in deference to the two elder wives' feelings and partly because of a new infatuation, his building project. He was a hard taskmaster who required his contractor and builders to work long hours. He could no longer wait patiently to move into his own premises. The rented shop in Cecil Street was hopelessly inadequate in every way. There was lack of storage space as well as sleeping room for his Burmese employees.

Aw Boon Haw was impatient to see the completion of his new dream. He was like a man possessed, a lover besotted. He arrived among the first at the building site each morning to personally supervise the construction of his new headquarters. He became more of a hindrance than a help, stepping on everybody's toes. He countermanded the instructions of the foreman and annoyed rather than assisted in his desire to ensure that every job was done right.

Every brick must be perfect and every beam of the best quality timber. The concrete must be mixed exactly as specified and, for good measure, he would shovel an extra quantity of cement into the mix. Driven to exasperation, a worker asked, "*Towkay*, why are you so fussy about everything?"

The reply was: "Because I want my building to stand for a thousand years." He gave the unfortunate man a withering look and added, "You don't have to come to work tomorrow." No worker ever questioned him from then on.

The contractor's capacity for absorbing Boon Haw's abuse was boundless. He was a youngish Teochew named Ng. Like many before him, Ng had migrated to Singapore with his parents who progressed from building sampans to godowns along the Singapore River. The elder Ng had some useful advice for his son before he died of malaria. "The rich often demand more than they bargained for. They like to show who is the boss. Treat their abuse like water off a duck's back and you will not feel the hurt. Humour them and they will part with their money more readily. Flatter them and they may even become friends."

The younger Ng had taken his father's advice. He listened stoically as Boon Haw ranted. His head nodded in seeming agreement when the *towkay* insisted that things should be done a certain way. But when the owner left, the contractor went back to doing things exactly the way he felt they should be done. It was the only way to treat a difficult customer.

Boon Haw was more difficult than any other client. But his was the most lucrative contract by far. Ng was not about to argue as long as progress payments were made promptly. Boon Haw paid in cash each time the architect certified the contractor's claim. In this way, work progressed steadily in spite of Boon Haw's daily interference.

The millionaire lived for the day when he could move into his new factory. The evening meal was never complete without an eloquent report on the day's progress. His sons, too young to share his enthusiasm, were indifferent. Piah Hong, who had shared his early striving, was as proud as any wife could be. Kyi Kyi was glad because it kept him in Singapore and diverted his interests from those involving other women.

Three lion troupes attended the opening of Aw Boon Haw's new headquarters. It was fitting that such a splendid building should be so honoured. The Hakka community provided a shaggy lion and a team of twelve men to prance to the heart-pounding beat of drums and shattering clash of cymbals. They were paying homage to one of their own kind.

Not to be outdone, the Hokkiens rivalled the Hakkas in celebrating the occasion with an equally monstrous lion of their own. Boon Haw might be Hakka, but he was also a son of their province. Ng, the contractor, felt that it was expected of him to contribute a lion too. He was, after all, the man who built the Tiger's new lair. It was also a gesture of gratitude as he had profited much in the contract. Ng's lion represented the Teochew community.

Each of the lions strove to outperform one another. The spectators cheered and clapped. They watched in anxiety as one after another the lions mounted a human pyramid to retrieve a prize hanging thirty feet above. The grand prize was a red packet containing one thousand dollars put up by Aw Boon Haw. It was his gesture of appreciation for the tremendous support. To his immense satisfaction, it was the Hakka lion which finally succeeded in winning the prize. One courageous, but foolhardy, lion dancer fell and broke a leg.

The new Eng Aun Tong, Aw Boon Haw's Hall of Everlasting Peace in Singapore, was indeed an impressive building. It was the biggest structure in the area at the time, situated at the junction of Neil and Craig Road. The most distinguishing feature was a cupola topping the building. Boon Haw had intended it to be a giant replica of a jar of Tiger Balm. The crowning glory was to be a metal cap painted the exact colour of the cap on the bottle of the actual ointment – a deep gold.

"This unique feature will advertise my medicine as no other medium could," the owner boasted. "Nobody can mistake the building for anything but the headquarters of Tiger Balm."

What was unique to the owner was a monstrosity to the architect. It would stand squat and ugly for all to see. But the latter was a tactful man and a prudent professional. He refrained from voicing an objection. There were other ways to show up the Tiger's poor taste.

The architect spent long hours building two scale models of

Eng Aun Tong. One carried Boon Haw's version of the cupola. As anticipated, it was a mutation of an otherwise pleasant-looking building. The architect had never been more repelled by his own handiwork.

The other cupola, as visualised by the architect, was an eye-catching piece of work. The tower-like structure supported an elegant roof gracefully curving up to an equally graceful rounded peak on which sprouted a flagmast which was to become Aw Boon Haw's standard bearer. It was hexagonal in shape just like the Tiger's precious jar holding his magic balm. This was the only concession the architect made to the millionaire's whim.

Both models were presented to the owner for approval. The man did not take long to decide which cupola would grace and which would disgrace his building. He allowed himself a rare smile and, with a rarer pat on the architect's back, said, "You are quite right. Yours is the better looking." Admitting he was wrong, even though obliquely, was perhaps the rarest of Aw Boon Haw's traits.

The interior of the cupola was to become his special preserve. He alone held the key to it. No one was allowed inside. It served as the depository for Tiger Balm's most secret ingredients. Trusted employees were taught to compound the ointment up to perhaps nine-tenths of the whole process. The vital one-tenth was prepared by Aw Boon Haw away from prying eyes. This was to ensure that no man would ever learn the complete secret of the original balm.

Reasonable quantities of the vital ingredients were prepared in advance and stored in the cupola under lock and key. Whenever required, an exact amount of the secret compound was added to a determined quantity of the mix prepared by others.

Many of the Tiger's new workers were Hakkas who were educated in Chinese. Many were placed in supervisory positions to the utter disgust of the Burmese who had loyally followed Boon Haw from Rangoon. Their knowledge of the Burmese language was of no practical use in Singapore and there was constant friction from the beginning, but none dared involve the boss with their bickering for fear of losing his job.

The third group of workers were the local-born. They were a mix of Hokkiens, Teochews, Cantonese and Hainanese. The Hainanese were also known as Hylams, a term they resented as it denoted a people who served as cooks, houseboys, waiters and other menial servants. Many of the local-born were educated in English. They were also proficient in the dialects and possessed a working knowledge of spoken Malay, the *lingua franca* of Singapore and Malaya.

As the vast majority of Eng Aun Tong's customers were Chinese, that language became the main medium of correspondence. This served Boon Haw well as he knew no other language but Chinese, besides spoken Burmese. But English was just as important even if it was not much used among the Chinese except out of necessity. The government of the day expected English to be the official medium of communication. Local firms employed English-educated clerks to attend to correspondence from the authorities. Aw Boon Haw's local-born non-Hakkas dealt with this foreign language.

Automation was still a thing of the distant future. In those days, every stage of manufacture was carried out manually, from stirring the Tiger Balm mix in huge cauldrons to packaging the finished product in packs of twelve. The whole operation was highly labour intensive, especially in the packaging department which employed eight out of every ten in the whole workforce.

Cheap labour was abundant. Women were preferred to men. They ranged in age from fourteen to forty – young girls helping to supplement the family income, housewives supporting lazy husbands and out-of-work *amahs* working to earn enough to send their pittance to hungry relatives back in China. The job called for nimble fingers. Not much muscle was needed. Nor brain. But a high degree of concentration was required to produce the daily quota expected from each. Apprentices started on twenty cents a day, gradually progressing to fifty cents when she could produce the set quota for an eight-hour shift. Paydays were on the fifteenth and last day of each month.

By far the most popular of the Tiger Brand medicines was Tiger Balm. It accounted for three-quarters of the total revenue. A crude assembly line method of production was devised for it. The women's part in its production commenced with filling the molten compound into tiny containers arranged in trays of fifty. One hand balanced the tray of rattling little jars while the other worked a tap attached to a steel cauldron holding up to ten gallons of liquid balm. It took a lot of dexterity to fill without spill. Only those women with steady hands were chosen for this job. The substance in the filled jars was allowed to cool and solidify overnight. The process of labelling and packaging began the next morning.

The packing women sat forty to a table fifty feet long. At exactly 8 am a lady supervisor swung a bell. Busy fingers began sorting out the piles of little jars of balm dumped haphazardly on the table into neat rows even before the last peal had faded. The clattering of glass on glass mixed with the chatter of a few hundred women created a continuous hum not unlike that in a busy marketplace.

The next step was capping the open containers. One hand grabbed a handful of caps from a basket nearby and the other steadied the bottle for a cap to be screwed on, one after another without pause until the handful of caps ran out. The process was repeated and in no time, the thousands of gaping jars were neatly crowned. The women took a break. Some wandered to open windows to smoke their conical-shaped cigarettes. Others sipped tea from the communal refreshment stand provided by the management. A few less seasoned workers agitated cramped fingers. The majority simply nattered.

After capping, the bottles were transferred to another table for labelling by another batch of forty women. This was a sticky job. The glue, prepared from rice flour, was applied with the finger, label by label and then stuck round the bottle. A "directions" leaflet, folded over six times, was then wrapped round the container. The leaflet contained indications and method of usage. It was printed in six languages – Chinese, Burmese, Siamese, Malay, Tamil and English. Each jar was then completely wrapped again in colourful paper. A circular seal on each end protected the product against imitators.

Finally, the wrapped articles were packaged in packs of twelve. Aw Boon Haw sold his products only by the dozen. Each package was decorated with pictures of the two brothers, each clearly identified by his own name. With sales in the millions it was little wonder that Aw Boon Haw became the most recognised man in the Orient.

By any calculation, such laborious and excessive packaging would result in an uneconomical and, therefore, unprofitable operation. The cost of labour and packaging materials exceeded that of the ingredients used. Yet, the unit price of each product was within the means of everyone. His distinctive packaging never failed to attract and to sell. This resulted in a phenomenal turnover. At its peak, Eng Aun Tong produced millions of jars of Tiger Balm alone each month. High volume, low price and availability combined to give profitability beyond the dreams of others. One product alone, namely Tiger Balm, was sufficient to make him a millionaire every few months. And those responsible for contributing so much in the building of the Aw empire were those faceless packaging women who sat huddled at their long tables eight hours a day.

Within one year of its opening, the Singapore factory produced ten times as much as Rangoon ever did. Aw Boon Haw's satisfaction for the moment would have been complete if only he had his brother to share his new office. But Boon Par chose to remain where he was. Boon Haw had no choice but to exercise patience. He was confident that he would succeed in getting the stubborn leopard over to Singapore soon.

Fourteen

There was harmony in the household. Piah Hong was less inclined to pull Kyi Kyi up for any infringement of the house rules she set. Kyi Kyi complained less and laughed more. She had recently adopted a son, Aw Hoe, on her first trip back to Rangoon. Boon Haw was not in favour at first. "You're still young, you have many childbearing years ahead of you," Boon Haw said.

Kyi Kyi insisted. "You owe me a favour in return," she said. "If you can have another wife, why can't I take a son?" Boon Haw had married Geik Cheah the previous year.

The child was four and came from a large family named Ang. He was the darkest of the siblings, but the cutest of the lot with twinkling eyes and a happy nature. The Tiger withdrew his objections when he saw how besotted his wife was with the boy. Kyi Kyi was transformed into a doting mother. The name, Aw Hoe, had been Boon Haw's choice.

Though the other boys, Aw Swan and Aw Kow, fought, then ignored him at first, they finally accepted Aw Hoe as one of them. They had little choice – Kyi Kyi lavished expensive toys on her son though Piah Hong had no intention of spoiling her boys. Aw Kow and Aw Swan went out of their way to be nice to the little fellow in order to share his playthings. Boon Haw could sigh with relief that there was now comparative peace in his household.

Ah Weng Dhobi was the best laundry shop in the Tanglin area where the Aws lived. The washing business had been a family trade for three generations. Ah Weng the proprietor continued the tradition when he migrated to Singapore from his native Canton many years ago. He washed and his wife ironed. His first customers were the British commercial types who persisted in going to their offices fully suited. As a concession to the heat they had their suits tailored in white cotton drill. They never really could keep cool even in white cotton. Clothes clung to sweaty bodies even under the whirling fan. People like Ah Weng profited when the white man sweated.

Each expatriate wore a fresh suit every day, sometimes two. Ah Weng didn't scrimp on soap, starch and labour to ensure the clothes were spotless and crisp. Stiff clothes creased less but also made the wearer perspire more, and therefore, needed more frequent washing. One could call him a calculating *dhobi*.

Ah Weng's wife was no less proud of her part in the family laundry business. She considered it a personal affront should any crease remain after struggling with the heavy iron so painstakingly heated over a charcoal fire. She was famous for the knife-edged creases on trousers and for jackets as crisp as a dollar bill fresh off the mint. The *tuans* were delighted and the *mems* recommended other *mems* to Ah Weng.

Boon Haw had discarded his tunic and now wore European-style suits to keep up with the times. The bane of his life when he first adopted the European style was the tie. He could never tie a decent knot and the silly thing often threatened to strangle him.

Until Ah Weng took over, Boon Haw's maidservant spent long hours washing and ironing his suits. But the results were not quite satisfactory to the big boss. The creases on the trousers were not quite straight; the jackets could do with a little more starch; the collar tips curled where they should be flat. The poor maid was often in tears. She threatened to leave. Piah Hong was not ready to lose the servant she had trained from the day the latter had arrived from China. She suggested that her husband's clothes be sent to a *dhobi* for washing. It was worth spending a few dollars a month so that the services of the hardest working member of the domestic staff could be retained.

Next door to the Aw residence was a vacant plot of some two acres. A poor Malay family had usurped a small area to grow tapioca. A Chinese market gardener cultivated vegetables next to the tapioca patch. The Aws obtained their supply of fresh greens from the Chinese. The rest of the neighbouring plot was taken up by poles and clothes lines. They belonged to Ah Weng the washerman. He had been using this free drying ground long before the Aws came onto the scene. The maidservant kept a lookout for Ah Weng the day after it was decided that a *dhobi* should wash her boss's clothes.

Ah Weng paid no heed to the woman's call as he bent beneath the huge weight of a big bundle of clothes. The woman called again. As Ah Weng walked on, he muttered about old maids having nothing better to do than attempt to seduce married men. Incensed by the *dhobi's* behaviour, the servant shouted over the fence, "You corpse head, why are so rude to me when I have business for you?"

Ah Weng dropped his bundle and went over to the servant bristling with indignity. "Why did you call me a corpse head?" he demanded.

"Because you are stupid."

"In what way am I stupid?"

"I have a millionaire's clothes for you to wash and you ignore me."

"Who's the millionaire?"

"My boss, the great Aw Boon Haw."

"Ah, I hear so much about him. Forgive me – I am happy to wash his clothes."

Washing a millionaire's clothes would not make a millionaire out of him. Perhaps some of the colossal luck millionaires were blessed with would rub off the rich man's clothes to rest on him. He would be contented to be just half a millionaire. He would expand his business and employ others to work for him and be spared the daily back-breaking labour. And his wife would have a woman to do her daily chores. From what he had heard, Aw Boon Haw was a generous man. He had contributed to schools and to homes for the poor and aged, donated large sums to charity and even paid the funeral expenses of the destitute. The millionaire might even grant him a loan to build up his business once he became acquainted with the excellence of Ah Weng's washing. His patronage would bring him great prestige among his peers. Indeed he would wash the Tiger's clothes. Aw Boon Haw would wear the whitest and crispest clothes in town.

The maid servant brought Ah Weng down to earth. She shouted at him, "I want you to start washing the *towkay's* clothes today, or I shall take them to another *dhobi*."

"Wah, you are such a fierce woman for a Cantonese. It must be due to working for Hakka people," the *dhobi* chided.

The maid shot him a withering look. "All right, all right, I will wash your *towkay's* clothes today," Ah Weng decided to pacify her rather than get another scolding from the fiery old dragon.

"I'll bring the clothes to you in a little while."

"No need. I'll take them now. As you are also Cantonese, I shall not only come for the clothes every day, but shall bring them back as well. I assure you of my best service to your *towkay*." It made his day when the maid gave him a smile.

Boon Haw had no more complaints. His clothes were whiter and smoother than they had ever been. The tips of his collars no longer curled up. He was happy. The maid was happy. His wives were happy as they no longer had to put up with his foul moods over badly-washed clothes.

But the episode of the impeccable raiment for the boss did not last for very long.

Ah Weng was delivering his washing as usual. He had come to look forward to the daily visit and to marvel at the lifestyle of the rich. Piah Hong handed over some money to the maid to pay him. She counted the money but the amount did not seem right for the number of pieces washed. "Ah Weng, am I not right to say that you charge five cents for each piece whether it is a coat, trousers or a shirt?" the maid asked the *dhobi*.

"That's right," Ah Weng replied.

"Then why are you charging my boss more than others? By my calculation you are charging him seven cents a piece."

"That's also right. I charge two cents more for collecting and returning the clothes."

"But that's not right. Your shop is practically next door to us. Moreover you offered to collect and return the clothes. You'd better explain it to my boss's wife. She will think that I am taking a commission from you and I will lose my job."

"I wouldn't worry about it if I were you. It is such a small matter nobody would mind or notice. Especially one so rich as Aw Boon Haw," the *dhobi* said and left.

But Piah Hong did mind. She had not forgotten their humble beginnings. Although dealing in ten-dollar bills was now an everyday affair, she had not lost respect for the coppers. Boon Haw did mind; even more so than his wife. He summoned the *dhobi* to account for the overcharging.

Ah Weng caught glimpses of the object of his admiration on a few occasions when he delivered Boon Haw's clothes to the mansion. The latter's wealth had been a source of inspiration. His visions of becoming a *towkay* himself appeared with disturbing frequency since the day he was contracted to wash the rich man's clothes. He was now actually about to meet the great man and to speak to him. He was confident of explaining away the matter of the two extra cents. Any man would be willing to pay more than two cents extra for the great care he and his wife lavished on his clothes. Ah Weng entered the Tiger's den with high hopes.

"Why do you charge me more than you charge the foreigners?" Boon Haw asked the *dhobi* as soon as he appeared. Only Europeans were foreigners to Boon Haw. He didn't regard himself as one although he came from Burma. "You are dishonest!"

Ah Weng explained his home delivery service but Boon Haw brushed the explanation aside. "You made the offer to my servant and no extra cost was mentioned. You are taking advantage of me and that is dishonest."

"I thought I was providing an extra service to make you happy, *towkay*. I don't collect or deliver clothes to any of my customers. You are the only one."

"But you did not say that you would charge me more for this service," Boon Haw insisted. "To do well in this world, one has to be honest. To judge by your high-handed action, you are not honest. If you need money that badly, I will lend it to you. I refuse to be cheated even over a few cents."

The *dhobi* refused to be intimidated. Far from being repentant, he shook his head in wonder and said, "*Towkay*, I really cannot understand how a rich man like you can be so stingy. Two cents won't buy me a cup of coffee. Why do you make such a fuss over a trifling sum?" It was a classic case of adding insult to injury.

The impudent *dhobi* could thank his lucky stars that Boon Haw's brawling days were over. The Tiger had acquired respectability along with great wealth. Long gone were the days when he was quick to pick a fight and fight to win. A tongue-lashing had replaced the fisticuffs. Many a wayward employee and such like underling had withered under his verbal assault. But the colossal audacity of the man rendered him speechless. With a superhuman effort he curbed his urge to lash out. He walked away muttering something about teaching a crook a lesson he would never forget.

Piah Hong was outraged that her husband should be subject to such humiliation. "How dare you speak to my husband in that manner," she demanded. But there was little she could do besides the obvious withdrawal of patronage. Kyi Kyi was no less scandalised. "Such disgraceful conduct deserves punishment," she proclaimed to no one in particular.

The punishment was swift and drastic. Boon Haw bought the land next door. He evicted all the squatters and built a fence around his new property to ensure they were kept out. The maid servant resumed washing her boss's clothes. No matter how hard she tried, she could not match the *dhobi's* skill.

But from then on, Boon Haw learned to be less fussy about his clothes.

Fifteen

Now that he had built a splendid headquarters for his business, Boon Haw began to yearn for an even more imposing structure for a residence. He had been living in houses built by others. Although extensive renovations were done at great cost on the homes he purchased , they were nonetheless second-hand homes. It was a humiliating thought. The ego which had developed with prosperity beyond his early dreams demanded a house never before occupied by others. The only way to achieve this was to build the house and live in it from the very first day.

The tiff with the *dhobi* had been a blessing in disguise. His lesson to Ah Weng had secured him an ideal plot to build his dream house. It was overgrown with weeds and was an eyesore. It was a breeding ground for mosquitoes and those who suffered most were the people who lived next door, namely, the members of the Aw household. Piah Hong grumbled and agitated him to sell it. "We will make a good profit," she said. "Let somebody build a house there and it will clear away the mosquitoes. I have suffered long enough."

"Woman, you do not know what you are talking about," Boon Haw rebuked his eldest wife. "A person's wealth is not measured by money alone. A man is never really rich unless he owns a lot of land. I want to buy more, not sell what I have. The more the better. Land becomes more valuable with each passing day. Money loses its value."

The weeds grew taller. The mosquitoes grew bolder. Piah Hong complained louder. Then came the day when Boon Haw told his long-suffering lady, "You can stop grumbling, my sweet potato. I

am going to build the grandest house next door for us to live in."
Piah Hong had grown fat with the idle years. Her husband called
her "sweet potato" in moments of affection. He also called her by
that not quite complimentary nickname when the urge to tease
her corpulence seized him.

Piah Hong expressed neither joy nor regret when she answered,
"About time you did something to it. It is going to waste." As an
afterthought she added, "It would be nice to live in a house of my own."

Boon Haw made no comment.

He wasted no time putting his idea to work. The construction
of his new residence took priority over everything else. The very
next day after announcing his decision he called the architect who
had designed his factory to prepare plans for a house that would be
"a showpiece" in Singapore. He had no definite idea exactly what
the house would look like. His brief: "My new house must be
modern yet traditional. Money is no object. Build me a house fit
for an emperor. But do not build an Oriental house."

Boon Haw took no chances in this project which was so close
to his heart. He commissioned three other architects to submit
plans for his house. "Modern yet traditional," he told each one.
"Don't spare the cash. It's my money. Whatever you may have in
mind, just remember one thing. It must be a house fit for Aw Boon
Haw."

Offered a blank cheque, the architects went to work with
uncommon zeal, each unaware that there were others burning the
midnight oil. In due course, at intervals staggered by Boon Haw, the
four hopeful men showed their drawings with great expectations. One
after the other, Boon Haw rejected their respective concepts. They
were too modern or too traditional; too big for the plot or too small to
do him justice. There should be enough land left over for landscaping
but at the same time the building should dominate the area. Not very
bright was what he thought of the professionals. He does not know
exactly what he wants, was the silent opinion of the architects.

"I have three others working on it," he finally told each

architect in exasperation. "I hope you will be the one to earn my money. There will be a bonus to the one who can satisfy me." With such competition and the promise of a fat fee, the architects returned to their drawing boards with renewed vigour. But again none was sufficiently inspired to produce an acceptable design.

The architect who was responsible for giving Aw Boon Haw so much pride in his factory building persevered where the others had given up in despair. He had a reputation to uphold. He also saw in Aw Boon Haw a source of many other lucrative assignments to come if he could satisfy the millionaire. If he could not do it on his own he saw no harm in enlisting the help of others. The main thing was to get the job done. Consequently he secured the assistance of an American architect who was seeking to establish himself in the colony.

Everybody had heard of the famous Aw Boon Haw. The gossip mill had circulated varnished tales of his exploits; each telling had added on to them a little more glamour and a lot more spice. The life of Aw Boon Haw had become a regular topic of conversation wherever and whenever friends gathered to while away idle hours. The American was fascinated by the exotic East, and the even more exotic lifestyle of the Tiger. He was an admirer of the so-called multi-wife tycoon for the glamour attached to his name. "I'll do my darndest to build the guy his dream house," he assured his Singapore friend. "He is really something again."

Neither could understand why Aw Boon Haw was against a building with an Oriental character. It was contrary to the taste of a man so steeped in Chinese culture and tradition. "What the heck," the American said. "It's his dough and what the Tiger wants the Tiger shall get."

The name of the American architect has long been forgotten. But his legacy, the masterpiece he erected for the Tiger Balm King, was to stand as one of the showpiece residences in Singapore. It was a splendid example of dignity, grace and distinction blending into one building that never failed to please the eye. The beautiful proportions made it appear larger then it actually was. Four tall fluted columns in front contributed to its elegant appearance. It was truly a house built for gracious living.

Perhaps the most distinguishing feature was a tower-like structure topped by a ribbed dome. The American must have noted the owner's delight with the cupola on his factory building. But this was no depository for his Tiger Balm secrets. It was a place for meditation. A retreat from the impositions of unwelcome guests.

Slabs of granite formed steps leading up to the reception room. On the right were three huge bedrooms. On the left was the main hall with its bay windows. Marble columns supported ceilings decorated with the most artistic designs human hands could render. Italian ceramic tiles covered the floor from wall to wall. The richness of the interior was more than a match for the impressive appearance of the exterior.

The Tiger mansion vaguely resembled the Washington White House, albeit on a much minor scale. This was probably due more by design than accident, considering the nationality of its creator. Aw Boon Haw had it painted white, which further reinforced this impression. From the day of its completion, his employees dubbed it the "White House."

The millionaire was delighted. He graced his home with the purest marble sculptures from Florence and the finest carpets from Tientsin. He acquired choice objects of art to complement the rich furnishings. Rare jade carvings in the shape of gods and goddesses of Chinese mythology vied with jade animals, birds, bowls, urns and vases for admiration. His jade acquisitions grew with the years and in time became the biggest and most valuable private collection in the world. His White House became known as the Jade House to the thousands of visitors from near and far who flocked to view the priceless collection.

The day for moving into No. 3 Nassim Road, the millionaire's new address, finally arrived. The house was completely furnished. Every item of furniture was custom-made. Conspicuous by their absence were the rosewood furniture so beloved of wealthy Chinese. This was in keeping with the owner's wish to avoid giving the house an Oriental flavour.

A soothsayer had picked the day deemed most auspicious for the move. It was midday, when the sun cast the least shadow. It was undesirable to occupy a new house accompanied by long shadows. One never knew what evil spirit might merge with the shadow to gain entry into the house. Boon Haw called out to his wives, "Piah Hong, Kyi Kyi, it's time to leave the old house for the new. Hurry, we must not hold up the ceremony."

Aw Boon Haw believed in luck. He heeded omens, good or bad. But more than luck, he believed in himself and had always maintained that fortune mattered little unless given a big push. Boldness was second nature to him. His daring had left a mark he would carry to his grave.

As a boy in Rangoon, he skipped classes one day and joined his rascally peers for a day of fun at the circus. The menagerie, which was out of bounds, proved exciting to this mischief-bent gang of scallywags as they taunted the caged animals. A tiger was feeding on a chunk of half rotten carcass. "Hey, Boon Haw," a scrawny Burmese boy cried out to him. "Now is your chance to live up to your name. If you are as brave as you are always boasting to us, I dare you to take the meat from the tiger."

Boon Haw could not ignore the challenge. His standing in the gang would suffer and he would lose his privileges. He approached the cage and stood before the snarling beast. A closer look revealed the tiger to be more ferocious than he imagined. He wished he had not skipped classes that day.

"Come on, what are you waiting for? Are you afraid?" came the taunt. Hurling an oath at the jeering boy, Boon Haw pushed his right hand between the bars to grab the meat. The tiger, riled by this rude intrusion, was equally quick. It unsheathed its claws and shot a paw out to strike the boy. Boon Haw sensed the danger in time and withdrew, but not before the tiger left its mark. Boon Haw was to carry this badge of courage in the form of a paw shaped scar on his shoulder for the rest of his life.

A troupe of lion dancers and a priest in yellow robes were waiting at the foot of the granite steps. Beside them was a table piled high with firecrackers to clear evil spirits and usher in the influence of good health, good luck and great prosperity.

"Why is Kyi Kyi moving with us?" Piah Hong asked. "I thought you built the house for me to live in and Kyi Kyi was to remain in this house."

"You potato, the house is too big for you to live alone. It would be better for all of us to live together in one house." It was never Boon Haw's intention to leave Kyi Kyi behind. There was no questioning his affection for his first wife. But he loved his younger wife as much. Kyi Kyi must also live in the house where he lived. And the White House was where he meant to live. He couldn't tell Piah Hong his true feelings because she still occupied a special place in his heart. They had shared hard times and he wanted her to enjoy the good times. Just then, the first string of firecrackers began exploding. The well-wishers had given the signal to take up formal residence before the moment of good omen passed.

"Come on, the both of you. Let's go now and not keep our friends waiting. I'll walk ahead and you follow quickly."

Piah Hong baulked. She had shared a house with another woman and tolerated her presence for four years now. Must she continue to undergo the vexation? Did she not deserve a house of her own again to do as she pleased and not to have her servants take orders from another? Apparently not. "You take Kyi Kyi with you," she pouted. "I am not going. I shall stay in this house."

"You have to make things difficult for me at the last moment," Boon Haw scolded. "I must go now before it is too late. You can do as you please. But don't say I didn't ask you." Boon Haw stalked off. Kyi Kyi followed.

A fit of pique resulted in Boon Haw acquiring a piece of land to build his castle. Piah Hong's anger robbed her of the satisfaction of being among the first to live in the very first home Boon Haw had built for them. This was also the second occasion where she had to take a back seat in favour of Kyi Kyi. She had come to live in the old house a year after the younger woman had moved into it. She was left alone to fret with no one but herself to blame.

There was in Boon Haw an almost insatiable urge to outdo and outshine others. He developed a brand of flamboyance which in others, would be interpreted as self-adulation. But if one looked deep enough, there was a certain logic in his show. Everything he did out of the ordinary was calculated to advance the popularity of his products. His showmanship in this direction was unequalled. One of his stunts bordered on the bizarre shortly after moving into the new mansion.

The Buick limousine he had acquired two years earlier was among the classiest cars available in Singapore. It cost a princely sum of two thousand and eight hundred dollars..

The young Indian driver Singaram maintained it in impeccable condition. He spent two hours every day flushing the undercarriage and washing off the grime and dirt with a rubber hose. Every speck of dust in the interior was carefully removed with a piece of yellow polishing cloth. The boss refused to ride in a car that was anything but spotless. He was quick to scold and just as quick to replace a driver. Jobs were scarce and twenty dollars a month plus living quarters had made Singaram the envy of other drivers. The Buick was immaculate. But there were others being driven around in the same model.

Boon Haw decided that his personal carriage must not only be the most outstanding but the most unique as well. But what could he buy that others with money could not? His fertile imagination supplied the answer in a flash. A tiger car. What could be more appropriate? He couldn't think of any. A tiger car would enhance his image. It would be compatible with the Tiger Balm King sobriquet his admiring public had bestowed on him and of which he was so inordinately proud. It would also be a reflection of his ego, said his critics.

Nobody had ever ordered a car in the shape of a tiger before. Nor one in any shape except that of the accepted kind. The motor agents were puzzled by the strange request. Puzzled and amused. Aw Boon Haw was deadly serious.

"Make me a car like a tiger and I shall pay you handsomely," he promised. But no agent was equal to the task. One by one they conceded defeat.

In desperation, Boon Haw turned to a contractor who had fabricated metal utensils for the preparation of his medicines. The artisan consulted other metal workers. Nobody dared undertake the job no matter what the millionaire promised. Their craft did not extend to tiger mock-ups mounted on a motor car. Boon Haw insisted it could be done and toned down his specifications. Pleasing the tycoon could generate great favours in return.

The contractor finally agreed to build a tiger car. Not a whole tiger, just the head.

Boon Haw had no alternative but to compromise. "We will paint the rest of the car with tiger stripes," he told the contractor. "That would give it more the look of a tiger." That settled, the next step was to shop for a suitable machine to be converted into a mechanical tiger.

A succession of salesmen touted the merits of their models. A bright spark from Cycle & Carriage, a newly incorporated company owned by a Chinese family, sang the praises of a car called the Overland Whippet. "The world's best low-priced car," he proclaimed. "Only one thousand six hundred and fifty dollars. They don't come any cheaper," he added with a confidence as though the deal was as good as closed. "Young man," replied the Tiger, "I don't buy cheap things. Your car is not for me."

Others made their pitch. "The latest in automobile refinement" called a Dodge Deluxe Sedan was offered by another firm called Central Motors. It cost two thousand seven hundred and five dollars. An invention known as magneto ignition was available for seventy dollars extra. A Chevrolet sedan from Borneo Motors carried a bargain price of one thousand eight hundred dollars if Mr Aw considered the Dodge too expensive. The salesman was shown the door for his impertinence.

The Ford Motor Company had been anxious to live down the flippant remark made years ago by its founder: "You can have any colour you like as long as it is black." Its illustrated brochure proclaimed: "Our cars now come with lacquer finish in three colour options." The local agents, Universal Cars, could make no impression on the man who sought distinction.

Upstart Cycle & Carriage returned with "the most beautiful production in Italian art," a six-cylinder car called the Ansaldo. Boon Haw was not persuaded.

Guthrie & Co. who had sold one Buick to the millionaire attempted to sell him another. The newest model would seat seven adults and would make a very big tiger indeed. The price was also big – five thousand two hundred and fifty dollars. But money was no object. Boon Haw decided against it because he didn't want another car of the same make. Another British firm, Malayan Motors, showed him a masterpiece in American engineering. The Packard four-door sedan was luxury on wheels. It was one of the longest cars on the road and cost even more than the Buick. Boon Haw was interested but his artisan talked him out of it. "The car looks like a hearse," he said. "Bad luck to use it."

The car finally picked was a German NSU. It was nowhere as beautiful as the Italian job or as commodious as the Packard. But the artisan made sense when he told the Tiger, "Big Boss, no car will ever look the same again once I'm finished with it." How right he was. He butchered the pride of Germany and in its place was born a monstrosity.

No animal, no matter how beastly, had ever been so maligned

as that grotesque specimen of a tiger. A boxy body painted in false stripes replaced the purposeful torso of the noble cat. Where the radiator once sat, an outsized head fabricated to resemble that of a tiger hissed steam when the engine roared. The jaws were permanently agape and the mouth extended to avoid overheating the motor. Each jaw sprouted two frightful fangs. Wire whiskers looked like displaced quills on the rigid snout. It was a most odd-looking tiger.

Aw Boon Haw was happy with his oddity. But he wanted a roar to go with it. The sound emitted by the horns was too feeble. The artisan scouted the island for a device to simulate a roar. He found a pair of klaxon horns and with some tinkering produced an unearthly sound which was not quite a roar but most effective in attracting attention which was what the whole exercise was about. It was during the night that the metal monster came into its own. In addition to the two powerful headlights mounted on the mudguards, Aw Boon Haw had two high wattage bulbs replace the tiger's eyes. These were painted red. Many an unwary soul was scared out of his wits when the shattering blare of the klaxons caused him to turn around to be confronted by an indescribable creature with gaping jaws and bloodshot eyes bearing down on him on a dark night. Nothing could be more terrifying than this unexpected encounter.

The tiger car became the talk of the town. Some were bemused by his idiosyncrasy. Others shook their head in wonder. Detractors ridiculed his bizarre brainwave. The owner was not the least bit concerned. His rationale:

"No one could help noticing. He would want to know the identity of the passenger, the man who manufactured the famous Tiger Balm. Who could resist a product which spawned such an unforgettable character? Thus would another customer be won."

None ever approached Aw Boon Haw's flair for promoting his products. The medium might be outrageously outlandish, but the impact was what counted.

Sixteen

When Sir Hugh Clifford succeeded Sir Laurence Guillemard as governor of Singapore in 1927, he remarked shortly after assuming office, "This colony is beyond my expectations. It is truly a capital outpost. I dare say it will one day rank as one of the greatest ports in the empire, a commercial centre for all to admire and to envy."

There was a lot going for Sir Hugh to enthuse over. The entrepot trade was bursting at the seams. Freighters from the world over awaited their turn for berths to unload their cargo from the industrialised West. Captains chafed with impatience to set sail again with produce from the Orient. Coolies laboured round the clock to fill holds with rubber, tin, timber, rice, copra, spices and a host of other commodities for the hungry factories in Europe and America.

Only a fraction of this prosperity benefited the ordinary worker. He was glad to get any job that paid regular wages. Merchants exploited cheap labour and made untold riches. Unions were unknown. There was no minimum wage. Hours were long. Working conditions were mostly atrocious. Still they came. Each boat from China disgorged more immigrants seeking work, heads filled with dreams of wealth and a life of ease and plenty.

The British administration imposed few, if any, restrictions on commerce. There was no immigration control. Everyone was free to come and go as he pleased. The Colony's laissez-faire brand of capitalism gave every man the opportunity to make whatever fortune he was capable of making. The more astute among the newcomers seized the chance and thrived. Many achieved success beyond their wildest dreams. With few exceptions, these achievers travelled a common road, that of rags to riches.

One of the greatest opportunists was an immigrant from Amoy. His name was Tan Kah Kee and he wheeled and dealed to become a legend in his lifetime. Tan Kah Kee was a typical example of the Chinese immigrant who arrived with great resolve and went on to amass a fortune which enabled him to acquire a stature matched by very few. Among his friends and contemporaries were illuminaries whose names today read like a roll of honour in the brief history of Singapore. Lim Nee Soon, Dr Lim Boon Keng, Lee Choon Guan and Lim Peng Hian, to name only a few, were among the many eminent Chinese leaders whose integrity and industry contributed so much towards the building of the modern metropolis that is Singapore today.

Tan Kah Kee came to Singapore from his native Fukien province in 1890. He was sixteen years old, a youth fired with the determination to make his mark in the world. Old family ties and a desire to acquire some education had prevented him from joining his father earlier. The father's failing health was a reason for his premature journey.

The elder Tan owned a rice dealership which had seen better days. He put his son to work straight from the boat. The boy possessed no business experience whatsoever. But he was willing, shrewd, industrious and ready to learn. The young Tan Kah Kee carried on working when others had gone home for the night. He suggested changes and made improvements. The father was sceptical, but his deteriorating health forced him to allow his son to assume the greater share of the burden. The business made rapid progress.

Tan Kah Kee was appointed manager of the family firm two years later. He never looked back from then on. The firm prospered. The young man, hardly twenty-one, assumed complete charge. Tan Kah Kee was not to rest on his laurels. He realised that diversification was the key to even greater prosperity and a safeguard against total collapse. And so he branched out into pineapple canning in a factory in Sembawang, a rural area in the north of the island. Canned pineapple was a new gastronomic delight much appreciated by the affluent West. It was an instant success.

It was not long after this that Tan Kah Kee redeemed an enterprise which his father had been forced to sell due to falling fortunes. He repurchased a pineapple plant which had once belonged to his father and thus erased the stigma of failure on the family name. This act gave him more satisfaction than all the money he had made so far.

To ensure that his factories would never have to depend on others for fruits to process, Tan Kah Kee bought five hundred acres of land in Johore, on the mainland, to grow his own pineapples. Suppliers were not above the practice of withholding fruits to force up prices or to shut down a plant for an eventual takeover. He would not expose himself to blackmail or extortion.

Though pineapple generated a high proportion of the family income, rice was still the mainstay of the budding business empire. Rice was the staple food. There was no substitute. Rich or poor, a meal was not a meal without rice on the table. There was a lot more money to be made out of it. Tan Kah Kee decided it was time to break into the monopoly of the rice importing and exporting trade held by a few merchants. He invested all the money he could spare to set up his own operation. The young man who set foot on the island fourteen years ago had arrived. He was only thirty but was already regarded as one of the shrewdest merchants in Market Street.

In 1877 an English botanist named Henry Nicholas Ridley obtained some rubber seeds from Brazil and experimented with its cultivation in the Botanic Gardens. Ridley was confident that the sticky fluid would soon be one of the most sought-after commodities in the world. It was also to make Malaya the world's greatest rubber producer along with tin.

The rubber plant from the jungles of South America found the soil and climate to its liking. It not only thrived in growth, but produced more latex than in its native environment. Then, as now, land-scarce Singapore did not have the acreage to grow rubber on the scale Ridley envisaged. Plantations rich in pepper, cloves, nutmeg, cinnamon and other spices were cleared to make way for the newcomer, but it was not enough.

There was land for the asking across the narrow Straits of Johore. The scramble for land in the Malay Peninsula became a stampede. The British saw great potential in the new crop, even more so than copra which flourished in the tropical Malayan countryside. Vast areas of jungle were cleared and land was made available to whoever wished to plant rubber. In the bid to cash in on the worldwide demand for the sticky fluid, owners tapped their trees to death. But for every tree that perished, a hundred took its place.

Ridley came to the rescue. He devised a method of tapping the tree in a herring-bone pattern. This ensured the tree did not bleed to death. Tappers now required just one day to acquire the skill of shaving the bark with a curved knife without damaging the tree. Though it was easy to learn to tap, there was soon a shortage of tappers. The workers, equipped with tapping knife and two pails, each slung from the end of a shoulder pole to collect the latex, ventured forth at dawn to brave mosquitoes and other hazards such as the deadly cobra. They caught the fever sooner or later. Their skin turned yellowish from taking quinine to combat malaria. It was a difficult job for a mere thirty cents a day.

Malays shunned the work, preferring to cultivate on their own land. The Chinese dominated the mining industry and many would rather scrape together some money to start their own smallholding or tap their own rubber.

The British solved the problem by importing labour. Droves of Tamils from poverty-stricken South India filled holds in steamers bound for Penang or Port Swettenham. From these entry points they were distributed in packed lorries or trains to estates crying out for workers. Like the earlier Chinese immigrants, wives and families were left behind. These men were housed in "coolie lines," so-called because the basic quarters to shelter them were arranged in long rows.

The invasion of the British and later other European managers spawned a breed of men commonly known as planters. These voluntary exiles from the West came with their future assured. They sailed to their distant postings in the luxury of a passenger liner and arrived to take up residence in a bungalow with every home comfort provided to help ease the weight of the white man's burden.

Many planters came without their spouses. The rigours of the tropics were not for the delicate roses of England. The survivors had to learn how to cope with the heat and humidity, and the ubiquitous Anopheles mosquito, the deadly carrier of malaria. Before long, the loneliness forced men to seek solace from the bottle when the day's work was done and the long night confronted them.

Spirits soon addled the brain and kindled passion. Liaisons between the lonely planter and local women developed. Many an alcoholic and blatantly promiscuous planter was shipped home in disgrace. There were many replacements eagerly awaiting to succumb to the lure of the exotic East where fame and fortune beckoned.

The rubber industry prospered as Ridley had predicted. The industrialised West clamoured for this raw material for which new uses were found and new patents taken out. Every ship leaving Singapore carried a cargo of rubber in its bulging holds. Chinese merchants acquired modest holdings and cashed in on the demand. Tan Kah Kee joined in the scramble. He bought one thousand acres of land in Johore in 1906 and planted it with rubber. His pineapple plantations were doing exceptionally well but rubber looked more promising. This was to be the greatest milestone in his business life and was to earn him the nickname of the "Rubber King."

The rubber boom exploded in 1909. The scramble to get into rubber accelerated into a mad rush. Tan Kah Kee's trees were a long way from tapping. A fellow rice merchant who was determined to be a rubber baron made him an offer he could not refuse. If taking money from a foolish man was ignoble, milking a rival was all part of the game. He sold his one thousand acres at a great profit. But far from quitting the rubber business, he promptly bought two more far larger pieces of land and planted two thousand acres with rubber and the rest with pineapple.

Tan Kah Kee became a millionaire by 1919, one of the few among his 250,000 compatriots in the colony. He was afflicted with a need to achieve and blessed with the capacity to strive. An inborn astuteness combined with a native shrewdness ensured success in most of his undertakings. His holdings included eight pineapple canneries, two large rubber estates and a rice mill, besides a number of other businesses at the outbreak of the First World War.

War was a time to make great profits. Shipping space was at a premium and he refused to be held to ransom by shippers who demanded exorbitant payment for shipping his goods. He overcame this by the simple but costly expedient of buying two steamers. He now had more than enough shipping space to spare. It was his turn to tell others to take it or leave it.

The greater part of his business transactions was with foreign buyers. This required English, a language with which he was unfamiliar and which he had no desire to learn. He could afford to engage the best man for the job and the best turned out to be a brilliant young man named Lee Kong Chian. The new employee, a linguist among his other qualifications, became an indispensable assistant almost from the day he joined Tan Kah Kee in 1916. He reorganised his boss's rubber business and arranged to sell the commodity direct to European and American buyers, thus cutting out the foreign agencies and realising even greater profits.

Rubber, like tin, was vital to the war effort. Demand skyrocketed. So did the price. A pineapple canning factory was converted into a second rubber mill. It soon ran out of capacity. Another mill was commissioned. The demand for rubber was insatiable. Rubber became as good as gold and infinitely more useful in fighting the Kaiser and his armies.

Tan Kah Kee was sitting on top of the world when Germany surrendered in 1918. He was the leading Chinese industrialist in Singapore and Malaya with interests as varied as rubber, rice, pineapple, shipping and a string of trading companies. Lee Kong Chian had proved himself to be more than an able lieutenant. He became Tan Kah Kee's right hand man. Admiration developed into affection. Such rare talent must not be allowed to leave the family. Tan Kah Kee offered his eldest daughter's hand in marriage. Lee Kong Chian accepted and became the tycoon's son-in-law in 1920. He went on to distinguish himself as a leading merchant and educationist in his own right.

Tan Kah Kee branched out into manufacturing the year he took Lee Kong Chian into the family. He converted a rubber mill into a plant to produce rubber goods. Canvas shoes with rubber soles were sold at half the price of their imported competitors. Every other student wore his shoes to school and to play. Every other bicycle was fitted with his tyres and tubes. He was also an inventor and his factory turned out a range of products that found ready acceptance. He held four patents for his inventions based on rubber.

As Tan Kah Kee's fortunes multiplied, so did his acts of benevolence. His biggest beneficiary was Chinese education. He was now in a position to contribute even larger sums towards his pet interest. It became almost an obsession to a man whose early circumstances had deprived him of the knowledge he craved. The illiteracy in China had haunted his moments of triumph in commerce. An illiterate people would always be exploited by others. He decided to expand his crusade on education to his motherland.

The schools he had helped to found and support in Singapore offered education up to high school only. He now aimed to set up an institution of higher learning. Dr Sun Yat Sen had overthrown the corrupt Ching dynasty in 1911. A new era had dawned on the Middle Kingdom, now a modern republic.

Tan Kah Kee offered to set up a university in China. The Republican government was more than receptive. The would-be benefactor was asked to pick the site. Naturally he chose his hometown of Amoy. Amoy University was born in 1921. Tan Kah Kee not only financed the project, but also established a large endowment fund to ensure its viability. For this magnanimity and others to follow in his lifetime, the educationist was bestowed honours never before accorded to any other overseas Chinese. Both the Kuomintang and later the Communist Party of China regarded him as a great patriot.

In Singapore, Tan Kah Kee's mantle of leadership in the Chinese community was a natural consequence of this largesse. His compatriots of all dialect groups accorded him the esteem which was his due. His fellow Hokkiens revered him. The colonial government sought his advice on matters bearing on Chinese affairs. But he never really enjoyed the full confidence of the administration. His chauvinism was too obvious, and his ties to China, too binding. Now known as the "Rubber King" for his extensive rubber interests, Tan Kah Kee was unconcerned by this mistrust. He commented, "Any little recognition by my country and my countrymen is more valued than the highest honour from outsiders."

The Ee Ho Hean Club was the most exclusive and prestigious of the many Chinese clubs in Singapore in the twenties. Its membership was limited to one hundred but this number was seldom reached due to the exceptionally high criterion set for prospective members. The president of this elite society was Tan Kah Kee. This position conferred a prestige second to none, and yielded an influence enjoyed by few.

The Ee Ho Hean Club was founded in 1895 by a group of Hokkien businessmen who sought a more congenial environment than that offered by clan associations or chambers of commerce. The original clubhouse in seedy Duxton Road moved into better premises in Club Street in 1910. Both addresses were conveniently close to the Chinese business district centred in Market and Telok Ayer Streets. A third address was found in Bukit Pasoh Road in 1925.

What started out as a purely social club offering a variety of diversions rapidly developed into an informal business exchange. Deals were struck over a pot of tea or game of cards without the benefit of a written agreement. A man's word was his bond. Woe betide him who dishonours it. He became a pariah.

The club was meant for Hokkiens. Teochews, Cantonese, Hakkas and the rest had similar establishments of their own. But the Ee Ho Hean Club emerged as the best. Its membership comprised the top layer of Chinese society in terms of wealth and business connections. An insider enjoyed advantages denied to outsiders. Non-Hokkiens who considered themselves equal or even superior to the Hokkien members sought to join the club. A few of the most prominent of these outsiders were eventually admitted.

"These people may not be Hokkien but they are Chinese nonetheless," conceded Tan Kah Kee. "And some of them are very rich, even richer than some of us. They will be an asset to our club." But the rule limiting membership to one hundred remained. An "outsider" was admitted only when a vacancy occurred; which was rare.

One of the earliest non-Hokkien members was Aw Boon Haw. He was less of an outsider than others. Though he was Hakka his father was born in Fukien province and he spoke the Hokkien dialect. His credentials were outstanding. His fame had preceded his arrival from Rangoon.

Aw Boon Haw did not really need the Ee Ho Hean Club to advance his business interests. His customers were mainly the poor and ignorant who found his medicines affordable and effective. He enjoyed a near monopoly of the ointment and analgesic market. Many an imitator had tried to cash in on similarly compounded medicines, but none had the Midas touch of the Tiger.

Aw Boon Haw recognised the value and eminence of the Ee Ho Hean Club. With every member well known as a lion in society, leadership of the group was tantamount to leadership of the whole Chinese community. He coveted Tan Kah Kee's status in the club and his envy led to a bitter contest for leadership which was never resolved.

Top*: Aw Boon Haw the Tiger ... a legend in his lifetime.*
Bottom*: Aw Boon Par the Leopard ... co-founder of the
Tiger Balm empire.*

Top: *Eng Aun Tong: the Hall of Everlasting Peace.*
Bottom: *The White House in Singapore where the famous jade collection was on show.*

Top: *The first Tiger car built in 1927.*
Bottom: *The second Tiger car in 1932 … just as fearsome. The lady is the third Mrs Aw (Ooi Geik Cheah).*

Haw Par Villa: where myths meet fantasies.

Aw Boon Haw with his three wives and three youngest children in 1936. L – R: Ooi Geik Cheah, Aw Jee Haw, Tay Piah Hong, Aw It Haw, Kyi Kyi, and Aw Sian.

Aw Boon Haw and his four wives. Seated L – R: Khoo Siew Eng,
Tay Piah Hong, Aw Boon Haw, Kyi Kyi and Ooi Geik Cheah.
Standing (1st row) R – L: Aw It Haw, Aw Hoe, Aw Swan, Aw Kow,
Mrs Aw Kow, Mrs Aw Swan, Mrs Aw Hoe (Chan Sau Yong), Aw Sian,
Aw Seng. Grandchildren are seated in front. The rest are relatives.

Top: *The debonair tycoon, Aw Boon Haw, at age sixty-seven.*
Bottom: *Family members were among the first depositors at the opening of Chung Khiaw Bank.*

First anniversary photograph of the Singapore Standard on 3 July 1951. Seated ninth from the right is S. Rajaratnam, twelfth from the right is Aw Kow, fourteenth from the right is the author, Sam King.

Seventeen

Good natured banter. The occasional joke. It was the usual Thursday gambling night. The session started off innocently enough. Harmless insults instead of high-priced commodities were being traded freely among the high-flying merchants. Refined speech gave way to coarse outbursts and colourful expletives whenever lady luck frowned. Propriety flew out of the window as losses mounted. The tycoons unwound their taut nerves and buried the past week's tensions of the market place in battles of a different kind.

The Thursday night gambling sessions had become traditional. Nobody knew how or when they started, and nobody cared. The tycoons were only glad there was a Thursday night. Stakes were high. Losers could afford to lose; and winners did not really need their winnings. They gambled for the sake of gambling.

The house imposed a five percent levy on each winning hand. It was the house which was the real winner in the end. The money collected went to a special fund to be disbursed as thought fit by the management. The yearly takings were considerable. A generous proportion of the collection was earmarked for charity. Men of substance were not always devoid of compassion for the downtrodden although these donors were involuntary contributors.

As far as gambling was concerned, Tan Kah Kee was an amoralist. He did not lay down hard and fast rules for those who indulged, but he insisted that members observe one condition. This was that they refrained from bringing in outsiders. He had no desire to see the premises turned into a common gambling saloon. It was not that he wanted to be a kill-joy. He was only being careful. The members accepted the ruling. Gambling was in their blood. As for Tan Kah Kee, he had other pressing matters on his mind.

The rubber balloon began to deflate in 1925. Prices tumbled the following year and many "rubbermen" went bankrupt. Tan Kah Kee suffered considerable, but not catastrophic, losses. His enterprises were too widespread. His hero Dr Sun Yat Sen had died in 1925 at the age of 59. His beloved China was in turmoil. Chiang Kai Shek was contending with Wan Ching Wei for leadership of the Nationalists. The warlords were carving out the country into domains of their own.

A suave young man named Chou En Lai was recruiting communists in the cities while in the countryside his ideological mentor and master, Mao Tse Tung, was organising peasants to rally under the Red Flag. Even as Mao and his followers were making a power-hungry Chiang believe they would fight alongside him against a threatening Japan, they were moving to unite the country under communism, a new order in which there would be no role for Chiang.

The communists scored their biggest victory on August 1, 1927. Chu Teh, the fiery young commandant of Nanchang Military Academy, attacked the city with some one thousand cadets. The Nationalist governor surrendered after offering token resistance. And so was born the Communist People's Liberation Army that was to force Chiang to flee to Taiwan twenty-two years later.

Tan Kah Kee saw his beloved motherland in danger of completely disintegrating. He feared that he would not see a strong and united China in his lifetime. The future of Amoy University, the culmination of a lifetime dream to better his countrymen, was at stake. It was little wonder that he showed no inclination to join his fellow members at the gambling tables. His thoughts were thousands of miles away when a commotion at one of the tables brought him back to the present.

The players at the mahjong table were an incongruous foursome.

The only common denominator was their wealth. One was a thin man given to the habit of spitting. The brass spittoon beside him bore testimony to his disregard for the disgust shown by his comrades. He was a rice merchant who owned two of the largest godowns by the Singapore River. It was said that he had sold the grain at highly inflated prices when there had been a shortage during the war. He was not the only merchant who had made his pile in the blackmarket and, therefore, was spared the accusing finger.

The second player was a fat copra trader who constantly chewed on a toothpick in between popping preserved plums into his mouth. Whilst his girth proclaimed his prosperity his mode of dressing did not. He wore baggy pyjama-type trousers overlapping his pot belly and a short-sleeved singlet rolled up to just below his sweaty armpits. Fat men do not take kindly to the heat. The swirling ceiling fan above produced insufficient cooling. He sucked on the liquorice plum as he agitated the toothpick between his thick lips.

The third man was a compulsive gambler whose fondest wish was to have every night turned into a Thursday night. He smoked as intensely as he gambled. The maid who served endless rounds of tea ensured there was always a large spittoon within his reach. Ashtrays were hopelessly inadequate for his stacks of half-smoked cigarettes. This *towkay* was a Peranakan, one of the very few local-born Chinese whom the immigrant tycoons grudgingly acknowledged as their peer.

He enjoyed the *ang mohs'* favour because he spoke their language well. His ingratiating manners secured him many lucrative contracts denied to others even though their quotations were much lower. Substandard goods supplied at inflated prices were overlooked because he knew which palms to grease. He was a teetotaller who ordered the best Scotch by the case during Christmas time.

The contractor had acquired two vices since joining the club. He was now indulging in the first and looking forward to the delights of the second. His *loh chai*, the much abused personal servant, had earlier whispered into his ear that all was ready for his opium session. Two comely maidens awaited his pleasure at the den in Keong Saik Road; one to roll the sticky substance into pellets for the smoking pipe, and the other to pander to whatever inclination that might arise when the drug took hold of his senses. Gambling, opium and women, not necessarily in that order, were the ultimate pleasures of a successful man. He considered himself a very successful man indeed. This Thursday night was especially wonderful. He had won more than enough to pay for the pleasures of many Thursdays.

The fourth player at the table was a well-built man whose glowing cheeks reflected his good health. He was a living example of the benefits of ginseng roots. He could afford the best and he thought nothing of paying a few hundred dollars for the shrivelled root to be steam-cooked with choice cuts of beef or preferably, with dog meat. He was a firm believer in the restorative properties of this Korean plant and attributed his vigour and virility to it. An aphrodisiac, no less.

He was nattily dressed, in sharp contrast to the others who regarded good dressing as secondary to moneymaking. Having discovered the elegance of sharkskin, this gentleman had discarded his cotton drill and now sent his suits to the dry cleaners instead of the washerman. His hair, still black at forty-five, was parted almost centre in keeping with fashion. It was sleeked down with lavender-scented brilliantine. The shine on his patent leather shoes matched that on his head. A frown masked his face. Aw Boon Haw had not played a winning hand all evening.

The scowl that marred his features unnerved the chain-smoker who kept on puffing. His reputedly foul temper added to the tension. The contractor swore never again to sit down at the same table as the Tiger from Rangoon. But, in spite of his nervousness, Lady Luck kept smiling on him.

"Game!" he shouted a sixth consecutive time which drew a silent oath from the much annoyed Boon Haw. The contractor felled his row of ivory squares face up for all to check his winning hand with a triumphant clatter. The losers glumly counted out token chips which collectively added up to over ten thousand dollars. The despised Peranakan had won sixty thousand dollars so far.

"I'm going to be the biggest winner tonight," gloated the contractor as he raked in the chips with effeminate fingers sprouting inch-long nails. He began to light another cigarette.

The flaring end of the Swedish matchstick broke off and landed on Boon Haw's lap. The unfortunate Tiger Balm King leapt up with a roar to reveal a neat hole burnt through his sharkskin. "You low-class opium addict, you are only fit to mix with rickshaw pullers and not gentlemen like us," he berated the contractor. The expletives that followed in Hakka were even more colourful.

"Master Aw, I apologise most humbly. Please do not be offended. And please do not be so offensive. It was just an accident."

The Tiger refused to be pacified. "You smoke too much. You local-born are all alike. You ape the foreigners and you have lost your Chinese heritage. What are you going to do about my trousers?" It all came out in one breath. Boon Haw was purple with rage.

"It is a small matter, hardly worth your anger. I'll pay for a new pair of trousers, I'll buy you ten pairs," the usually mild contractor replied with spirit. "What is the cost of a pair of trousers to a man as rich as you?"

"Nothing! You can keep your tainted money. I don't need your charity. But I demand some other satisfaction from you."

"What will satisfy you? A virgin girl? That would cost a mere five hundred dollars. Would that be sufficient satisfaction?"

"You are crude like the rest of your kind."

"If I am crude to mention it, what do you call a man who actually uses a virgin and then casts her aside?" The contractor was surprised at his own boldness. He was not an aggressive man, but he could sense that the sympathy of the others was with him. Thus encouraged, he continued, "What do you say, Master Aw? My *loh chai* is here and he can get you a virgin tonight to make you forget your losses."

Boon Haw was not to be baited. Even if he did sleep with virgins he had no intention of advertising the fact. Gossip about his private life could not be avoided. Every man of any prominence was fair game. But he refused to give substance to gossip. He changed the subject.

"I demand some other satisfaction," he repeated. "Are you man enough to cut a deck of cards for fifty thousand dollars? Or don't you have the balls for it?" Crudeness.

It would take considerable kowtowing to the colonial masters and bribing many officials to secure a contract which would yield fifty thousand dollars. But his reputation was at stake. Though it pained him to the core to stake fifty thousand dollars on the turn of a card, there was no way out if he wished to retain his fellow members' esteem. He would otherwise be shamed into relinquishing his membership.

The games at the other tables had come to an abrupt halt when Boon Haw spat the epithet "you low-class opium addict." Such words uttered with such scorn had never before been heard in the club. They might be humble in origin, but wealth was a great leveller which also served to give an aura of refinement to once gauche immigrants. A quarrel that smacked of the gutter was taboo. Everyone in the room was shocked into silence.

The chain-smoker stared into space to gather his wits. He debated within himself if it was worth fifty thousand dollars to be considered a peer of these men from a country he had never seen nor wished to see. But they were good company, even though their behaviour at times was obnoxious and their culture incomprehensible. Rough people in spite of their wealth. But it flattered his ego to mix with them.

"What's the matter? Are you afraid to accept my challenge after so much big talk?" Boon Haw rudely broke into his thoughts. "Did your English education not teach you to match your words with deeds?"

"Master Aw, I have been taught to behave like a gentleman by the foreigners. My ways may not be yours. Nor yours mine. But as a gentleman born and bred in Singapore, I shall give you the satisfaction you demand. I shall give you the opportunity to win back what I fairly won. But I still say it is a foolish thing to do; to gamble fifty thousand dollars on one card."

Boon Haw was not a man to be lectured. The impertinent *dhobi* had paid for his impudence. Now this common sycophant had the audacity to call him foolish. He bristled with indignation; and made to lunge at his tormentor. The fat copra trader grabbed the Tiger by the arm and in doing so nearly choked on his plum. He spat out the offending fruit and said, "Master Aw, please control your temper. You will surely kill our friend if you don't. Let us proceed with the game."

Boon Haw glared at the trader and looked around the room. The watching members glared back at him. The Tiger knew where their sympathy lay. Discretion overcame valour. It would be a disgrace for him to be expelled for unbecoming conduct and bringing the club into disrepute.

"Ah Joo, bring me a new deck of cards," the Tiger shouted across the room. The head boy came running.

"Be so kind as to shuffle the cards," Boon Haw requested the fat trader who had forsaken both toothpick and plum to devote all his attention to the exchange between the arrogant tiger and the despised contractor. "One can't really trust a man who deals with foreigners."

The contractor ignored the insult. He was more concerned with fifty thousand dollars. The trader shuffled the cards with a dexterity quite unexpected of his plump fingers. He slapped the deck on the table and asked, "Who will cut first?"

"I give the honour to the man with the big mouth," Boon Haw sneered. "Cut!" he ordered his antagonist.

The contractor drew a three of spades. The spectators groaned. Fifty thousand dollars was as good as gone down the drain. Boon

Haw could not resist a snigger. "Now is my turn to slaughter you. And you will be more respectful to your superiors in future."

But it was not to be. The Tiger turned up a two of hearts. The spectators either cheered or jeered, depending on which camp they belonged to. The club had never been more noisy.

Tan Kah Kee had a private room in the premises. Here was where he did most of his work, designed and planned his projects. The noise outside disrupted his concentration. He left his room to find out what the commotion was about.

The contractor stared at the cards in disbelief. His mental abacus told him that the evening's loot had totalled one hundred and ten thousand dollars. He broke into a wide grin in sheer delight, to the great annoyance of the Tiger, the would-be slaughterer who had become the slaughtered. The contractor lit a cigarette. Nicotine never tasted sweeter. Boon Haw fumed as the smoke curled towards him.

"Master Aw, do you have enough money on you to pay me now?" the contractor asked innocently enough. Boon Haw froze with anger. "I don't mind waiting until tomorrow or any time you wish."

"What makes you think I am giving in now? You must be fair to me. Or don't you know how to play fair? I demand another game. And we will double the stake. One hundred thousand dollars to the one with the higher card. Are you man enough? Or do your balls shrink!"

"Do I have a choice?"

"Yes. Prove that you are an honourable man or show everyone that you are just a running dog."

The contractor's occupation had rendered him immune to taunts and insults. He had been called worse than a coward and a running dog. His living depended on his ability to absorb insults and never to retaliate where it might hurt his pocket. But he was obsessed with the determination to hobnob with the elite and to remain a member of the Ee Ho Hean Club. Moreover, he would still be ahead by ten thousand dollars should he lose the next round.

"I'll match my words with deeds," the contractor announced with aplomb. Ah Joo, bring us another deck of cards." He could not resist a smirk at taking the wind out of Boon Haw's sails.

The fat trader intercepted the cards and shuffled without being asked. He placed the deck before the contractor who pushed it towards Boon Haw. "Master Aw will have the honour of cutting first." He was enjoying himself at the expense of the Tiger.

Boon Haw drew the queen of clubs. The contractor turned up a knave.

"All's fair and square now," the fat trader said. "One winning hand each. Let us continue with our game." The thin man concurred.

"I have not finished yet," Boon Haw protested. "There must be a third draw to decide who is the final winner. I propose two hundred thousand dollars for the final draw."

Tan Kah Kee had had enough of watching this scant regard for money. He had earned his the hard way and he had lost a fortune when the price of rubber took a nosedive the previous year. That was a calculated risk. Huge sums being tossed about like cigarette butts were obscene. He shuffled up in his China-made slippers and wagged a finger at the contractor. "You will stop swallowing the bait if you know what is good for you. It is disgraceful!" The contractor accepted the admonition without a murmur, relieved at being spared the possibility of losing a sum that could buy him a lifetime of opium and sensuality.

Many self-made millionaires equated wealth with breeding. But in spite of their material success, they did not really succeed in shedding their coarseness in speech or in manner. They spat, swore at the slightest excuse, displayed table manners expected only of coolies, and possessed a demeanour which advertised their background. Tan Kah Kee was one of the few exceptions. He was careful to cultivate the social graces and refinement that were the mark of a Mandarin. He was self-made in wealth as well as in breeding.

The Tiger Balm King stared in fury at the Rubber King for the interference. Tan Kah Kee sensed the hostility. He was also aware of the resentment Boon Haw harboured over his standing in the Chinese community. He determined to avoid being baited by the younger man for he had great respect and admiration for Boon Haw's achievements and philanthropy. They were alike in this respect; both were generous towards the less fortunate and contributed freely to Chinese education.

"Master Aw, please do not be offended if I offer some advice as an elder brother. We may make small fortunes by gambling, but we should not lose all by gambling. Gamble by all means, but let us do it within reason. We play for fun and to pass the time but please let us not get reckless and give our club a bad reputation. The authorities will close it down and we will not have such a desirable place to meet and talk."

The brotherly advice from Tan Kah Kee was interpreted as insufferable scolding by Boon Haw. The aroused Tiger saw neither gentleness nor reason in Tan Kah Kee. "Who gave you the right to assume the role of an elder brother?" he snapped. "I do not need anybody's advice. It is my money and I shall gamble as I please, where I please and with whoever I please."

Tan Kah Kee remained unruffled by the outburst. A quarrel was furthermost from his mind. He abhorred such confrontations. "Please do not be angry. We are friends and friends should look out for one another. Young men coming up in business should not indulge recklessly in this risky pastime," Tan Kah Kee continued in a fatherly manner. "They will lose their business and all they own. Gambling can be even worse than being a slave to opium."

Tan Kah Kee's position in Chinese society was a constant source of irritation to Aw Boon Haw. Each was brilliant in his own sphere. One had the foresight to diversify his business interests and thus prevent ruination when rubber collapsed. The other possessed the talent to exploit his one enterprise to the fullest. Tan Kah Kee was fifty-three years old; Aw Boon Haw was forty-five. To be regarded as a young man at his age implied immaturity in Boon Haw. And he considered it an unforgivable slur on his character.

Both were public images but Boon Haw's flair for capturing the limelight easily made him the most colourful personality of his day. He aspired to be not only the leader of the Hakka community, but that of all the Chinese in Southeast Asia. He resented Tan Kah Kee and all that he stood for.

"You are being condescending and I don't like it," he retorted with heat. "You are the one who has lost a fortune in rubber but I am richer than ever. I shall give you the chance to make up your losses. I shall play you in any game you choose for any stake you care to make." Boon Haw had never thrown a more reckless challenge.

"I do not take money from foolish people," Tan Kah Kee replied in a tone bordering on contempt, and turned away. For once in his life Aw Boon Haw was left speechless. Tan Kah Kee stalked back to his room, shaking his head in wonder at a man regarded as a pillar of society, who could display such recklessness. Dismayed, Boon Haw sat and stared at the retreating figure. The bad blood spilled on that Thursday night between these two men was to last for the rest of their lives.

The tension was relieved by the appearance of an old man with an even older fiddle. He wore a long loose gown and from under his black silk skull cap hung a scrawny queue. A toothless grin wrinkled his gaunt cheeks and shuttered his beady eyes. He was a relic of the court musicians of old China.

The old man was accompanied by two exquisite maidens whose tender ages were reflected in their nubile forms. The girls were dressed in brocades of silk in colourful patterns. Their outfit consisted of a blouse with cloth buttons and a skirt reaching down to the ankles. Their tiny but unbound feet were encased in daintily beaded cloth slippers. Lustrous jet-black hair was arranged in twin buns, one each side of their heads. They walked with mincing steps. Both were heavily powdered and rouged as befitting the sing-song girls that they were.

The old musician was the grandfather. The girls' parents had been killed by soldiers of the warlords who pillaged and ravaged their village in China. The grandfather had escaped with the terrified girls, and they had found their way to Shanghai. There a kindly British captain of a coastal tramp offered the refugees free passage to Singapore. He gave the old man a small stake on landing. The musician's regard for foreigners changed. There were kind souls after all among them.

The old man was an accomplished musician and well-versed in the folk songs of his country. He was also a good teacher. His granddaughters learned all they could from him to help him earn a living the only way he knew how. The trio began entertaining homesick immigrants for pennies. As their popularity grew so did their takings. They now entertained only in the better clubs and at private functions.

The old man scraped his fiddle and the girls launched into a song in high-pitched tones and stylized movements. Its origin was long forgotten, but the lyrics evoked such nostalgia that even these hard-bitten exiles found it hard to banish the mist from their eyes.

The contractor was enthralled by the lovely sisters. His thoughts wandered and he wondered if his opium girls were as beautiful. Or as desirable. Could they make up for the one hundred thousand dollars he had won and lost? He suddenly needed opium and female company more than at any time in his life. The thought of the pleasures awaiting him bucked up his sagging spirits. His pain was already lessened.

He beckoned to his *loh chai* standing by the staircase. His rickshaw had been waiting all evening, he was told. The opium room was ready, smoking lamp lit and six tubes of his favourite brand of opium secured. The girls were young but well-trained in the art of pampering opium smokers.

A naturally friendly person, the contractor turned to Boon Haw and said, "Let us forget what happened. You are the winner and I am the loser. Come with me and let us enjoy ourselves in Keong Saik Road. My *loh chai* can find you anything you want."

Boon Haw was grateful for the unexpected gesture. His self-esteem was at its lowest ebb. Tan Kah Kee's snub in the hearing of so many devastated his ego. He had been too shocked to react and had recovered only when the contractor spoke to him. There was at least one person who did not ignore him. The antagonism of a few moments ago subsided.

"Thank you," he said with unusual graciousness. "But I must not intrude into your private pleasure. Please go ahead. I will find my own pleasure. But I will walk down with you."

The two reconciled antagonists walked down the stairs side by side. The contractor climbed into his rickshaw. Boon Haw stepped into his tiger car and headed for delights of his own. He needed a lot of consoling to forget the humiliation of the evening.

The thin man and the fat trader were left sitting at the table. The former spat into his spittoon and said, "Let us go somewhere for other enjoyment. I've had enough gambling for one night."

The latter spat out his toothpick and asked, "What do you have in mind?"

"Do you like your bones pressed?"

"It all depends."

"On what?"

"On whether it is a man or a woman who does the pressing."

"Have you been to the Massage Hall in Victoria Street?"

"The Japanese place?"

"Yes, I go there often. The Japanese girls are very good."

"I hear they are also very beautiful."

"And very fair-skinned. Mrs Haru is a very good masseuse. But everybody wants Miss Hana. She is young and the prettiest."

"Do they only press bones and nothing else?"

"My good friend, why do you pretend to be so innocent? A woman who touches your body is also prepared to let you touch hers."

"I'm curious about the beautiful Miss Hana."

"Let's go then."

Eighteen

Ah Lan found life with Boon Par difficult. She had cause to fret.

"He cannot see a woman without entertaining thoughts of enjoying her body," Ah Lan complained. "I would be far happier living in a hut and eating gruel and salt fish with a poor but faithful husband than living in a palace with a womaniser." She nagged when he was home and she ranted when he was not.

Boon Par was finding life with Ah Lan just as difficult. Ignoring the woman brought some relief. "No man can be a slave to a woman," he declared. "I would go crazy responding to her wishes."

Unlike his younger brother, Boon Haw was made of sterner stuff. He was also very much a chauvinist. "A wife's duty is to obey her husband, and to share his bed whenever he pleases," he told his sister-in-law. "You have only yourself to blame if your husband seeks consolation elsewhere. I am sick and tired of all this squabbling. It will only bring bad luck to the family."

It was, of course, not a view Ah Lan shared. To friends who cared to listen, she said, "Both brothers are alike. All they can think of is woman."

Consumed with jealousy, she would confront her husband, hands on hips, and demand which woman he was going out to meet. And when he returned home, which one he had seen.

Boon Haw was in Rangoon to bring his brother up to date on the Singapore operation. "It's become impossible to attend to all the important matters myself. You can't trust anyone as much as a brother," Boon Haw told the younger man, who in turn unloaded his problems with his fiery, quarrelsome wife.

Boon Haw was exasperated. "I'll teach the wretched woman a lesson," he promised himself. It was a lesson only an arrogant man like himself could deliver. He found another wife for Boon Par. Teo Hong Yin was another woman from Penang, but not a Peranakan Nonya. She was Hakka.

Boon Par was reluctant at first. Another wife was not in his reckoning. In fact, there was already another woman in his life, another family which, for reasons of his own, he had kept from the brother with whom he had no secrets until now. It was not yet time to reveal this affair.

Boon Par found peace with his new wife. She was amiable and pliable. She never questioned his comings and goings and was grateful for any small favour he chose to bestow on her. But to poor Ah Lan, the new woman in the house was the most painful insult to a string of injuries. She became even more bitter and unforgiving. There was to be no reconciliation. She was a woman scorned, the more galling because a third party was the cause of her final downfall. In the end she returned to Penang where she was to spend the rest of her life, alone and abandoned, except for a house and living expenses.

But even the rich were not immune to pain and misery. Boon Par fell ill. The doctors in Rangoon did not enjoy his confidence, professionally or otherwise. He had no desire to add to the considerable gossip going round over the nature of his illness. It was whispered that Boon Par was inflicted with the debilitating "women's disease." The millionaire embarked for England with a male nurse in attendance to seek a cure.

He returned to Rangoon after consulting several specialists with little evidence of recovery. There was distress in his step and a hesitancy in his movements.

Aw Boon Haw suffered for his only living brother. More than anyone else, he understood what it meant to be deprived of the joy of a chase and the satisfaction of its fulfilment. He insisted that

Boon Par leave for Singapore without delay. "You are the only brother I have left. It is my duty to look after you."

Boon Par realised he could hold out no longer. He needed his brother's resolve and confidence; he wanted to be near his brother for the dependence the latter could provide. He had missed Boon Haw greatly these last few years. He could not dissuade Boon Haw from leaving; now he could not persuade himself to remain in Rangoon. But he did not know how to begin to tell what he had to tell.

It had begun years ago when their mother was still alive. It was because of his desire to avoid hurting her that Boon Par had kept his liaison with a Burmese woman a close secret. Even after Mother's death he found no occasion to confide in Boon Haw. Not even after the woman had borne him three children. Boon Haw did have more than an inkling of his brother's life away from the family, but he respected Boon Par's decision to keep this to himself.

Boon Par lit a black, fat cheroot which he puffed for effect rather than for pleasure, and looked with brotherly affection at the Tiger. "Jee Ko," he began softly, "you're the best brother anyone could ever have. I was so sad when you went to Singapore; I could not join you for a very good reason, a very dear and personal reason."

"I think I understand." The Tiger's words were very gentle.

If Boon Par was surprised he showed no sign of it. "Daw Saw has been a very good wife. I am happy with her." Boon Par paused. He continued when the expected comment was not forthcoming. "We have three children. The eldest is a girl. Cheng Hu is thirteen. Another girl, Cheng Sim, is seven." Boon Par noticed the anxiety on his brother's face. He smiled. "The third child is a boy. Cheng Chye is my youngest; he's four years old."

The Tiger flashed a wide grin, as much in delight as in relief. Every man must have at least a son to inherit. So much the better if the son is of his own flesh and blood. "Cheng Chye is a lucky name. I am very happy for you and your family. You must bring them with you to Singapore."

But it was easier said than done. Boon Haw's attempt to convince his Burmese sister-in-law of the advantages in moving to Singapore was of no avail. Daw Saw refused to be persuaded. "I have lived in Rangoon all my life and I could never fit into a foreign land. I am old and it is hard for me to change." She was actually thirty, a still slim and attractive woman. But like many Burmese women, she considered herself old after bearing three children.

"Will you then allow your children to go?" Boon Haw asked with some effort to conceal his annoyance. "They will have all the advantages there. It is the children's place to be with their father."

"You can take my man away from me but you can't take my children. What's to become of me when I am old and feeble? Who's to take care of me?"

"You shall not suffer from want of anything. I shall see to it," Boon Haw promised his sister-in-law. "You shall have a house to live in and money to spend for the rest of your life."

"No, my children stay with me!"

Boon Haw persisted. He cajoled and threatened. Finally, Madam Daw Saw said, "You can take Cheng Hu and go. Cheng Sim and Cheng Chye must stay with me. You cannot take everything from me. My life will be so empty."

"Your life need not be empty. You are still young. Many women don't marry until they are thirty or older."

"Women who marry at thirty don't have three children like me. Please take Cheng Hu, and go before I change my mind. I was born here and I shall die here!"

Boon Par came to live in the house that Boon Haw had vacated the previous year. With him were his third wife, Hong Yin, and eldest daughter Cheng Hu. He occupied the room below because his infirmity did not allow him to climb the stairs. Boon Haw walked over each morning to enquire about his brother's condition, and after the morning meal, helped his brother into his tiger car for the drive to the office.

"This is so nice," Boon Par commented as he surveyed the office he shared with his brother. "It is like old times to work together again in the same office. But this office is so much better, this building so much grander. We are really important people now, I wish I had come earlier."

Boon Haw beamed at his brother's approval. "The important thing is you are here at last. We have always worked as a team. And as a team we shall conquer the world. Everything here as elsewhere is as much yours as mine. We shall keep it in the family for a thousand years. Our father would have been so proud of us."

The seeds of a Haw Par dynasty were planted and the brothers gloated over their possessions. Boon Par then suggested consolidating their business. "It is time for us to slow down the pace. You have been working too hard, and I am not what I used to be."

Gently, Boon Haw replied, "Not yet. I have many plans. We must keep going or we shall lose our touch, and be overtaken by others."

"What do you have in mind?"

"We are going back to our motherland."

"But I am in no condition to travel."

"I know. But you are not going. You will be more useful here to keep an eye on things while I expand into China. Our people need our medicines. They are poor and our products are cheap and effective. We will sell them even cheaper than here. We must help our people."

The potential market in China was even greater than the combined market of Southeast Asia. Five hundred million and more against some two hundred million. A fabulous opportunity indeed to make an even more fabulous fortune.

Boon Haw was not one to let the grass grow under his feet. He went to Hongkong the same year Boon Par came to Singapore.

With money to pave the way, he had little difficulty renting a shop within a week. It was a well-situated outlet on Bonham Strand East. Every shop was owned and every house tenanted by a Chinese of the working class. Tiger Balm and its sister products were already well known in the colony of about a million inhabitants. Then, as now, ninety-nine percent of the population was Chinese.

Labour costs in Hongkong were even lower than in Singapore. But not low enough to make his medicines affordable to everyone and yet retain a high profit margin. His aim was a consumer price below that of Singapore. The solution was not difficult to find. The inexhaustible labour market on the mainland begged to be exploited.

Boon Haw picked Swatow to set up his first factory in China. This location would serve to supply not only Hongkong, but as much of China as possible. A chain of sales outlets along the coast followed shortly. Shanghai emerged as the top branch in terms of sales. It was to be the springboard for further expansion into the north just as Hongkong was a springboard into the south.

The launching in Hongkong met with instant success. A jar of Tiger Balm now cost half the price of the previously imported product. City dwellers bought two jars where one used to serve. One jar was carried on the person and the other left at home for the family. Peasants stocked up on the ointment and analgesic powders. Self-medication cost much less than a herbal prescription. Western medicine was beyond reach or was suspect. The widespread acceptance was no surprise to Boon Haw. He was confident from the start that the Hongkong and China operation was another gold mine. "Give the people what they want at a price they can afford and they will come back for more," he boasted. "Of course, your products must also be effective, like mine are."

Though Boon Haw was quite happy to exploit the China market, he had no intention of living in the country, even temporarily. The land was in constant turmoil. Warlords refused to be subdued. Communist influence was spreading. Corruption was rife. Chiang Kai Shek's Nationalists were divided into contending factions squabbling over whatever spoils they could lay their hands on. A militaristic Japan was knocking at its door. China faced domination by an Asian power after a century of humiliation by the West.

Hongkong was to be his second home, Boon Haw decided. It was also the best placed to direct the China operation. "The British are arrogant but they understand business. They don't interfere as long as you are legitimate," he told his compatriots when asked why he chose another British colony as his base. "They live by trade and they understand a trader's needs. Patriotism is a noble thing but patriotism towards my pocket is just as important. How can I help my countrymen if I am deprived of the opportunity to make money? Big money, not the kind that a shopkeeper makes."

Huge posters, printed as well as hand brushed, extolling the virtues of the instant cures, were pasted on every conspicuous wall space. Poster boys roamed the city to scout for strategic locations. One team covered Hongkong island. Another disfigured walls in Kowloon. Posters torn down by vandals or outraged house owners were replaced the next day. A few dollars usually placated the owner. The more stubborn were persuaded after a "discussion" with tough-looking protectionists. Each poster boy was paid a dollar to put up twenty posters. The springing tiger soon became as ubiquitous as the rickshaw.

The Swatow factory strained to meet the ever-growing demand. More workers were recruited. Production supervisors were instructed to increase the workers' productivity. Bonuses were offered for output beyond a set norm. The factory introduced double shifts from eight to four, and four to midnight. The late shift workers were provided with a free meal but no hardship pay. Many worked double shifts to earn extra income for simple luxuries such as more meat on the table or a bicycle.

Not surprisingly, Shanghai soon became the biggest outlet for Hongkong. Its population was twice that of the colony, and the Shanghainese were the most affluent among the Chinese. They were shrewd, industrious and thrifty. The free-spending habits of the large foreign community of many nationalities which carved up the great port city into their respective spheres of influence did not rub off on them. Medicines of every description from the West were freely available, yet Tiger Balm replaced Zam Buk, and Tiger Headache Cure outsold aspirin.

Big money began to flow in almost from the first day the Swatow factory opened. Half the output went to mainland consumers. Unwieldy-looking junks meandered their way along the two hundred-odd miles of winding coastline carrying Tiger brand medicines as far north as Shanghai. Junks were slow but cheap. Overland transportation ran the risk of hijacking by highway robbers. Peasants turned to banditry when harvests failed and families went hungry. Not all *taikongs* were honest captains. But Boon Haw ensured their loyalty with generous bonuses and promises that their families would be well looked after should pirates maim or kill the breadwinners.

If all else failed, a friendly call from a triad chieftain would bring the most rascally *taikong* into line. The arms of the triad reached everywhere. Boon Haw's early patronage of the Rangoon chapter had reached the ears of the Swatow underworld. If the law fell short, there was another to be bought. The most important consideration was the safe delivery of the cargo and the consequent profit.

Boon Haw lived in a rented house just outside Hongkong's notorious Wanchai district. The area adjacent to the island's commercial district was a hotbed of crime. The triads divided Wanchai into sub-districts, each under a *tong* leader. Policemen seldom ventured into the gangsters' domain, certainly never at night . The foolhardy ended up floating in the harbour. Periodical police raids netted only the small fry, the sacrificial "soldiers" offered as token prisoners to appease the Commissioner. Pay-offs in return for tips on impending raids were made regularly. Station sergeants grew rich. District Commanders grew grey in frustration.

Successive anti-crime campaigns only seemed to spawn more crime. And more gangsters. Hoodlums from Canton muscled in when they heard of the rich pickings to be had in the colony. The result was gang warfare. The police often turned a blind eye to the mayhem in Wanchai. "It saves us the trouble of exterminating those vermin," commented a senior officer. "Let them kill one another all they want. We will just clear up the bodies after the slaughter is over."

There was no end to the clearing of bodies. For every thug eliminated, two others took his place. Truces were broken as often as they were called. The racketeering continued. More tips were passed on. More sergeants grew richer.

Opium and prostitution in Hongkong thrived side by side. Opium dens doubled as brothels. Girls who rolled opium beads for pampered patrons were also prepared to satisfy their baser needs. It was expected of them and encouraged by the den masters. The house took half the girls' earnings. Opium dulled the senses and aroused passion. It was a foolish girl indeed who did not take advantage. The more greedy would have no qualms rolling the man for what he was worth, and leaving him to rue the night he had indulged when day broke.

Gambling was illegal in a community where the urge to gamble was in the blood. But there was little the law could do to curb it, let alone to suppress the widespread practice. *Fan tan* was the commonest form of gambling and mahjong the latest craze. Black *fan tan* oblong tiles vied with white mahjong squares to produce the louder clatter in gambling dens, homes, clubs, five-foot pedestrian walkways and just about anywhere there was a flat surface and some shade.

Extortion spawned protection. Extortioner and protector often worked hand in hand. The shopkeeper's lot was a choice between getting beaten up by the extortioner or having his premises wrecked by the protector. As neither choice was palatable, he had no alternative but to pay both extortioner and protector.

As in Rangoon and in Singapore, Boon Haw was not subject to open extortion. He did not pay protection money as such. His method of ensuring personal as well as business security was more subtle. Among his first acts was a very generous donation to "charity."

"Distribute the money to whoever you consider deserving," he instructed the self-appointed headman of Wanchai. After deducting his "fee" for services to be rendered, he "donated" half the money to the chiefs of the Hongkong and Canton triads. The other half was distributed to the genuinely poor and destitute. Even the triads would think twice before doing harm to a champion of the underprivileged.

To be in Hongkong was to meet Cantonese everywhere you turned, hear the dialect spoken wherever you went, and to do business with Cantonese whether you liked it or not. Boon Haw changed his attitude towards this glib-tongued people from Canton and put aside his mistrust of the unfortunate *dhobi's* compatriots. He had no choice if he wanted to succeed. They were second only to the Shanghainese in their flair for business. As a consequence, his Hongkong branch employed mostly Cantonese.

Boon Haw needed someone who knew Hongkong intimately and who could be relied on to do his bidding without question. His two expatriates from Singapore knew the Tiger Balm business as well as any employee he had. But they were quite lost in Hongkong. They did not speak the dialect and this rendered them quite helpless. And useless for the Tiger's purpose. He hired a succession of Cantonese assistants and fired them with equal haste. It was not that they were incompetent. He just did not understand their mentality. "They talk too much," he complained. "They are argumentative, stubborn and sly. They can't get along with people." It did not occur to him that the shoe could fit the other foot.

Nineteen

A Cantonese in his early forties walked into the Bonham Street store a few months after the opening and asked to see the big boss. "The boss is busy," the clerk said and attempted to brush him aside. "If you are seeking a donation, I'd advise you to write in."

"I am not here for charity. I'm giving Eng Aun Tong business. Big business."

"The boss does not take orders. I do. How much medicine do you want?"

"I don't deal with clerks. I want to see your boss. I am Leung Sin Loong."

"Never heard of you before."

"You will hear a lot of me in future if you continue to be rude," the Cantonese replied.

It was noon. Boon Haw came out of his temporary office from a backroom to go for lunch. A rented Humber rumbled impatiently. The Chinese chauffeur stood by to open the door. "*Chow san, tai si tow,*" Leung greeted the big boss as soon as he saw him. "Have you eaten?"

"I am on my way. Who are you?"

"I am Leung Sin Loong, your servant. Will the big boss give me some face to take him to lunch?"

"I like to eat alone."

"I know a place which serves the best *sum sum* stew in Hongkong. Also bird's nest soup in Korean ginseng."

The mere mention of the dish stirred his interest. He looked at the brash man and saw Western clothes draped smartly over a spare frame. A bright red tie was knotted the way he would like to knot his, but which he never mastered. The slight scowl he gave the intruder was returned by a smile which lit up the face and revealed longish white teeth anchored to receding gums. Boon Haw's instinct was to brush him aside. But there was something beguiling about the man. His impeccable Cantonese betrayed his origin. People from Canton were always pushy. Cantonese were not really fanciers of dog meat. An occasional bowl for its purported health properties perhaps, but never as common fare. It was a tempting invitation. Boon Haw had not eaten the health-giving dish since his arrival in Hongkong.

Emboldened by a silence where a rebuke was expected, Leung continued, "I came to talk business with the big boss. Big business. As much business as your factory can offer."

Another one of those tricksters who live by their wits, Boon Haw thought. But he sounded earnest. He looked prosperous. Besides, a helping of dog meat cooked in fragrant herbs was just what he needed to buck him up. The past few weeks had not been easy. Setting up a business was an energy-sapping task. He had a great need for some tonic food to restore his vitality.

"Is it far to the three threes restaurant?" Three threes add up to nine which has the same sound as "dog" in Cantonese. Dog eaters could be subtle in speech if not in eating habits.

"Very near. Ten minutes by rickshaw."

Boon Haw hesitated. It was not a good enough excuse to go out with a stranger just to dine on dog meat. "What sort of business do you have in mind, Mr Leung?"

"Ai ya, big boss. There's time enough for that. We can discuss better on a full stomach. I, too, am very fond of dog meat and it would be so much more satisfying eating it with an illustrious person like you." Actually, he loathed the dish.

"Let's go in my car."

"As the big boss pleases. I shall sit in front with the driver."

Boon Haw liked the man's flattery. He liked his humility and,

197

most of all, he liked the respect shown to him. He stepped into the car and sank into the soft seat. The Cantonese closed the rear door after the big boss with one hand and opened the front with the other. He jumped in and took his place beside the driver. This Cantonese knows his proper place, thought the proud Hakka.

Leung Sin Loong directed the driver to a side street off Queen's Road. It was steep and narrow. It was lined with hawkers peddling vegetables, fish and assorted meats. Flies buzzed on pale chunks of fatty pork and then transferred their attention to slabs of bloody beef hung on bamboo poles. Fresh water fish swam in wooden tubs while fish from the ocean lay lifeless on wooden crates. A woman reached into a bamboo basket cramped with chickens and pulled out a squawking hen by its scrawny neck.

"How much for this half-dead bird?" she asked the vendor.

"Fifty cents."

"Corpse's head! Why so dear?"

"This hen is young. Lay eggs only two seasons. Still very tender."

"Thirty cents."

"Ai ya! You want to bankrupt me? Forty cents. Last price."

"Thirty five cents."

"I'll sell you a rooster for thirty five cents. Weighs twice as much."

"Your rooster is as old as your corpse's head. You eat it yourself. I'll have the hen. Very dear."

"Very cheap. It's a bargain."

The hen would cost twenty cents wholesale. Overheads cost next to nothing. How else could street vendors become shopowners in a short time? Daily marketing was a dreary chore relieved only by the joy of haggling and the self-deluding satisfaction of outwitting the unbeatable vendor.

Sin Loong peered through the windscreen as the Humber inched its way uphill. He tapped the driver's shoulder and said, "Stop, we're there." Over the doorway of a not-too-clean eating shop hung a signboard boldly painted with the numerals "333."

"Big boss, this is the shop that serves the best stew. They cook only the meat of young dogs. Tender and tasty. I know the proprietor. He will serve us personally. I'll introduce you."

Aw Boon Haw needed no introduction. The skinny owner instantly recognised the man in the big black car. He came out smiling and kowtowing. "To what do I owe this great honour of your patronage, Mr Aw Boon Haw? Please come into my humble shop so that I can serve the great philanthropist personally."

Boon Haw was persuaded neither by the man's grovelling manner nor by the blatant flattery. His nostrils distended as the aroma of delicately spiced meat wafted towards him. The vision of pinky tender morsels swimming in thick gravy was persuasion enough.

"I represent a syndicate which obtains all kinds of produce from the mainland," the Cantonese said as Boon Haw ate. "But the peasants and villagers demand Tiger Balm in part payment. Your medicines are very popular, but they are available mostly in the coastal districts and not in the interior where they are very dear. My principals cannot get enough supply. They therefore cannot buy as much produce as they require. With Tiger Balm they can. Tiger Balm sells for many times the price in Swatow. Tiger Balm could buy us many times the quantity we can now obtain and make us many times the usual profit. If you can supply us all we want, my principals are prepared to share their profit with you. Very good business for us. Very good business for Eng Aun Tong. You like our proposal?"

The Tiger did not like it. He saw through the ploy. They wanted to corner the Tiger Balm market and create an artificial shortage and then sell the ointment at grossly inflated prices at the expense of the poor consumers. And at the expense of Boon Haw's reputation. He suddenly lost his appetite and plonked down his bowl of rice on the marble-topped table. The bowl broke. The Tiger swore. The Cantonese jumped in fright.

"Big boss, did a bone stick in your throat?"

"Something did stick in my throat. But it certainly was not a bone."

"You don't like what I said?"

"I don't like people who try to cheat poor people."

Leung Sin Loong changed his tune. He was too shrewd a man not to realise that Boon Haw had seen through the game. "I did not like the idea myself. But I am just a paid servant who does as he is told. A man has to make a living one way or another."

A likely story, thought Boon Haw. Probably a schemer who employs other people's money for his personal profit. A rascal in respectable clothing. A nimble mind which could turn adversity into a blessing.

"I could kick your bony backside in front of all these people," the Tiger threatened.

"I deserve a thousand kicks."

Boon Haw suppressed a smile. This scoundrel in fine clothes appeared to be a man who could serve him well. The Tiger was partial to a person who was ready to admit guilt and to grovel in penitence. A survivor with a glib tongue and a talent to wriggle out of uncomfortable situations. A useful man to have in his entourage of flunkies.

"But I am not going to kick you."

"You are truly a man of great understanding, big boss. I thank you. I wish I could do something for you in return."

"You can."

"Good, good. Tell me what I can do to be in your favour again."

"I want you to cut all your connections with whoever employs you and work for me."

"It will be a great honour to work for a great man. But what can I do? I am not familiar with the medicine business."

"You can do a lot by doing just as I say."

The Cantonese liked the idea of working for this proud and impulsive Hakka. He had become disenchanted with his backers who used him as their front man in their shady deals.

"Your offer flatters me more than I know what to say. Please do not think I am ungrateful if I ask how much you will pay me."

"How much I choose to give you depends on how well you please me. At any rate you shall have more than enough to keep you in fine clothes. Do you want to work for me or don't you?"

"I am your servant. I know you are a fair man who will not treat me like a beggar."

"One thing more. Who is your tailor?"

The Cantonese flashed his toothy smile at the oblique compliment.

"I will bring him to you after we have finished eating. Will my new big boss allow me to order him another bowl of rice? And another bowl of hot stew?"

Leung Sin Loong also ordered for himself another helping of the stew he detested. He must show he liked what the boss liked. This was the first lesson he had learned when he set out to live by his wits at the age of sixteen.

The new employee was an invaluable "Man Friday" to his capricious boss. He seldom said no and would attempt anything for his employer, even though he knew the job would surely fail. He became known as the "yes man" among the Tiger's employees. He took their sneers in good humour and was not backward in returning their jibes with interest. "Your wives will seek other men if you allow your manhood to wither with jealousy," he once countered partly in jest but mainly in malice. But he did not forgive the clerk who treated him with such scorn. The man was eventually fired. Sin Loong had plenty of opportunity to plant the right word in the boss's ear.

Boon Haw's vision at forty-six was as clear as any man's his age. But he fancied spectacles. All the very rich men he knew wore spectacles. And he was richer than most. "Sin Loong, how would I look with spectacles?" he asked his alter ego one morning on their way to the store.

"Even more distinguished than you already are, big boss," came the quick reply. "Provided you get the right spectacles." He was just as quick to qualify his opinion.

"And what do you think are the right spectacles for me?"

"Gold spectacles, of course. Gold signifies wealth. Gold brings good luck. Gold for the *tai pan* with the golden touch."

Boon Haw liked the sound of *tai pan*. It had the same meaning as *tai si tow* – big boss. But *tai pan* had the ring of power and authority, attributes he understood and respected. He was an authoritarian and he demanded respect from everyone. The term had been associated mostly with the powerful foreign merchants since the days of the opium trade more than a hundred years ago. But Boon Haw considered himself to be more qualified than foreigners to receive that form of address. He would soon be a greater captain of industry than the conniving traders from the West, he promised himself.

"Where do you think I could get spectacles worthy of a *tai pan?*"

"I know a man who makes the best spectacles in Hongkong. He is *kwai loh*, but a very good craftsman. My *tai pan* will have the best twenty-four carat gold spectacles money can buy."

Joseph Ezekiel sat on the bench provided for customers. He was a fair and well-built man of indeterminate age. His mane of light brown hair was greying at the temples but his face was unlined and his eyes alert. They darted everywhere as if on the lookout for pursuers. It was midday. He had waited an hour. He was hungry.

On Ezekiel's lap lay a valise containing specimens of spectacle frames. It was his stock in trade. Resting on the bench beside him was a small brown paperbag. It contained his lunch. Ezekiel looked at his watch for the umpteenth time and finally decided to appease his hunger.

The valise placed flat on his lap served as a dining table for his spartan fare. A small flask of tea, a chunk of unleavened bread, a block of cheese and an apple was the menu. He was not a poor man, his trade served him well, but to be parsimonious was a trait that had sustained his scattered people for two thousand years.

Ezekiel half-filled the flask cap with tea and took a bite of his cheese. At that moment Boon Haw walked in followed closely by Sin Loong. The millionaire stopped and looked in surprise at the man on the bench. What was this European man doing here among the locals instead of some lofty place lording over his minions? More amazing was the fact that he was eating on a bench like some coolie by the roadside. Eating food that could hardly fill the belly of a child. Boon Haw stood and stared.

Sin Loong hastened forward and said, "Big boss, this is the man I've asked to come about your spectacles. He is highly recommended."

Boon Haw recovered and nodded. "Ask him to come into my room."

Ezekiel carefully returned his food into the paperbag and followed Sin Loong.

The Tiger invited the optician to take a seat. He was intrigued by this European who did not behave like one. He did not even dress like one. No tie and no jacket. Just a pair of grey trousers and a white shirt, short sleeved. Unable to hold back his curiosity any longer he asked, "Why does a European like you do such a humble job selling spectacles?"

Ezekiel smiled. "It is a living."

"But Europeans are not contented with just making a living. They want great wealth and power."

"Many do. Many can. Many cannot. The honourable Mr Aw is already a rich man and will soon be a great man. To be rich is to be powerful. I may be a rich man one day myself. I may not. It does not matter. For the present I shall help people to see better."

"But all Europeans do not think like you."

"All Europeans are not like me. Nor I like the Europeans you see."

Ezekiel brought out his test lenses. He fitted one after another into a dummy frame to test the Tiger's vision. None suited. He fitted a non-magnifying lens. The Tiger smiled and nodded his head. The man did not need glasses but insisted on being fitted. Ezekiel obliged. Boon Haw chose an oval frame from the many specimens laid out on his desk. "Make it in gold," he instructed. "Solid gold, not plated. Make sure it is twenty-four carats."

"No, no. It is too soft. Your spectacles will bend. At most, eighteen carats."

Boon Haw was not convinced. Gold was not gold unless it was pure gold.

"Are you sure you can't make it in twenty-four carats?"

"I can but it will not be good and you will blame my workmanship. Fourteen carats is even better."

"No, no. Make it eighteen then. The more gold the better. How much?"

"It will depend on how much gold is needed. I can make you a pair for one hundred dollars or another costing twice as much."

"Make me a two-hundred-dollar pair. Here's the money."

Ezekiel accepted the advance payment and said, "I'll come back next week with your spectacles. It will be the best pair I have ever made."

Boon Haw was eating his lunch in his office when Ezekiel returned one week later. The previous night's carousing had given him a sluggish liver and he had decided against going out for a regular meal. A bowl of beef and noodles was all he wanted. Sin Loong peeped in and announced, "The spectacles man is waiting outside."

"Send him in, you wooden head!"

Ezekiel apologised when he saw the strands of noodles dangling from the Tiger's mouth. "I'll come back later."

Boon Haw sucked in the offending strands with a whistling sound and replied, "Sit down. Are my spectacles ready?"

"Yes, Mr Aw. I have them with me."

"Have you eaten?"

"Not yet."

"Did you bring your paperbag?"

"I always do when I go out."

"Then please eat while I eat."

"The *tai si tow* is very considerate."

"Eating is a very important function of life. Even kings stop affairs of state when it is time to eat."

Ezekiel produced his flask, bread, cheese and apple.

"You had the same food last week. A cat eats more. Do you eat the same food every day?"

"I have no one to cook for me. This is a simple but nourishing meal."

"Surely it is not enough for a big man like you?"

"Enough, I only eat to live."

And I live to eat, besides making money, thought the millionaire.

"Can I ask my man to order you a bowl of noodles?"

"No, no. Thank you very much. I only eat our food. We call it kosher food."

Boon Haw had no idea what the man meant. To him, food was food. The Buddhists did not eat beef. The Muslims shunned pork. He would eat anything that moved, provided it tasted good. Or was supposedly good for his health.

Boon Haw wolfed down his noodles while Ezekiel nibbled at his cheese and bread. When the apple was eaten down to the core, the optician put it into the paperbag, dusting invisible crumbs off the desk and said, "Thank you for sharing your meal with me."

"But you ate your own food."

"To share your time with me is the same as sharing your food with me. I am grateful you did not make me go hungry."

"You are a most unusual person. I have never met anyone like you."

"I am a Jew. We are a much misunderstood people. And often maligned. For instance, we practise parsimony and are accused of miserliness. To us, to be parsimonious is to be thrifty and not mean."

"You do not behave like the other Europeans. They are so arrogant."

"If by European you mean someone born in Europe then I am one."

"They have no time for the others except when they can make a lot of money out of them."

"The Europeans have little time for us too. We are refugees. We are victims of the Bolsheviks because we are capitalists. We are not Russian aristocrats who also fled Russia for their lives. They are the white Russians. But because we, too, came from Russia we are regarded as one of them. Please forgive me, I'm afraid I bore you."

"No, no I'm not bored. Please go on. So you are not a Russian although you were born in Russia."

"I am, or was, a Russian by nationality but a Jew is a Jew wherever he is born. Like many of my people, I am now a stateless person. We were driven out of our rightful land two thousand years ago. We are all survivors waiting for the day when we shall return to the land of our forefathers. Our promised land. The dispossessed shall repossess. Not as usurpers but as legitimate claimants to what is rightly ours.

"In the meantime, we are unwelcome guests of whichever country we happen to be in. Jews among gentiles. We dispersed to survive. We survive to return home. We will meet again next year in Jerusalem or the next and the next. But we shall return. Shalom."

Ezekiel's expression grew radiant as he talked. His mind was thousands of miles away in a yet to be reborn Israel. There was no bitterness nor despair. He was reminding himself of his people's plight and renewing the promise they had made to themselves. A people scattered, persecuted and humiliated, but never losing faith.

"We are alike in some ways," Boon Haw said. "We Hakkas do not have a province of our own in China. Hakka means 'guest people.' Imagine a Chinese living as a guest in his own country."

"We will be all right as long as we have faith in ourselves; faith in our individual endeavours. Faith and determination. Now may I show you your spectacles?"

Boon Haw put on his spectacles and studied his reflection in the hand-held mirror provided by the optician. He looked at the painting of his namesake on the far wall and nodded in satisfaction. He looked at the tiger again without his glasses and said, "The picture is as clear with spectacles as without."

"Quite so," the optician agreed. "I told you that you did not need spectacles but you insisted."

"I may not need them but I want them. I think I look good with them on."

"Very good, big boss," added Sin Loong who was standing behind Ezekiel. "You look even more distinguished, especially with the gold around your eyes."

Ezekiel smiled slyly and said, "As you are named after the tiger, I've taken the liberty of putting a tiger on your spectacles."

"Good, good," Boon Haw smiled back in delight as his finger caressed the springing animal carved on the bridge of the frame. "You are a very good spectacle maker."

"The gold cost one hundred and sixty five dollars. I charge only thirty dollars for my work. Here is the balance from the two hundred you gave me."

"You are a very good and honest spectacle maker. Please buy yourself some apples with the five dollars."

The millionaire and the optician understood each other perfectly even though they could converse only in fractured Cantonese.

Twenty

Colonel Ivan Petrowski became a casualty of the Russian Revolution when the Bolsheviks toppled Tsar Nicholas and proclaimed his kingdom a socialist republic. He lost everything he treasured. Vast tracts of land which the family owned for generations were confiscated along with those of the other members of the Russian gentry. Most of all, he lost the one thing he valued most: his position in the royal household.

As were his father and grandfather before him, Petrowski was privy to the Tsar's confidences. He was senior officer of the household guards in St Petersburg, and rubbed shoulders with royalty like he was one of them. He was born into a life of privilege that was the birthright of the ruling class.

But with the dawn of the irresistible Bolshevik uprising, he was lucky to escape with his life, thanks to a faithful retainer who hid him and his family in his country house. His only son Stefan, whom he was grooming to succeed to his exalted position, was killed by the mobs. Olga, his wife, was inconsolable. His daughter Tanya, a sheltered twelve-year-old, was too young or too terrified to understand why their world of glitter and abundance had suddenly come tumbling down.

The Kaiser's army blocked escape to the west. Petrowski bundled his heartbroken wife and weeping child into a donkey cart and set out east. They were disguised in peasant clothes provided by an old retainer. Everything was left behind except for some jewels sewn into the lining of an old camel hair coat. The gems would ensure their survival unless apprehended by the communists or robbed by peasants in the now lawless countryside.

Petrowski had no idea of his destination. His one aim was to flee the terror. To leave Mother Russia and the anarchy as far behind as he could. The old retainer was faithful to the end. He was their servant, guide and friend during their three-year trek across the hostile Siberian wastes. The little party met hundreds of other White Russians in similar plight. Many perished or lost the will to survive.

Deliverance of a sort came when the Petrowski family crossed the border into Mongolia. It was foreign soil, out of bounds to pursuers real or imagined. The band of refugees, which at one time numbered some two hundred, had dwindled to less than half. Many were too sick to continue. The dispossessed aristocrats sold their jewels to pay their way to Tientsin where they hoped to receive succour from the large European community in the port. Instead, they were ignored.

Petrowski headed for Shanghai. The great port was already host to a larger number of displaced White Russians. The welcome to these refugees by their white compatriots had worn thin by the time the Petrowskis arrived. The colonel knew of no profession other than soldiering. The family survived by prudent disposal of the few remaining pieces of jewellery. Olga pined for the life they had left behind. There was no longer the will to live when she fell ill. Ivan succumbed to extreme depression when his wife died, and he, too, followed her shortly after. Tanya was left to face the world alone and unprepared.

The child who had fled her homeland and all the privileges into which she was born had grown into a beautiful child-woman of sixteen. Deprivations had not arrested her blooming. Shabby and ill-fitting clothes did not conceal the form that promised of even greater seduction. Tanya's dignified bearing betrayed her aristocratic blood. Her poise and composure were inherited attributes. Her crowning glory was her head of golden hair which cascaded down her shoulders like cornsilk over a tender ear of maize. The girl was unaware of the beauty that drew admiration from the refined and lust from the coarse.

Her father's death left her in a daze. She was cast adrift to face a world she dreaded. The sparsely furnished flat she lived in offered nothing but bitter memories. She was destitute. Tanya locked herself in the flat and refused to receive fellow White Russians who called to enquire about her welfare.

Hunger drove her out of her cocoon one week later. She wandered downstairs and knocked at the door of the tenant below. A peroxide head appeared through the partly opened door, recognised her and called out, "Oh, Tanya my dear child, we have been so worried about you. Come in, come in, you poor, poor dear."

Tanya hesitated when she saw the plush interior of the apartment. It had been a long time since she lived in comfortable surroundings. Her lot had been terror, cold, mud, hunger and living in wretched hovels. The comforts of home had become alien things.

The woman gently pulled Tanya into the room and swiftly closed the door. The hungry Russian girl just stood and stared at the rich furnishings. A chandelier sparkled with the reflection of a hundred crystal prisms. Two beautiful European girls each occupied an overstuffed armchair while a third stretched a languid form on a ten-foot couch. Under the half-starved orphan's feet spread a Tientsin carpet with a Ming motif and silken pile an inch thick. On the far wall was a built-in bar with a bewildering array of bottled spirits over a glass-fronted cabinet full of the finest crystal ware. A statue of the Virgin Mary and Child occupied an arched recess above the door. Purple velvet curtains hanging from ceiling to floor shielded what went on inside from prying eyes.

Though below the standard of luxury into which she was born, Tanya was reminded of her home. She burst into tears. She wept for her paradise lost forevermore. She wept for her brother and for her parents. She wept for her present circumstances and for what was to become of her. She wept copious tears and found some relief. The freeing of pent-up emotions loosened her taut nerves. The need for sleep became overwhelming. She collapsed on the floor and did not wake up until the next day.

Madame Arlette was a French woman who did what she did best: pleasing men. Her series of affairs in Paris had resulted in divorce. When her current lover asked her to accompany him to Shanghai where he was to take up a new posting in the French Settlement, she had accepted without hesitation. Life in Shanghai for the high income expatriates was a continuous round of champagne parties. And easy liaisons. Her lover was recalled home when war broke out. Arlette chose to stay put.

She had become enamoured of a dashing, but naive, young American. She was ten years his senior. She enjoyed his youthful exuberance as much as she enjoyed giving him the benefit of her experience and sophistication. Arlette was left once again without a lover when America entered the war in 1917. He left Shanghai to enlist in the navy.

There didn't seem to be much future in devoting her time to any one man. The war in Europe had taken away men of romance and generosity. A lover of this breed had become a rare commodity. But there were many who were less able-bodied but more discreet who sought liaisons with no strings attached. Older men with money. Willing to sow late oats and paying handsomely for the effort. Arlette became a social escort.

She was still an attractive thirty-three, full of life and vivacity, an accomplished mistress in the art of pleasing men, young or old. She decided to change her appearance with a change in profession. Her dark brown hair became a shriek of blond. Her cheeks were more generously rouged to recapture the bloom of youth long gone and her crimson lips boldly advertised her availability. Her flair for dressing set her apart. Deft alterations here and there, and well-chosen accessories, transformed her old Paris garments into high-fashion clothes as if they were fresh out of the designer's workroom.

Arlette was an instant success. Men clamoured for her time.

Stodgy ageing merchants coaxed stiff joints to match her nimble feet on the dance floor. In a society of unscrupulous adventurers, there was nothing like having a lovely woman in one's arms to revive one's lost gallantry. Men fought over her. Women feared her. But they needn't have bothered. Arlette was having too good a time and making better money to consider setting up another love nest.

In spite of her spendthrift ways, Arlette had a sizeable nest egg stashed away when war ended. The ravages of a fast life began to show on her face and her figure. Hours of preening before the mirror could not hide the crow's feet. Corsets were little help in containing an expanding waistline and a sagging bosom. "I'll give the old goats two more years of my life and then I shall pack up and return to Paris," she promised herself. But Arlette changed her mind when 1920 arrived.

Shanghai had become a sanctuary to thousands of White Russian refugees. Many were destitute. Many daughters of the dispossessed aristocracy were also beauties who drifted in in such numbers as Shanghai had never seen before. There was gold to be mined in those unfortunate girls.

Each time she had to disappoint a man who sought her favours, Arlette was asked to introduce another girl to fill the bill. She obliged but her substitutes were never satisfactory. They were all young and pretty, but being Chinese and of an alien culture, the girls lacked the social graces demanded. They were bedded but seldom escorted to social functions to be displayed.

But the Russian girls would be more than just right to add lustre to the dull social scene. Arlette wasted little time. Within a week she had recruited four girls, all under twenty and every one a peach. She housed them in her apartment and dressed them in stylish clothes. With proper shelter, food and restored confidence, it did not take long for the girls' breeding to resurface in public. Arlette was pleased. Her wards were grateful.

Arlette's became the most exclusive address within a short

time. None but the favoured and generous were admitted into her close circle of social escorts. She ceased to entertain the many patrons who still preferred her sophistication and devoted all her time to her new business. She became mother, counsellor, friend, teacher, confidante and, occasionally, disciplinarian to her wards. Most of all, she relished her role as mistress of her classy brood. She kept half the girls' earnings in return for all the essentials and many luxuries a girl could ordinarily need.

Not surprisingly, some girls developed more permanent liaisons and moved out. She recruited replacements and additions. Only the best and most attractive crossed her portals. There was no shortage of young ladies of high birth. They all wanted a life of ease after the ordeal of flight and resettlement. The girls were on call to men who could afford their price and who met with Madame Arlette's approval.

Tanya woke up in semi-delirium. Another day had passed without food. She was too weak to get out of bed. She called out for her nursemaid who had deserted the family in the first days of the revolution. She called for her mother and then her father. But no familiar face appeared. She cried in despair. Caterina, the only one left of the original four girls recruited, came into the room. Her heart reached out to the hapless girl. She was one of her own kind. The older girl understood more than Arlette or any other non-Russian could, the feeling of utter hopelessness that afflicted the abandoned. Caterina befriended Tanya and promised to help her as much as she could.

It was only to be expected that Tanya become a member of Arlette's establishment when she recovered. There was nowhere else she could go. She had no skills but was blessed with uncommon beauty. Her only friends were Caterina and the other girls in the apartment. Moreover, Arlette was kind and considerate. When she asked Tanya what she would like to do, the girl answered without hesitation, "Why, work for you, of course." It was a way of paying her debt and making a living.

Tanya was sixteen, the youngest and prettiest among the bevy of beauties. She became the most treasured gem in Arlette's collection. Her company was available only at a premium and only to those personally approved by the French woman. Once again, life was secure. She had always been dependent on others. She now had Arlette to depend on.

Tanya had just turned twenty-one when she met Robert, the Englishman. The years of being constantly in the company of men from disparate backgrounds and different inclinations had turned her into a woman who mistrusted men. None had attracted her until Robert came into her life. She was disarmed by his boyish charm and insatiable zest for life. He was extraordinarily attentive and unreasonably jealous. A tipsy member passed a rude remark about "Russian scum" when Robert showed off Tanya in the club in the British Concession. Robert punched the man and was in turn punched into senselessness.

Tanya helped her lover back to his flat and spent the night with him. It was against Arlette's rule which required every one of her girls to return to her apartment no matter how late she was kept out. But there were exceptions to rules. Tanya was in love and any rule could be broken for the sake of love.

On an impulse Robert proposed marriage the next morning. Tanya accepted. She moved in with him one week later. Tanya was extremely happy, but little did she know that Robert was running out of money. He was a remittance man. His wealthy father in London was quite happy to send him a generous monthly cheque as long as the black sheep son could be kept away from dipping his sticky fingers into the family till. The gambling debt his father had settled prior to his banishment was sufficient to pay a king's ransom. Tanya, the escort girl, longed to become Tanya, the respectable wife, as soon as possible.

"Wait till we get back to England and I promise you a grand wedding with all my family present," Robert assured her every time she popped the question of marriage. Promise followed promise.

They were living on borrowed time. Two years passed in blissful abandon.

When the first waves of passion had subsided, Robert resumed his visits to the clubs to drink and gamble. He drank more than he should, and gambled with a fervour as though there were no tomorrow. He pledged remittances yet to come and his losses mounted. His creditors threatened to break his arms for dishonouring his pledges. Shanghai became too inhospitable a place to continue his exile.

Robert charmed his way into the confidence of the American captain of a freighter and was offered free passage for both him and Tanya to Hongkong. Tanya's beauty captivated the good captain. Robert's tale of losing his job due to office politics earned him the seaman's sympathy and charity. The captain introduced Robert to his ship's agents in Hongkong with the request that they assist the young couple in any way they could. Before parting the American pressed some money on Robert. "Here's some dough, pal. It ain't much but it should see you and that honey of a girl of yours through for a spell." Five hundred dollars was a godsend to the down-and-out Robert.

Robert and Tanya checked into the Peninsula Hotel across the bay from Hongkong island. Only the best would do even if the means were meagre. It was more in keeping with the lifestyle into which Robert was born. Tanya was delighted.

"Do you know of a *kwai loh* who is prepared to undertake a little job for a lot of money?" Sin Loong asked the shipping manager.

"What is it that you require this *kwai loh* to do?"

"Oh, nothing much. Just to take a suitcase from Macau to Hongkong."

"And for that he's to be paid a lot of money?"

"Who are we to be concerned if the people involved are prepared to pay whatever they want to pay? Look, there's a hundred dollars bonus for you if you can find the right man."

Sin Loong was well known to the shipping manager. He was a frequent caller to arrange for various shipments on behalf of whoever employed him. There had been no complications. Moreover, a hundred dollars was nothing to be sneered at.

"Yes, I think I know someone who is willing to take the suitcase. He is an Englishman who is temporarily out of work. I can't promise I can get him but I will try. How much is the job worth?"

"One thousand dollars."

"That's a lot of money to carry a suitcase."

"That's a very special suitcase."

Sin Loong took out a wad of notes. He peeled off five crisp bills.

"Here's half your bonus. Fifty dollars." He counted out another ten. "And here's a hundred for the *kwai loh*. The other nine will be paid when the case is delivered. Together with your fifty."

Robert was overwhelmed. It was a most unexpected windfall. He did not bother to ask what the case contained. Never look a gift horse in the mouth. He would have travelled to Timbuktu and back for half the money. It was too good to be true. But a hundred dollars in his pocket told him it was true.

Sin Loong was introduced to Robert in the manager's office. The Cantonese approved of the Englishman's fine bearing and impeccable manners. It would be difficult to find another more respectable-looking European in all Hongkong. He invited Robert to dinner to get better acquainted. Robert brought Tanya to sample proper Cantonese cuisine. Like the American captain before him, Sin Loong was captivated by Tanya's beauty when she walked into the expensive Chinese restaurant on the arm of the handsome Robert.

Robert spent the first day in Macau idly placing small bets in the casino. A Portuguese Eurasian approached him on the second day and whispered, "The suitcase will be delivered to your room tonight. You will leave by the first ferry tomorrow morning."

The ferry tied up at the pier and the mainly Chinese passengers rushed to disembark. Robert beckoned to a porter to carry his bag. Gentlemen did not carry their own baggage. A customs officer together with a British police inspector and three constables stood at the landing and eyed each debarking passenger. Robert walked towards the landing some distance behind the porter. His instinct warned him of danger. The customs officer stopped the porter and opened the suitcase. He lifted out a parcel wrapped in hessian cloth. He sniffed the parcel and exchanged a few words with the inspector. The policeman unhitched a pair of handcuffs from his belt and snapped them smartly around the wrists of the protesting porter.

Robert disappeared into the milling crowd. A nattily dressed Chinese nearby nonchalantly walked towards a waiting rickshaw and urged the puller to hurry off. Sin Loong and Robert would have been caught with the parcel of opium if the police party had waited a few more minutes.

The Cantonese and the Englishman met in the shipping manager's office that afternoon. "Mr Robert must leave Hongkong immediately," Sin Loong said in a panic. "The porter must have told the police about Mr Robert by now and they will surely find him soon. And I, too, will be arrested."

"And me, what about me?" wailed the manager. "Ai ya! Mr Leung, why do you have to smuggle opium? I would never have recommended Mr Robert or anybody else if I had known."

"How can we get Mr Robert out of Hongkong?" Sin Loong asked. "The sooner the better."

The shipping manager was just as panicky. He induced Robert to sign up as an ordinary seaman on a steamer bound for Europe that night. Robert was easily persuaded. He did not relish the idea of languishing behind bars in a foreign jail. It was too risky for him to cross over to Kowloon to explain to Tanya. "I shall see her tomorrow. Tell me what you want to say to her," Sin Loong volunteered.

Robert scribbled a short note, asked the manager for an

envelope, put the note and some money into it and handed it to Sin Loong. "Give this to my lady. You got me into this mess. You've got to help her in any way you can."

Tanya read the note and cried her heart out:

"My precious Darling ... something dreadful has happened. I must leave immediately. But I am all right. Take heart, my love. I shall send for you as soon as I am able. Eternally yours ... Robby."

Months passed before Tanya heard from Robert again.

"... though I am in England, my heart and my soul are with you, my dearest princess. I think of you by day and dream of you by night. The pater has been mean. I have no job and I live in the family country house with only a pittance. Surely there must be some silver lining on our miserable cloud. I shall do all I can to send for you, my dearest. Chin up and be brave ..."

Tanya cried her heart out again in despair.

Leung Sin Loong held no official position in Eng Aun Tong. But he was kept busier than most other employees. Whenever anyone came to the boss with a problem he was told, "Get Sin Loong to attend to it." Where others failed to obtain anything in urgent need, Sin Loong would succeed in ferreting out the article from sources known only to him. Most of all, the Cantonese was useful to Aw Boon Haw as a social relations man. And as a household manager.

It was Sin Loong who transformed the rented house into as comfortable and congenial a home as the boss would like. He sacked the household staff and engaged two new *amahs* to keep the house spick and span. He dismissed the Hakka cook and replaced him with a Cantonese who specialised in exotic Hakka dishes. The Tiger could always rely on Sin Loong to get him whatever his heart desired.

Living on his own so far away from home left a lot of idle time on Boon Haw's hands. But the absence of family constraints gave the Tiger ample opportunity for his sexual peccadillos. The merest mention of a desire for female company would see Sin Loong disappear for an hour or two to return with a candidate who almost always met with the boss's approval. Aw Boon Haw was no scrooge with women who pleased him. They, in turn, showed their gratitude to their "agent" in the form of a fat *ang pow*. Sin Loong never accepted services in return for services rendered. Cash in hand was better than temporary comfort in bed.

Sin Loong, the man of few principles, was at the same time a man of conscience. He felt responsible for Tanya's plight. He was the only friend to the stranded girl.

The money which Robert had left for Tanya was barely sufficient to cover the Peninsula bill. Sin Loong suggested she move to more modest quarters. He pulled strings and got her into a hostel for working girls. There Tanya was delighted to meet up with Caterina again. The girl had given in to an impulse to lift the wallet of a gentleman client. Arlette expelled her from her establishment and Caterina was forced to leave Shanghai.

The girls fell into each other's arms and wept over their misfortunes. They decided to share a room for old times' sake and to keep each other company. Sin Loong felt it was his moral obligation to pay Tanya's rent.

Caterina's fortunes had fallen a long way. She was forced to accept a job as dance hostess in a cabaret. European girls never worked in cabarets. Not even the lowliest tart from Soho. The slightest suspicion of any indiscretion would result in a one-way passage back to their country of origin at the expense of the colonial government.

The White Russian girls were a different breed. They could not go back to Russia. The colonials sneered at them as so much white trash. They were a disgrace to the white race. "We have to live with this blight in our society as there is nowhere we could deport them to," said an immigration official. Added another, "It would be more palatable if only they were not so infernally fair-skinned."

It was only because of their complexion that they were so much in demand in Hongkong as elsewhere in the Orient. Where a

Chinese taxi dancer received a twenty-cent coupon for each dance, a Russian received three. The management deducted half the value when the coupons were cashed each week. What extra income the girl could earn depended on her personal inclination.

Tanya became a cabaret girl two weeks after moving in with Caterina. It was the only way she could keep body and soul together until her Robert could send for her. Sin Loong continued to pay her rent and visited her once a week to enquire about her well-being. His heart ached each time he saw her face cloud when he could give her no news of her beloved Robert.

He would gladly provide passage money to enable her to sail for England. With her out of Hongkong he would not be constantly reminded of his self-imposed responsibility. His conscience would be free. But Sin Loong was a spendthrift. He looked prosperous but it was all show and no substance. He toadied to Aw Boon Haw hoping for an opportunity to strike it rich and then to strike out on his own.

The boss looked cross when Sin Loong presented himself one morning. Sin Loong never failed to turn up. It pleased his ego to be seen arriving at the shop with the boss even if it was only riding beside the driver and having to open the door of the car on arrival.

"Sin Loong, from which back street did you find the girl last night?" Aw Boon Haw growled even before the lackey could sing a "good morning."

"She had an offensive smell and she behaved like a peasant!"

"That cannot be, big boss. She is fresh merchandise. She has just taken up the profession. Only fifteen years old."

"Fifteen or fifty, she is low class. She didn't know how to talk. She didn't know how to please. And she certainly did not wash."

"A thousand apologies, big boss. She is truly new, and a country girl. Her parents are dead. An uncle brought her over from the mainland to live with an aunt. The woman said she must earn her keep. So she put the girl to work. I think you are only her third patron."

Sin Loong expected the Tiger to take the last statement as a compliment. But Aw Boon Haw was not impressed. "A dish tastes better with seasoning. Next time be sure I do not have to teach a girl how to please a man. Unless she is a virgin." Sin Loong did not ride to work with the boss that morning.

Sin Loong decided to give the office a miss to allow the Tiger time to cool down. He went to the shipping manager's office. They were friends again. It had been many months since Robert made that furtive night flight in a sampan to board the steamer for England. The danger had passed. The police had run up a dead end with the disappearance of the Englishman. The manager was no longer afraid to be seen with Sin Loong. Moreover, the man was now working for the Tiger Balm King and the respectability rubbed off on him.

"There's a letter from our foreign friend," the manager said as they sipped scalding tea. "I hope he is sending some money for the girl to join him. I don't really feel secure until she has left Hongkong. Love drives men to do crazy things. Robert might come back to join her. We will be in danger again."

"You are right. The man is capable of doing desperate things. I'd better take the letter to the Russian girl now. There may be a cheque inside."

But there was no cheque. And no good news for Tanya. Robert could not raise the fare and he had no idea when, if ever, his father would allow him to work in the family business again.

Tanya was shattered. Sin Loong shared her misery. Both were desperate. One had to get away from her wretched life. The other had to make her go away so that her presence would not entice Robert back and expose him to arrest for smuggling opium. An idea began to germinate in Sin Loong's fertile brain.

Would Tanya please the Tiger enough to earn her passage for the lovers' reunion? More important, would she agree if he propositioned her? He knew she had been keeping herself for Robert. Why else would she head straight for the hostel after the band struck up the last tune? Why would she turn down her friend Caterina's constant urging to make a foursome for fun and profit? Perhaps in her despair, she would give less regard to her virtue.

It was a delicate matter. Sin Loong mulled over different approaches. He finally decided that bluntness would be easiest. "Miss Tanya, would you sleep with a man if he gave you a lot of money? Enough for you to go to England and be with your Robert again?"

Tanya ceased sobbing in surprise. It was so unexpected coming from her friend. In all the months she had known him, he had never made a pass at her. "You mean become a prostitute?"

"Not exactly. Just once for a lot of money and no more."

"Is any man worth that sacrifice?"

"I can't give you an answer. I am not a woman."

"No, you are not. A man can love one woman and sleep with another."

Tanya considered the alternatives. To be true to her man and most likely never to see him again. To sleep with another and earn his scorn. Carry on as she had been doing and endure an indefinite purgatory in Hongkong. She was at a dead end.

"Mr Robert would understand. You sleep with a man just once not because you are a bad woman. It is your great love for him. It is your greatest desire to be with him again. And he with you, I am sure."

Yes, she yearned to be in her lover's arms again. To love and be loved. To belong to someone and for him to belong to her. There was no one else in the world she could call her own but Robert. Tanya allowed herself to be persuaded.

They went to Aw Boon Haw's house in separate rickshaws. Sin Loong paid off the pullers and asked Tanya to wait outside while he let himself in with his key. It was a distinct honour for him to hold a key to the boss's house. The Tiger was seated in his favourite armchair fanning himself. "Where have you been all day, you stupid man?" he growled as soon as the Cantonese appeared.

"Didn't you know I was not at all pleased with your peasant last night!"

The Cantonese smiled. "So sorry, big boss. I have been busy all day trying to make up for your disappointment. I have a surprise for you. I have brought you a Russian princess."

"You must be smoking opium all day. Princesses don't become prostitutes."

"This one is not a prostitute. She is a good girl who is stranded in Hongkong. It is not easy, but as you know, I always try to please *tai pan*."

"White girls have rough skins, even your opium princess, I'm sure. Their face and body are disfigured with spots and they don't wash often. Even worse than the peasant girl."

Sin Loong was not about to be put off by a prejudiced boss. Certainly not after all the trouble he had been through. "Won't you take a look at her to see how beautiful she is? The girl is waiting outside."

"You can't keep a woman waiting outside my door at night. What would people think?"

What would Aw Boon Haw think was even more important as far as Sin Loong was concerned. His approval would probably mean Tanya's deliverance from her purgatory. And his freedom from the threat of arrest.

Tanya allowed herself to be led in like a lamb to the slaughter. Confronting her was a robust Chinese with the biggest pair of ears she had ever seen. His sharply creased trousers were held up by braces over a silk shirt. The tie was askew. Her eyes strayed to the glittering object on his finger. It was a solitaire diamond ring reflecting the light of the ceiling lamp and magnifying its brilliance a thousand times. Tanya no longer wore diamonds but she was still familiar with the precious stone. The one on the man's finger must be at least five carats in weight. She surmised he must be a very rich man indeed.

Aw Boon Haw was expecting a blowsy *hong mo moi* with a

demeanour to match. But this red-haired girl turned out to be slender and refined looking. She was quite beautiful and looked younger than he expected. The woman was timid in her approach but possessed an hauteur quite out of character. Her fair hair shimmered under the light. Her skin was fairer than he imagined and free of the spots he despised. The Tiger sensed that this was no common whore. Her dignified bearing convinced the millionaire that this was a woman of high birth now in low circumstances. He forgave Sin Loong for describing her as a princess.

The master of the house indicated to his visitor to sit next to him. She was glad to do so as she was weak with hunger. The slice of bread and stale cheese which had served as her lunch had long been digested. It was nearly midnight. Caterina would soon return to the hostel where they usually shared a midnight snack washed down with half a bottle of cheap wine. The thought reminded her of her great thirst. She asked for a drink. Sin Loong poured out a half-tumbler of Hennessy XO. Nothing but the best for his princess. It was nectar to the girl who had not tasted such fine brandy for a long time. She sipped and some colour returned to her cheeks. She drained the tumbler hoping to overcome the shame that had haunted her all evening and promptly threw up.

Tanya began to cry. She buried her face in the silken cushions and great sobs heaved her body. Aw Boon Haw was nonplussed. He had half a mind to throw her out. But even a tiger sometimes has a softer side to his rapacious nature. The pitiful weeping of the girl with the golden hair drew a sigh of sympathy from the would-be predator.

The Tiger shouted for the servant. Ah Kee came running with a cup of Chinese tea. "No more, please no more," Tanya protested when she saw the amber liquid. "No more cognac for me. I want some food. May I have something to eat, please?"

The servant brought a tray of steamed buns and dumplings left over from her boss's supper and a steaming pot of coffee. The girl devoured the food and drained three cups of coffee. Her hunger appeased, fatigue followed. Tanya leaned back on the chair and closed her eyes.

"Big boss, I think I should take the girl back to her hotel. She is good for nothing tonight," Sin Loong said.

"You insensible man, can't you see the girl is in no condition to go anywhere? She can sleep in the room downstairs."

Sin Loong asked the girl if she would like to go to bed. "I'll take you back to your hostel tomorrow morning."

Tanya sat up in panic, "I won't! I can't!" More tears followed. "I don't want to earn the money no matter how much. Please take me away now." To bed meant only one thing to her – to sleep with the Chinese man, for that had been her mission.

Sin Loong in his best English and as simple Cantonese as he could utter calmed the girl and assured her that the rich gentleman did not want her to sleep with him. She could rest in the bedroom by herself until the morning. It was now very late and there were no rickshaws available.

Tanya looked at her intended patron but could see no passion in the man's expression. The Tiger gave her the flicker of a smile and said, "Rest." Whatever desire he might have had earlier was doused by the weeping of the distraught girl. A pity, he thought. It would be an experience to determine for himself if European women were as uninhibited as his friends claimed. But not tonight.

Ah Kee, the servant, had served many of her boss's women visitors but not a *hong mo moi* or one as beautiful and innocent looking as this. She kept muttering *"ko lian, ko lian"* (pity, pity) as she watched the proceedings. The Tiger was annoyed. He scolded her, "You good for nothing woman. One would think you were being raped. Go to the kitchen and make another pot of coffee." He started to leave when Tanya said, "Thank you, sir. I am sorry to have given you so much trouble." She spoke in halting Cantonese, having picked up a smattering of the dialect in the dance hall. "Hmm," the Tiger acknowledged her thanks. He was not a man given to affability. "I owe you an explanation, sir. Please sit down. I shan't cry anymore." Tanya had a compulsive need to relate the tragedy of her life. She had never told her full story to anyone, not even to Robert. She did not want to cloud their happy relationship with her sad tale.

The Tiger sat as bidden. He gestured to the girl to take the sofa. Tanya gratefully complied and lay down exhausted.

"I was born the daughter of a Count," she began. "His Imperial Majesty the Tsar was a friend of the family ..."

Aw Boon Haw had intended to stay only a few minutes to humour the girl. But he listened to the end. Tanya was not so much telling her story as reliving her life. Her face, in turns, assumed an expression of joy or sadness, anxiety or terror, love or hate, expectation or disappointment, each depending on the part relived. Throughout the telling she kept her eyes closed as if in a trance.

"... and in desperation I came here tonight to do a shameful thing. But I am afraid I must beg your understanding. I must continue to endure the ache in my heart ..."

Tanya lapsed into sleep as her painful recounting tailed off. She was physically and emotionally exhausted.

Aw Boon Haw looked at the sleeping girl and thought of the honest optician. Both were creatures of circumstances beyond their control and both had suffered persecution under the same tyranny. Ezekiel's faith in himself had served him well. The sleeping girl had always been dependent on others and was now in the depths of despair. Was there anything he could do to inject some confidence in her?

Sin Loong took Tanya back to her hostel early the next morning. He handed her a bulging envelope at the door.

"What is it?"

"Why don't you open it and find out?"

Inside the envelope was a wad of notes. Tanya's fingers trembled as she held it. "Why do you give me so much money?"

"It's not from me."

"Who, then?"

"The gentleman who did not want to sleep with you."

"But why?"

"He's a man of compassion."

"He's my saviour."

"He wishes you a safe journey and much happiness."

"Please tell him I am very grateful. I do not deserve his generosity but I accept his compassion."

Sin Loong smiled in satisfaction. He had achieved what he set out to do. His princess would soon be on her way to join her lover. She would be free of her uncertain existence. He would be free from the threat of arrest. The Cantonese allowed himself his first familiarity with the Russian. He ran his fingers through her golden hair in a gentle caress and said, "Good luck."

Tanya ran to her room in joyful flight. She threw herself on her rumpled bed and held up the money to look at it in disbelief. It was incredible that her deliverance should come from a complete stranger. She counted the money. Five thousand dollars. Incredible indeed. So much money for disappointing a man.

Twenty-one

Aw Boon Haw tossed aside the newspaper he was reading and paced the floor in agitation. Aw Boon Par folded his copy and placed it gently on his desk. "Jee Ko, is there something in the news that bothers you?" he asked, looking slightly puzzled at his brother.

"No, not bothered. Disgusted! The whole paper disgusts me. That damned *Nanyang Siang Pau*. It nauseates me the way it carries on."

"But it's supposed to be a good paper. It carries a lot of news and enjoys a wide circulation."

"What do you know? You don't read Chinese. You'd be disgusted, too, if you did."

Aw Boon Haw read only Chinese, and depended on the *Nanyang* to keep abreast of events. His brother Boon Par, on the other hand, read English. He had a choice of three English language newspapers: the *Singapore Free Press*, the *Straits Times* and the *Malaya Tribune*. He favoured the *Tribune*. The *Times* "prints more advertisements than news" and the *Free Press* was "free only where it concerns British interests."

"What is it about the *Nanyang* that you find so offensive? You have been reading it for as long as I know. Has it suddenly changed its policy?"

"I read it because there is no other paper worth reading, not that the *Nanyang* amounts to much. The *Lat Pau* is a rag. The *Nanyang Chung Wei Pau* (Union Times) is not much better. The amount of prominence the *Nanyang* gives to that *sinkeh* Tan Kah Kee makes me ill."

Aw Boon Haw was jealous of his rival's access to the widely read Chinese newspaper. He was also envious of the newspaper's commercial success. The *Nanyang* favoured the Hokkien community to which Tan Kah Kee belonged. And for good reason: the paper was Hokkien-owned, and employed mostly Hokkien talent. Most of all, it was a constant source of irritation to him to be reminded daily that Tan Kah Kee enjoyed the full support of the only influential Chinese daily in Singapore.

"I suppose it is only to be expected that a Hokkien newspaper should sing a Hokkien tune," Boon Par commented.

"Precisely. A Hakka newspaper, our newspaper will, of course, sing our tune."

Surprised, Boon Par looked directly at his brother. "What are you driving at, Jee Ko?"

"We must have an influential, quality newspaper of our own. I have wanted to own one for a long time, ever since that day when the 'red hair devils' raided our house and put us to such humiliation. A paper could counter those who oppose us. To correct injustice and to promote the Chinese cause."

Boon Par made no comment. He knew his brother and how impulsive he was inclined to be. Many a hasty decision had borne unhappy results.

Boon Haw continued, "We must start a quality newspaper. The sooner the better."

Boon Par pretended to be engrossed in his newspaper.

"The only way to influence people is to own a popular newspaper. Like Tan Kah Kee and his clique. Even other communities listen to whatever rubbish they say. They behave like they represent all Chinese. How ridiculous it is. It's time we had a voice for Hakka people, for all other people."

Carried away by his oratory, Boon Haw was entertaining a vision. "We must think big to be really big. One newspaper is not enough. We shall publish a chain of newspapers, wherever our business takes us. Not only will the Chinese in Singapore and Malaya listen to us, but also all those in Southeast Asia. What do you have to say, younger brother?"

"But our business is medicine. Our fortune comes from medicine. We have no experience in running newspapers."

"We can buy experience. We can buy other people's brains. Money can buy anything. Even people. Everything has a price. There are people who can be bought cheap."

Boon Par still had his doubts. "But where can we buy a newspaper? The *Nanyang* is not for sale. Even if it were, I don't think they'll sell it to us."

"I don't want to buy the *Nanyang*. I want to compete with it. I want Tan Kah Kee to listen to what I have to say. He has been expounding his views for too long. It has to be my turn."

Having settled down in the countries in which they resided, and in many cases, prosperously, the Chinese still regarded China as their motherland. Perhaps more than anywhere else, this feeling was strongest among the Chinese in Southeast Asia, especially in Singapore and Malaya. They were more concerned with events in their distant motherland than in the countries of their domicile. Of particular concern at the moment was the attitude of the Japanese towards a disunited China. Tan Kah Kee was a leading light in gathering support for the Chinese government and countering Japanese designs. In Singapore, the Ee Ho Hean Club became a nerve centre of Chinese nationalism. Members met frequently to plan and raise funds for China, and to organise a boycott of Japanese goods.

Aw Boon Haw wanted to show he was as patriotic as any other Chinese. He wished to be elected a committee member of the China Relief Fund. He offered an initial subscription of five thousand dollars to the fund. It was to be the most substantial single donation. To his great disappointment, the offer was turned down by Hokkien members. From then on, he withdrew his support for all pro-China projects in which his rival Tan Kah Kee was involved.

The British were unhappy over the political activities of the Chinese. They wanted to be seen as neutral in the brewing quarrel between the Chinese and the Japanese. It was an image difficult for the British to maintain as anti-Japanese sentiments mounted. The *Nanyang Siang Pau* seized every opportunity to condemn Japanese arrogance. It played up Chinese grievances, real or imagined.

The Colonial Secretariat recommended censorship. The governor, Sir Hugh Clifford, reflecting the British sense of fair play, found it obnoxious to gag the Chinese press whilst the British press enjoyed complete freedom. The *Singapore Free Press* and the *Straits Times* exercised as much impartiality as practicable on the growing Chinese-Japanese conflict.

It was left to the Chinese Protectorate to request the *Nanyang Siang Pau* to tone down its anti-Japanese reports. This was largely ignored. The lack of more drastic action served to encourage more anti-Japanese agitation. In this uncertain climate, it was not unexpected that Aw Boon Haw's application for a printing permit was officially turned down. "One rabble-rousing newspaper is problem enough," one colonial official commented. "Another would be an insufferable headache."

Aw Boon Haw was not a person to be easily thwarted. "If I cannot get in through the front door, what is there to prevent me from going in through the back?" he told his brother.

It alarmed the Leopard. He stuttered, "How … what do you mean?" Was the Tiger up to some tricks that could lead them into serious trouble with the British? "We have to be careful not to annoy the authorities too much," he cautioned. "It may affect our business." The house search in Rangoon was still fresh in the mind of the younger brother.

But it seemed that Boon Haw's mind was already made up. "We will not go far if we are timid," he said. "But do not fear, younger brother. I am not about to commit a crime. All I want to do is to publish a good newspaper to serve our people, and to carry the voice of the Chinese in this region for all to hear." Unsaid, but apparent to the younger Aw was his brother's overriding desire to hit back at his rival.

Teng Lee Seng owned a modest printing shop. His main source of income came from odd jobs such as printing handbills and pamphlets advertising cinema shows. Teng was a literary-minded businessman whose secret ambition was to publish a newspaper. But publishing handbills and the occasional journal with little or no readership appeal are not the stuff for dreams to come true. Until Aw Boon Haw changed his life.

The denial of a printing licence goaded the millionaire into a search for the takeover of an ongoing printing business. He offered to buy the firm which printed his medicinal leaflets. "You name the price, and I shall meet it," he propositioned the printer, but was told that the business was not for sale.

The Tiger retorted, "I shall take my business away from you." The bulk of the printer's income came from Eng Aun Tong. The printer spoke the truth when he moaned, "But I will be ruined ..."

"Not if you accept my offer."

"I am not a wise man like you or one who makes money easily. The only business I know is printing, and I shall continue to print and make a modest income for the rest of my life. I beg you as a fellow Hakka, spare my business."

"I shall give you a month to find me a printing shop or my patronage will cease. Make sure it has a good licence to print anything, especially a newspaper."

Teng Lee Seng's business was faltering. His customers were behind in paying their bills, and he himself was in arrears with his suppliers. Further supplies of paper and ink were already withheld. Teng was a desperate man. But he was unwilling to sell the business.

The printer whom Boon Haw had first approached learnt of Teng's plight. Teng said he would consider taking in a sleeping partner who could inject money into the firm and was delighted when the man returned the next day to tell him he had found someone who would like to be his partner. He was overwhelmed when he learnt that it was none other than Aw Boon Haw. Not only could he expect an unlimited flow of funds but his business would gain immeasurable prestige from its association with the famous millionaire.

Of course, Aw Boon Haw had no intention of being just a partner. But this was the back door he had to take in order to achieve his aim.

The deal was made. "Pay all your debts and stock up on all the supplies you need," Boon Haw instructed his associate. "I suggest you employ more staff to expand the business. Never mind the expense. I will finance you as much as you need."

Given a free hand, Teng Lee Seng began upgrading his operations and even gave the building a badly-needed coat of paint. Business picked up. The flow of funds continued. The Tiger was only giving his unsuspecting partner enough rope to hang himself.

Two months later, the Tiger offered to buy out Teng, lock, stock and barrel. Teng baulked. He had spent a lifetime building up his business, and he could begin afresh with the generous offer Aw Boon Haw made, but there was no certainty he could obtain another licence. In fact, he was certain the licence would be denied, especially after having transferred his to another person.

Aw Boon Haw did not mince his words. "I will withdraw my support, and you will be thrown out on the street," he told Teng. "You will be a beggar."

Teng stood his ground. "I will borrow, or beg to keep my business. I will seek support elsewhere."

"But you will never be able to borrow enough to repay me. I have put in many times what your company was worth. You will be made a bankrupt. Why fight me when you can do something else with the money I am prepared to give you? Name your price."

"I don't want your money," Teng shot back.

"Then I shall bankrupt you."

"You can do what you like. But you will never get my licence. I will return it to the government and have it cancelled," Teng was fighting mad.

The show of guts rattled the Tiger's confidence. The printing press was of no use to him without the licence. Was he to be thwarted again?

Boon Haw had not expected the printer's intransigence. Obviously, Teng was one man his money could not buy. He had to change his tactics. If money could not buy him, perhaps glory would sway him. Boon Haw swallowed his pride – and the effort nearly choked him. There was no choice. Better to suffer humiliation this time than to be continually upstaged by Tan Kah Kee every time.

Softly, the Tiger purred. "What is it you want, Mr Teng? I will consider it if it is within reason."

"All I want is to remain a partner."

"Would you like to be the boss of a newspaper?"

"What newspaper?"

"The best newspaper in Singapore"

"Whose newspaper?"

"Mine."

"But you don't own a newspaper."

"I intend to start one. Better than the *Nanyang*. I am prepared to put a lot of money into it. Even a million dollars, if need be."

"How can I be the boss if you are the owner?"

"I will own it, but not run it. I am not a printer. My business is medicine, the best medicine in the world. But I need someone who knows the printing business to take charge of it. Say, someone like you."

Teng's ears flapped. But he was still sceptical. He looked the Tiger in the eye. "Why me?"

"Why not you? I think you are very qualified."

"It is very tempting ..."

"You will never get another opportunity like this."

"How do I fit into the newspaper? I know printing as much as anyone else but I am not a journalist."

"Your job will be more important than that of a journalist. Even more important than the editor. You will be in charge of the entire operation outside of the editorial department."

"But you will need a printing licence."

"I do."

"And you don't have one."

"You do."

"Do I remain a partner?"

"You don't."

"Then I will have to consider it."

"I want your answer now! I can apply for a licence but it will take time. I can also look for another printing press to buy but it will waste time. It is stupid to wait when we can make a lot of money now."

Teng did not know that a printing press licence had been denied the Tiger.

"I will appoint you managing director. And pay you more than anyone else in addition to a big annual bonus. Just think of the prestige you would have as the boss of a big newspaper. You will be famous. Everybody will be your friend."

Fame was the spur to Teng's decision. He imagined himself a respected man of influence instead of a struggling printer with an uncertain future. A well cut custom-made suit like the millionaire was wearing, instead of the ink- and grease-stained baggy overalls. And driving about in a car instead of haggling with rickshaw pullers over fares.

"You will appoint me managing director?"

"I am a man of my word."

"I will be the highest paid?"

"You will deserve it." This was said with little conviction.

"How much bonus do you have in mind?"

"How much will depend on how much profit the newspaper

will make. And how hard you work."

"And I have to give up everything to look after your newspaper?"

"You will have everything working for me. You will be a *towkay* and I will compensate you twice as much as you have put into your business. Join me and you will not regret."

"You drive a hard bargain ..."

"I am also losing my patience. Do you or do you not want to be my managing director?" It was not a question. It was an ultimatum.

"I accept your offer." All the fight had gone out of Teng.

"Good. You've made a wise choice. Now please excuse me. I have many urgent matters to attend to."

"Well, younger brother, we've got ourselves a printing licence." Aw Boon Haw announced as soon as Boon Par came in. "I leave it to you to attend to the details. We must have the paper out as soon as possible."

The Tiger left for Hongkong shortly after acquiring the licence.

On the voyage back on the P & O liner, *Macedonia*, Aw Boon Haw thought of little else but his new paper. He had even decided on its name: *Sin Chew Jit Poh*, loosely translated into "Singapore Daily News." It was to be the most successful in a chain of newspapers under the grouping "Starnews."

An encounter on the second day out of Hongkong had given him much satisfaction. The first-class dining room was filled with elegantly dressed passengers. Men in black dinner suits and women in flowing gowns glided to the strains of the *Blue Danube*. Aw Boon Haw was conspicuous in that he was the only non-European and the only one in lounge suit. And the only unescorted gentleman. It did not bother him at all. He had no desire to be dressed in black. What did bother him was the cutlery.

The millionaire was struggling with a steak. The knife was blunt and the meat was tough. He wished Westerners were more civilised in their way of dining. Why couldn't they cut up the meat in small pieces before serving? Why did they have to attack it with knives and hoes instead of picking up little pieces with chopsticks? Why must a right-handed person transfer food to his mouth with his left hand? He was hungry though. He liked beef and he attacked the steak with renewed vigour. He sawed until the fine bone china squeaked. He was about to swear when he sensed a presence before him.

Boon Haw looked up to see a lovely young lady standing opposite his table. She gave him an apologetic smile and said, "Good evening, sir."

Boon Haw did not welcome the intrusion, but the beginning of a frown turned into a smile when he recognised Tanya.

"May I sit down?"

Aw Boon Haw enjoyed female company in private, but avoided being seen with them in public.

Tanya smiled. "I want to thank you for your great kindness."

Boon Haw gave another of his rare smiles in return. "Have you eaten?"

Tanya took it as an invitation to join him, and she sat in front of her benefactor.

"Yes, thank you. I do not eat much. I am too anxious to meet my man again, and I am too happy, thanks to you."

Boon Haw waved his hand, "It is only a small matter."

"It may be small to you, sir, but it means the world to me. And I did not earn it."

"It is not necessary to do something in order to earn a reward. There are times when a person deserves help without having to ask for it. Or to debase herself."

"You are an unusual man. I do not understand you but I am truly grateful."

"I hope you will be a good wife and bear many children." Boon Haw did not know what else to say, and he resumed his sawing.

"Please allow me the great pleasure of doing you a small service in return." Tanya had noticed her benefactor's difficulty in handling the cutlery. She reached out for the plate and with deft strokes cut up the meat into pieces. "Never mind the knife now, sir. Hold the fork with your right hand and eat the way the Americans do."

Boon Haw finished the steak, bade Tanya goodbye, and returned to his cabin. There was no sense in generating gossip and being exposed to the disapproving stares of his fellow passengers. But he was glad he met her again. It pleased him to know that the Russian waif would soon be reunited with her lover.

Twenty-two

The chance encounter with Tanya kept him in a happy mood. The Hongkong and China operation had gone better than he had hoped. Helping the hapless girl find happiness again had given him more pleasure than his many donations of far larger sums. His new newspaper was all set to make its appearance. So eager was he to be brought up to date that he instructed his driver at the Tanjong Pagar wharf to drive straight to his office instead of home.

Boon Par was equally delighted. "Things must have gone well in Hongkong for you to be in such good humour, Jee Ko."

"I always make sure that things go well. Tell me, are we all set to bring out the paper?"

"Yes, we are only waiting for you to give it a name."

"*Sin Chew Jit Poh.* That's what we'll name it. What do you think?"

"An honest name. A newspaper does not have to brag. Its readers are its judges. I'll tell the editor. He and Teng have suggested a few names. But I told them to wait for you."

"Tell them now. And tell them I want the paper out without further delay."

"There are some important documents to sign. And some senior appointments to confirm."

"You sign them and you confirm whoever you judge fit."

"No, Jee Ko, the paper is your cherished project and it is your pleasure to put the finishing touches. And to give it your blessing."

"Very well. You have been such a help while I was away. I really don't know how I can get on without you."

"You have some problems at home," Boon Par mentioned casually. "You should go home now. The paper can wait a little longer."

"What problems?"

With the Tiger so often away, Piah Hong assumed the role of head of the family. The servants would take instructions from no one but her. It was she who doled out the marketing money to Ah Boon, the cook, each morning. Piah Hong had just reduced the food allowance. Since the master was abroad, there was no need to buy expensive food, she reasoned. Piah Hong was a frugal woman who never forgot the early days when money was tight and there were many mouths to feed.

The children learned to obey her. Aw Kow and Aw Swan, at fourteen and thirteen years respectively, were not too old for punishment when they misbehaved. A thin rattan cane was always within reach and a few lashes on their posteriors promptly settled any quarrel. Kyi Kyi did not approve of such chastisement.

Aw Hoe, at seven, was as prone to pranks as anybody his age, and his mother was protective. At the slightest sign of trouble between the older boys, Kyi Kyi would gather Aw Hoe and take him into her room. "You must not play too much with your brothers. Otherwise, you, too, will get a caning from the fierce mama," she advised her son.

But boys being boys, advising Aw Hoe to keep clear of his brothers was like telling ants to avoid sugar. He was a very playful boy, full of fun and laughter, and not disinclined to participating in some mischief at the instigation of his brothers. He was generous with his toys which his adoring mother kept well supplied. Aw Kow and Aw Swan seldom possessed expensive playthings. Their mother considered them a waste of money. Aw Hoe's toys were the best from Robinson's. He shared them with his brothers out of generosity and a need to be accepted by his elders.

A fight broke out between Aw Kow and Aw Swan following a tussle over one of Aw Hoe's toys. The younger boy broke into tears on seeing his brothers wrestling on the floor. The innocent bystander received a lash on his rounded rump after Piah Hong had finished caning her boys. It was her way of showing fairness. Aw Hoe cried at what he thought was injustice. This upset Kyi Kyi and it hurt her more than the boy.

She rebuked her elder. "You can cane your boys as much as you like but leave Aw Hoe alone. He is not naughty like the others. I have never caned him and you should not either."

Piah Hong was taken aback by the boldness of the younger woman. Kyi Kyi had always deferred to her since the day she arrived in Singapore. The younger woman's disrespect angered her. She lashed out at Kyi Kyi.

"You have no right to speak to me like that. Why, I'm old enough to be your mother. I am the eldest wife and all the children, including Aw Hoe, are my children. I can discipline anyone of them as I think fit. Don't forget, other than Jee Ko, I have authority over everyone, Even over you."

Kyi Kyi was fragile. Piah Hong was nearly twice her size.

She decided not to reply. She bundled Aw Hoe and his toys into her room and locked themselves in.

The quarrel occurred in the morning. Boon Haw was due to return in the afternoon. Early in the day, Piah Hong had given the cook, Ah Boon, extra marketing money, instructing him to prepare a welcome home dinner. "There will be many guests for dinner, so be sure you do not disgrace the bosses," she told the cook.

"The money may not be enough, *towkay neo*," Ah Boon said.

"More than enough. You buy in the local market, not in the *ang moh* store." Market meat, like everything else, costs half of what they charge in Cold Storage. "Can you get some dog meat, too?"

"Hard to say. It is not sold openly."

"Get a catty, if you can. I'll give you some ginseng to steam with it. Your boss has been away a long time and he needs a tonic."

Piah Hong rarely stepped foot into the factory these days. Her contribution to the business had long ceased. Her mother-in-law's kitchen, which served as their factory, seemed like another world. It was a world which gave them the start to travel the long road to success. The start where countless bottles of Tiger Balm began to emerge and to build their wealth. Boon Par was there, of course. But he was only a brother, and there could never be a brotherly bond as binding as that between man and wife. It was this bond and the knowledge that she had played such an important part in her husband's success that sustained her when Boon Haw allowed one, and then another woman to intrude.

Piah Hong looked forward to her husband's return with great eagerness. She wanted to hear what further progress he had made in Hongkong and how much profit had been generated. Eng Aun Tong was her pride and joy.

Jealousy gnawed at Kyi Kyi's waking moments and uneasy dreams marred her sleep. She could not banish her dread. It was foolish to be jealous of non-existent women and suffer sleepless nights, she often told herself. But her unease persisted. She trembled at the thought of yet another woman coming into her husband's life, another threat to the affection which she so desperately wanted to monopolise. He had married Geik Cheah because of his need for someone to look after him. Did he also need another to look after him in Hongkong? Look after indeed, she snorted.

And so Kyi Kyi fretted and sulked. The sulk turned resentful after the tongue lashing from Piah Hong. Her mind was in turmoil when the grandfather clock chimed midday, and the usual snack was served. In deference to Piah Hong's seniority, she always waited for the older woman to take her seat before she sat down to eat. And like all dutiful secondary wives, it was her function to pour the tea and invite her elder sister to eat before she helped herself. But today was a day of rebellion. "She knows the time, and she is not a cripple to be served hand and foot," Kyi Kyi grumbled to herself as she took a bite of the steaming bun.

Slippered feet padding on tiles approached, and a voice demanded, "Why didn't you call me before you stuffed yourself?" Piah Hong, as usual, was agitating a string of prayer beads. Incantations switched to angry words even as thumb and forefinger kept busy as they moved from one ivory bead to another.

"I thought you were asleep and did not want to disturb you."

"You know I never take a nap until I have eaten. What's wrong with you? Do you have to put on such a funeral face on the day Jee Ko is coming home?"

Kyi Kyi kept silent. If anything, her sulk deepened. She was quite tired of being scolded like a child. She took a defiant sip of tea, and stared into the distance.

"Now do your duty and pour me some tea. Didn't your mother teach you manners?"

It was just too much for Kyi Kyi. She stood up abruptly to leave. Her chair fell over and landed on Piah Hong's toes. The table tilted and spilt some tea on her *sarong*. "Pour the tea yourself," Kyi Kyi hissed, and made to leave. She was not fast enough. Piah Hong pulled her over the table and thumped her on the back. "I'll teach you a lesson your mother never taught you, you bad woman. I'll teach you to respect your elders." Another two blows followed.

Kyi Kyi screamed more in rage than in pain. She wrenched herself free from the stronger woman, and ran, still screaming, into her room. "I'll tell Jee Ko. I'll tell him how you ill-treated me and Aw Hoe while he was away. I am not a child to be beaten by you, you fat one."

One of Aw Boon Haw's little pleasures was to frequent a fruit shop in Albert Street. He loved fruits and he bought them by the basket.

"Everybody should eat as much fruit as possible," he would tell his children. "Fruits are good for your health. They don't give you constipation."

Once, either out of weariness over his father's observations or an inherent dislike of fruits, his son, Aw Swan, had remarked, "But Papa, our Chinkawhite Wind mixture will get rid of constipation easily."

"True," the father answered fondly, "but isn't it nicer to eat delicious fruits than to swallow bitter mixtures?"

The son replied, "But if everybody eats fruits, there won't be anyone left with constipation to buy our medicine."

Such childish logic stumped the Tiger. He gave his son an affectionate pat on the head, and grinning widely, said, "You'd make a third-rate lawyer some day."

On his way home, Aw Boon Haw decided to call at his favourite fruit shop. The proprietor, sixtyish but as vigorous as anyone half his age, greeted the millionaire like an old friend. Though poles apart as far as wealth was concerned, the two men shared a common denominator. Each had three wives. Over the years, ever since Aw Boon Haw moved his family to Singapore, Ah Lek had been supplying fruits to the man he addressed as *tua towkay*. They became good friends in spite of their vastly different status. One was admired for his achievements and philanthropy, the other for his honesty and family harmony.

Ah Lek's three wives lived under the same roof in the apartment above the shop. The eldest was fifty and uneducated. She was fifteen when she came to Singapore to marry a man she had never met. Like many Chinese women of her generation, she had bound feet which no amount of persuasion could induce her to free. The second wife, now thirty-five years old, was the widow of a second cousin whom Ah Lek married out of a sense of duty as she was also an immigrant from Swatow and had no other relatives. The youngest wife, Say Choo (Little Pearl), was orphaned at sixteen, and taken in by the eldest wife to help with the children. Say Choo was obedient and submissive to the extent that, at eighteen, she was made pregnant by Ah Lek. When her baby boy joined the four other offsprings, Ah Lek did the honourable thing by recognising her as wife number three.

On that day, Aw Boon Haw ordered the fruits he liked in a desultory manner. He was thinking of home. He was all too familiar with Piah Hong's fits of temper, and Kyi Kyi's intransigence when she did not have her own way. Why couldn't his wives co-exist as peacefully as Ah Lek's?

"*Tua towkay*, you do not seem to be your usual self today," the fruit seller commented. "Anything the matter?"

"Yes. Women."

"Ah, have you taken another wife? You should be happy then. May I offer my congratulations?"

"No, not another. The ones at home are a problem enough."

"They fight?"

"How did you know?"

"I have three myself, remember?"

"Tell me, friend, what makes your wives get on so well with one another?"

Ah Lek laughed, and shook his head. "Not at first. My eldest wife was a tyrant to my second wife when I brought her home. Poor Siew Lan had to do all the work. She cleaned and cooked and washed, and when it was time to eat, she ate only after everybody else had eaten. I was angry at first, but the old woman was stubborn and fierce, and there was little I could do."

"Another woman would have left you."

"I know. But not Siew Lan. She had no place to go. She suffered in silence. She had been taught obedience to her elders and she never talked back. Seeing that nothing could change the first woman I married, I decided to try shaming her into liking Siew Lan."

"How did you do this?"

"Simple. I told Siew Lan to be even more submissive. 'Show your elder sister you are a better person', I told her. 'Every time she scolds you, offer her a cup of tea, and apologise for making her angry.'"

"But that's not fair to Siew Lan."

"I know. But what else could I do? Siew Lan was prepared to do anything to keep the peace. And peace finally came to my household. My old woman's skin was not as thick as I had thought."

"What about Say Choo? Did she have to undergo the same treatment? She would have two women sitting on her."

"Yes, but I had coached her well. My old woman started her nonsense soon after Say Choo gave birth. She offered her tea of penitence, and the old woman was reminded of her treatment of Siew Lan. Say Choo was even cleverer. Every time she offered tea to her eldest sister, she poured a cup for her second sister as well. They now love her as a sister."

"She could be mistaken for your daughter."

Ah Lek laughed. "She has, many times. My eldest son, Too Kia (Little Pig) is only a year younger than Say Choo. They are mistaken for brother and sister whenever they go out together."

"You are a lucky man, indeed, to have such a happy, peaceful household."

"I know, the gods have answered my prayers. I go to the temple every festival day to give my thanks."

Aw Boon Haw was deep in thought as his tiger car turned into Selegie Road for Orchard Road, leading to his mansion where a *dhobi* once hung out his washing to dry. He could not imagine Kyi Kyi offering tea every time Piah Hong raised her voice. He did not want her to; she was his wife and not anybody's servant.

Ranjit Singh, the watchman, opened the car door, "Welcome back, *sahib*," he said in Hindi. Aw Hoe ran up to his father and embraced him. "What have you brought me?" he asked. Boon Haw patted the boy. "No time. I'll give Mama some money to buy you what you like."

Aw Kow and Aw Swan greeted their father by shouting, "You're home, Papa." They considered themselves too old to indulge in a more affectionate form of welcome.

"Where's Mama?" Boon Haw asked the boys.

"In her room, crying," Aw Hoe promptly replied.

Piah Hong, who was standing near the doorway, said, "You must teach that woman to show me more respect. She was very rude. She splashed hot tea on me."

"And what did you do?"

"I taught her a lesson."

"I meant what did you do to make her splash tea on you."

"I scolded her, of course, when she started to eat before me. And when I asked her to pour me a cup of tea, like she always did, she not only refused but also jumped up in a temper and spilt tea on me. Hot tea which scalded my thigh."

"And what lesson did you teach her, you potato?"

"Naturally, I beat her."

"You are a real potato. Why must you be so fierce?"

"I would have beaten her more if I was really fierce."

Kyi Kyi burst into tears as soon as she saw her husband. "Jee Ko, we were ill-treated while you were away," she sobbed. "Aw Hoe was caned, and I was punched." It seemed her tale of woe would never end.

It angered Boon Haw. "There is nothing worse than to come home and be greeted by tears. Tears are for the dead. Tears bring bad luck. If you must cry, then wait until I am dead."

The outburst shocked Kyi Kyi out of her tears. A servant approached with a pair of house slippers, and knelt to take off the boss's shoes. Kyi Kyi pushed her aside. "Let me do it, Jee Ko," she offered in atonement.

Boon Haw saw the opportunity to adopt Ah Lek's unique way of restoring harmony in the home. "Before I allow you to take off my shoes, there is something you must do first," he told the repentant wife in a gentler tone.

"What is it that Jee Ko wishes me to do?"

The boss turned to the servant and ordered, "Ah Woon, go bring a cup of tea."

"Give it to second mistress," he said when Ah Woon returned. Turning to Kyi Kyi he said, "Now I want you to offer this tea to your elder sister and apologise."

Kyi Kyi was perplexed. Had her husband gone crazy? What he was asking added insult to injury, the wronged apologising to the wrongdoer. Shouldn't it be the other way round?

"Do as I tell you," Boon Haw said when Kyi Kyi was about to protest.

Dazed by the turn of events Kyi Kyi took the cup and walked towards Piah Hong with reluctant steps. "Elder sister, I was wrong. I apologise," she choked out the words.

The older woman was even more amazed. She had expected a confrontation, but instead her victim was making a peace offering. Piah Hong drained the cup in two gulps. She felt more uncomfortable than elated. "All right, the matter is forgotten," she said with as much graciousness as her surprise allowed.

Aw Boon Haw watched the proceeding with great satisfaction. Ah Lek may be only a humble fruit seller, but he is wiser than I am with women, he thought. Putting his own finishing touch to the dispute, he said to Piah Hong, "Now, I want you to tell Kyi Kyi that you won't beat her again. It is your privilege to correct those younger than you are, but it is unbecoming to resort to violence. Remember, you are the eldest wife of Aw Boon Haw and you must not disgrace the name."

Piah Hong accepted the lecture in silence. With an unaccustomed meekness she said, "Kyi Kyi, let's not have trouble between us again. What is past is best forgotten." She was relieved that her husband did not demand an apology. Aw Boon Haw, ever the traditionalist, was only observing the proper relationship between wives. It was unthinkable for a senior wife to apologise to a junior under whatever circumstances.

Peace of a sort was restored. After a bath and a change of clothes, the Tiger gathered his family around him to tell them only what he thought they needed to know about his venture into Hongkong and

China. "I shall take all of you there one day," he promised.

The dinner gong shattered the evening peace. Family members trooped behind the Tiger as they made their way into the dining room. As they walked past the kitchen, Piah Hong pointed to a bubbling clay pot over a charcoal fire and said to her husband, "That's for you before you go to bed. I put a whole root of your best ginseng into the pot with the meat. Another hour or so of stewing will bring out the best from the herbs. You don't look so well. Did you miss your tonic in Hongkong?"

But the Tiger never looked more vigorous, or felt less in need of the rejuvenating brew. Sin Loong saw to it – his regular servings of "three threes."

The *Sin Chew Jit Poh* saw the light of day on 15 January 1929, the eighteenth year of the Republic of China.

The *Sin Chew* quickly established a reputation for wide coverage and hard-hitting editorials. It soon became a thorn in the side of the British administration which now had two extremely chauvinistic newspapers to contend with.

Twenty-three

The newly appointed Tiger Balm agent in Penang was a Hokkien named Ong. Born in Fukien province in China, he had come to Malaya with his father when he was ten years old. The Chinese in Penang were mainly Hokkien and, therefore, a Hokkien agent was a practical appointment. Ong, however, could not shed his *sinkeh* accent. His attempts to speak the Baba dialect often brought derisive laughter from those around him. But he was good-natured, and laughed with those who maligned his speech. In so doing, he earned their goodwill. And their business.

The small Hakka community felt slighted because an outsider had been given the agency which they coveted. They took every opportunity to create trouble, and they wrote and fabricated reports on how badly the business was managed. Boon Haw decided to find out how true the reports were. The launching of the *Sin Chew* had taken so much of his time since his return from Hongkong. But with the apparent success of his publishing venture, the Tiger decided to visit his third wife.

"About time, too," his brother commented when Boon Haw spoke of his intention. "I think sister Geik Cheah has been a very patient wife. And a good one. I have never heard her complain."

"What is there to complain? I provide her with a house and money, and I don't demand much from her. All she has to do is to be there when I go. And to behave."

Boon Par softly reminded him, "She has been your wife for five years, and no woman has seen her husband less in all these years."

"You know I have been very busy. The business takes so much

of my time, and we cannot afford to relax. I am not complaining. Kyi Kyi is the one who complains whenever I go anywhere without her. I expect her to grumble again when I leave."

"Aren't you taking her?"

"You should know better than to ask. She can't and won't go to Geik Cheah's house. And how can I see Geik Cheah when I am stuck with her in a hotel?"

"Please do not be offended with what I have to say, Jee Ko. I could not help thinking: neither sister Piah Hong nor Kyi Kyi has given you a child. Do you think sister Geik Cheah will be different?"

"I don't know. I have done my duty."

"How old is she?"

"Twenty-one or two, I think."

"Five years a wife and not a son or daughter to bear your name."

"It's still not too late."

"I hope not, Jee Ko. We need many sons to carry on after we are gone."

"You should not say such things. It is bad luck to talk about our own deaths. We have a long life ahead of us. Anyway we are not without heirs. You have two daughters and a son. I have three sons. Who knows how many more there will be? I know there is still a lot in my loins. And in yours too, I'm sure. As for Geik Cheah, I shall spend more time with her. Another reason I don't want Kyi Kyi to come."

As expected Kyi Kyi protested. "You promised to take me on your next trip after you return from Hongkong. I do not want to be beaten again. I feel like a prisoner here."

"Nobody is going to beat you. Piah Hong is not a tyrant. She will love you if only you would show her your love too."

"But I need a change. I like the mainland more than Singapore. So many people here and all unfriendly. They stare at me every time I go out. They whisper among themselves and I know they are talking bad things about me."

"How do you know what they are saying when they only whisper? You are Aw Boon Haw's wife and you must expect people to talk about you. They will tire of it soon enough. And they will only bite their tongue if they speak evil."

Kyi Kyi's intransigence was vexatious. But Boon Haw could never really be angry with the child-bride he had married. Theirs was a special relationship. He was her husband, protector and father all rolled into one. Kyi Kyi actually liked the country north of Singapore. The jungle awed her. The endless rows of rubber trees fascinated her. She was intrigued by the immense wooden troughs supported by spindly legs in the tin mines, and the army of coolies labouring in the muck to extract the precious ore. Most of all, she derived great satisfaction basking in the deference accorded her when they were entertained by her husband's dealers. She was the one and only Mrs Aw Boon Haw when they were on their own, away from their home. Such homage paid to one sheltered all her life was to be relished to the fullest.

"This trip is all business and there will be little time to relax. It will bore you."

"I have been on your business trips before and I did not find them boring."

"This is different." Boon Haw reached into his store of wits and came up with an instant qualification: "I'm taking the tiger car into the towns and villages. The people there have never seen anything like it. It will arouse their curiosity as nothing else would. Everywhere we stop, people from all around will flock to see it and we will distribute samples to those who are not yet customers. You may be hurt if the mobs turn unruly."

The Tiger allowed himself to be carried away with his flash of inspiration. His pride and joy was the metal tiger. "Just imagine: everywhere we pass, people will stop to look in surprise. Everywhere we stop, people will rush to stare and touch and talk about the wonder from Singapore. Everybody will think of my Tiger Balm. It is the best kind of advertisement I know. We will be dealing with big crowds and it's just out of the question for you to be with me. Next time."

"Next time. Next time!" Kyi Kyi pouted. "I will be old before I see your next time."

Boon Haw's road show set out for the Malay Peninsula two days later. Who else but the Tiger riding his metal namesake could be the most fitting person to lead the caravan. A three-ton van, suitably painted with pictures of his medicines in colours matching the rainbow following on the heels of the monster vehicle, was loaded to the hilt with Tiger brand products. Tiger Balm took up two-thirds of the space. The cars carrying helpers and other paraphernalia of the trade completed the convoy.

The caravan made its first stop in the centre of Johore Bahru, a fair-sized town at the southern tip of the Malay Peninsula. "Singaram, sound the horn," the Tiger commanded his driver. The ever-smiling Indian obliged. The beast-on-wheels snarled the weirdest roar ever heard by any Malayan. Passers-by stopped in their tracks. Shoppers ceased their haggling and rushed out to see what the commotion was about. Children screamed and clung to their mothers in fright. A crowd quickly gathered. The Tiger stood up on the seat, and surveyed the scene. He waved his hand to acknowledge the attention, and then sat down on the folded hood to absorb the wonder of the crowd.

He would dearly love to make a speech and sing the praises of his medicines of which many in the crowd were already loyal users. But the medicine man was not used to making speeches. Giving lectures was more his forte. Moreover, he would have to speak not only in Chinese but also in Malay and Tamil to get through to the multi-racial throng. The most effective message therefore was to distribute his samples.

There was a near stampede to get the medicines. The Tiger was rudely jostled and nearly knocked off his perch as toughies began fighting over the samples. But instead of blowing his temper, Boon Haw was delighted with the response. All too soon, the quota for

Johore Bahru ran out. The order was given to pack up and move on, with the unlucky ones chasing after them.

The same scene was repeated elsewhere. The monstrous tiger car attracted crowds in Ayer Hitam, Batu Pahat and Muar. In the scramble for samples, it was inevitable that fights would break out. It was only his hard-earned cloak of respectability that prevented the Tiger from chastising the bullies. "No more samples," he announced. "Let's drive on to the next town for the night."

Malacca was one of the component territories forming the Straits Settlements. Having been occupied by two powers before the British established their sovereignty, Malacca bore many signs of early Portuguese and Dutch influences.

Only the rest house was typically British, introduced in Malayan towns for the benefit of British civil servants and merchants. These houses were run more like clubs than hotels, with their chummy atmosphere made cosier by the eternal *stengah* (Scotch and soda) or gin and tonic.

Boon Haw did not feel that the lodging houses befitted his exalted position in society. He sought accommodation at the rest house, but his young assistant, a Chinese named Soon Sit Aye, was turned away when he approached the reception clerk.

"Do you know who wants to stay in your miserable hotel?" demanded Soon.

"I don't care who, as long as he is not a European," the clerk retorted. "This place is for *ang mohs* only."

"Aw Boon Haw will buy this place and kick you out if you do not give him a room."

The manager, a middle-aged Hainanese writing at his desk some distance away, heard the name. He came over, "Did you say Aw Boon Haw?"

"No one else."

"Where is he?"

"Waiting outside. Impatiently."

The manager ran out and greeted the Tiger with profuse

apologies for having kept him waiting. He booked the Tiger personally in the rest house's best room, and sent for refreshments. "I know the big boss is tired. Please drink your tea. I shall send a girl to massage your weariness away."

"I don't want a massage."

"Anything you want, boss. Steak, pork chop, lamp chop, chicken chop. Anything."

"Three threes?"

"No, boss. Very sorry. I'll get the sack if I serve dog meat. The Europeans are very strict."

"Or very ignorant. Very well then. Send up some fried noodles. I'll eat in my room. And another pot of Chinese tea."

The manager left. He was glad the proud Hakka did not choose to eat in the dining room. He was risking his job taking in a non-European, even one as distinguished as the Tiger Balm King. As for Boon Haw, he wasn't inclined towards any country girl as the long awaited reunion with his third wife was so near.

The triumphant procession almost turned into a tragedy on the way to the Malayan capital, Kuala Lumpur. The vehicles stopped at a little town called Kajang to buy petrol. As usual, a crowd gathered around the tiger car. Free samples were distributed. Chinese, Tamils, Malays, all clamoured for "*minyak chap harimau.*" It was a most unruly crowd. They pushed into the van. To prevent any looting, an assistant pressed the tiger horn, and the fearsome blare froze the crowd.

It startled the wits out of an old Malay woman who was stroking the tiger's head and marvelling at the wonder from the big city. Life in the village among the paddy fields was dull and uneventful. Her granddaughter had run home to tell her of the beast, and the old lady had trod her unsteady way along the mud banks to see the "*kreta harimau.*" The monster's roar caused her to jump back in fright, and she tumbled into a monsoon drain.

The frantic cries of the old woman's grandchildren brought a Malay man rushing to the scene. The woman huddled in the drain was his mother. On learning how she got there, he invoked the name of Allah and unsheathed the *parang* he carried. He was the village *penghulu* (headman), and he was bent on teaching the "infidel" a lesson for subjecting his mother to such indignity.

The *penghulu* spotted Soon who stood rooted in amazement at the old woman in the drain. The headman advanced, *parang* raised, murder in his eyes. Soon jumped and ran towards the petrol station with the Malay on his heels. The station proprietor intervened. He was a friend who had given loans to the headman from time to time.

"What is wrong, *dato?*"

"I'm going to teach that ill-bred man a lesson he will never forget."

"Are you going to chop him with your *parang?* You will kill him."

"If it's the will of Allah, so be it."

"But *dato*, that's murder. Surely, there's another way out for you to seek satisfaction. You are the *penghulu* and should uphold the law instead of breaking it."

"What other way is there?"

"I am sure the *towkay* will compensate your mother generously. He is a very rich man."

"Five hundred dollars."

"That's too much for falling into a drain."

"Ask the *towkay*."

The proprietor asked. Boon Haw swore. "I'll give the robber fifty dollars or I will call the police," he finally said.

The headman had had time to cool off. Fifty dollars was many times more than what he was paid for settling minor disputes among the villagers. A lot of money for just drawing a *parang* and running a few steps. He accepted the money with a smirk. City folks were such easy pickings.

Being held to ransom was the last straw for Boon Haw. He became tired of his circus. The trouble wasn't worth it. He instructed the team to return to Singapore, and ordered Singaram to drive to the Kuala Lumpur railway station. There he boarded a train for Prai to catch a connecting ferry to Penang. A gharry took him the rest of the way to Geik Cheah's home.

The unheralded visit caused some consternation in the Ooi household. Four *bibis* were engaged in a game of *chi ki* in the living room, and three more were helping to cook lunch for the gamblers. Children chased each other or wiped sticky fingers on the upholstery. Boon Haw did not welcome guests whenever he visited. He frowned at Geik Cheah's greeting. "Jee Ko, what a surprise. We were not expecting you." She had not heard from him for months except for the regular registered letter containing money for household expenses.

"I do not have to give notice to come to my own house. I am very tired. Is my bedroom ready?"

"Nobody sleeps in it when you're not here, not even I."

Boon Haw's feelings were ruffled. He had looked forward to a quiet reunion. Instead, a houseful of tittering women and shrieking children were there. He marched upstairs to seek his rest.

Geik Cheah followed a few minutes later with a cup of tea. Bibi Ooi tactfully shoved her guests off. She was upset that her son-in-law was annoyed. His rare visits were like someone bearing gifts which were never delivered. To her, the greatest gift was a grandson. Five years married, and her daughter was still barren.

Friends gossiped, and the more intimate offered suggestions. Temples were visited, prayers said, and joss sticks burnt. A medium envisioned offspring in his trance but Geik Cheah was still as slim at twenty-one as she had been at sixteen.

Bibi Ooi was a troubled mother. A son for Geik Cheah would be the bond to tie Boon Haw to the family for the rest of his life. She had no illusions about a rich man's nature, especially that of her proud son-in-law. He was very rich, in the prime of his life, and his fondness for women was well known. More wives could enter his life later, but Geik Cheah would be provided for if she bore her husband an offspring, or preferably three in case evil spirits claimed the first-born when young. Then it would be hard for him to bear the disapproval of his peers should he abandon a fruitful wife. Bibi Ooi prayed. She wished Geik Cheah was like her elder sister Geik Heoh who had borne two sons in three years of marriage.

The next morning, Boon Haw was in a better mood. Geik Cheah left her husband's room and went about her household chores. She was definitely embarrassed. Five years married, and she still felt like a day-old bride whenever her husband visited. Bibi Ooi was pleased to see the couple resume married life as a married couple should.

The Tiger extended his week's visit to three. The day after his arrival was devoted to business. He sent for Ong, the Hokkien agent, and after hearing him out, and forming his own conclusions over the interference of his fellow Hakkas, he told the agent, "I don't care what you do or how you deal with troublesome people as long as you improve on your sales each month. Your main concern must be profit. I don't want to be bothered by anyone from now on until I leave."

Bibi Ooi's elder daughter came to visit and to show her new baby three days after Boon Haw's arrival. In her mid-thirties, robust and forward in her manners, she was unlike Geik Cheah who was painfully shy. The Tiger had met her twice before, and had taken a liking to his sister-in-law for her competence and happy disposition. "Brother-in-law, you're looking well," she greeted him as soon as she stepped into the house with the baby in her arms. "Did you bring your wives with you? I would like so much to meet them," she said, in all innocence.

"Not this time," the millionaire chuckled. I would not be here talking to you if I had, he said to himself. "I see you have another baby. Boy or girl? How old and what's his name?" he said, quickly changing the topic.

"Oh, this is Ah Kim. Three months old. Very naughty boy."

Actually he was a good baby with his mother's disposition. But it would be unbecoming to praise one's child. "By the way, where's Ah Nya?"

Ah Nya was Geik Cheah's pet name for the family. A common enough name. A girl was Ah Nya to anyone who didn't know her name. It was a polite form of address, like "miss." Geik Cheah inherited the name not out of formality but for convenience. No one could agree on the many names suggested for her.

"Your sister is in the kitchen. I asked her to prepare some medicinal soup for me," Boon Haw said, and added, "Baba people are ignorant of the benefits of Chinese prescriptions. I asked her to double boil my best ginseng with dog meat but she made every excuse to substitute it with beef. Can you persuade her to change her mind?"

"Here, you carry the baby, I'll see what I can do." Geik Heoh thrust the baby into her brother-in-law's arms, and went to the kitchen. She had not the slightest intention of changing Geik Cheah's mind. Their mother would throw a fit if she knew that dog meat was cooked in her kitchen.

Holding an infant was not exactly what the Tiger was trained to do. He was more used to handling bundles of crisp dollar bills. He looked at the baby. The baby looked at him, undecided whether to cry or go to sleep in an uncomfortable, strange embrace. Ah Kim settled for a few gurgles which melted the Tiger's heart. One of the few occasions he lived up to the "Boon" in his name. He was unusually gentle as he rocked the baby in his arms and made baby talk.

It was Bibi Ooi who came to his rescue. Coming down the stairs to oversee the preparation for lunch, she was surprised to see her son-in-law rocking a baby, unaware yet of her daughter's visit. Such domesticity from Boon Haw was something she would never have associated with a man who employed a servant for every child.

His normally stern visage assumed a benign look which made

him less intimidating. The old woman's surprise turned to amusement when the Tiger's baby talk sounded so much like gibberish. She watched the unconscious display of paternal feelings. More than ever she wished Ah Nya would give him his own baby to lavish the affection he so jealously guarded. There was, after all, a softer side to the nature he chose to show the world. She sensed his longing for a child of his own, and she was confident the love he would have for his baby would flow over to her daughter.

Bibi Ooi coughed lightly to announce her presence. She asked Boon Haw whose baby he was carrying.

"Your other daughter's."

"Is Geik Heoh here? I didn't hear her coming."

"She's at the back with Ah Nya. Please take the baby to his mother. He has wet me; so much water for so little a person."

Boon Haw's baptism of water raised a longing in his breast. His own flesh and blood by a wife, and not one by proxy. Boon Par would be so pleased. He had spoken with such brotherly feelings before Boon Haw left Singapore.

Yes, he said to himself, a son of undisputed origin to bear his name. He was certain the offspring he would sire would be a male. It was then that he decided to prolong the reunion with his third wife. An extended stay could reveal if Geik Cheah was indeed barren. He himself was supremely confident of his potency.

Boon Haw gave Geik Cheah a three-carat diamond at the end of his visit. She was more pleased with his affable mood than the gem.

Even more delighted was Bibi Ooi. She looked at the gift as a token of her son-in-law's love and esteem for her daughter. As for the Tiger, his thoughts switched to business ahead in Singapore the moment he stepped out of the house.

Twenty-four

"Did you stay in a hotel?" Kyi Kyi asked as soon as her husband came home.

"What a silly question! Why should I put up with the inconvenience of a hotel when I have a home of my own?"

"You go away again and again without me, and the first thing you do as soon as you come home is to scold me. You are cruel."

"And you're being childish. I was not scolding you, just telling you the truth."

"The truth! Huh! You're a different man since you married that Geik Cheah. She must have cast a spell over you." Kyi Kyi walked away in a huff.

Piah Hong later approached with a cup of Chinese tea. "Jee Ko, drink this and take a rest. You must be very tired. How was your trip?"

"As you thought, it was tiring. But a good trip. The tiger car was a sensation everywhere we went. How is everything at home?"

"I did not beat your Kyi Kyi, if you want to know. Did not even scold her. But the boys were naughty. Aw Kow and Aw Swan were lazy with their school work. They quarrelled and I caned them."

"And Aw Hoe?"

"I don't know. He was mostly with his mother. Did you see my mother in Penang? Did you give her some money?"

"You know I always do whenever I go."

"How is Geik Cheah?"

"She's well. But shy as a cockroach."

"What a name to call a person," the eldest wife laughed.

"You'll agree when you meet her. White cockroach would be an appropriate name for her. Her skin is as pale as ever."

"So now you have a potato and a cockroach for wives," Piah Hong bantered in good humour.

The mood passed. The Tiger said sternly, "You'd soon turn into a pumpkin if you keep on eating as you do." He was back in good humour and he teased her, "Imagine a pumpkin here and a cockroach there."

From then on the two called Geik Cheah "Peh Ka Chua" (white cockroach in the Hokkien dialect) whenever they had occasion to refer to her. The name stuck, and Geik Cheah became Peh Ka Chua to her peers.

Kyi Kyi learned of Geik Cheah's pregnancy through Piah Hong. They were having afternoon tea and snacks. The episode of the spilt tea had long been overlooked, if not forgotten. Casually, she said, "I hear Peh Ka Chua is pregnant."

Kyi Kyi stopped eating, and frowned, "How did you know?"

"Tai Sook (eldest uncle) told me."

Geik Cheah was an unhappy mother-to-be. Her delight, and that of her mother, in the early days of the pregnancy, had turned to bitterness. Word had reached them of gossip doing the rounds in Singapore alleging that the third Mrs Aw Boon Haw had been carrying on with other men whenever the Tiger was not around. The implication that Boon Haw was not the father of the baby due was all too obvious.

Bibi Ooi was shocked by the wicked lies. Her prayers had been answered when her daughter conceived, but now the blessing would be hollow if her son-in-law believed the gossip. She was too old and feeble to take the long train ride to Singapore to clear her daughter's honour. She was also a gentle woman who detested confrontations of any kind.

All she could do was to offer more prayers and burn more joss sticks in the Ayer Itam temple, and beseech the intercession of the Goddess of Mercy.

The subject of the gossip could do little but weep. The pain of being falsely accused of sleeping with another man was like a dagger in her heart. But even greater was the anguish at the thought that her unborn child could possibly be rejected by its father.

Her pent-up bitterness poured out in accusations against her mother. "It's all your fault, matching me with that man," she sobbed, when Bibi Ooi came with a tray of food. "I would rather remain an old maid or marry a beggar who trusts me rather than sleep on a bed of diamonds. What will become of the baby? Tell me, Mother, what is to become of a child without a father?"

Equally grieved, the mother softly replied, "Nya, I did what I thought was best for you. How was I to know that evil tongues would wag and wicked people would wish you harm? What is important now is for you to look after your health and ensure the baby is born strong. Now eat like a good girl, and try to understand your mother who loves you very much."

"I wish I were dead."

"Don't say that. The baby is innocent. We must not wish it harm. Besides, how can you be sure that Boon Haw believes the falsehood? He may not even have heard the evil talk. Let heaven be the judge. There is little we can do but pray and hope for the best."

Boon Haw had indeed heard the gossip. It amused him at first. Too much had been said about him to make him easily susceptible to malicious talk. Moreover, he knew Peh Ka Chua only too well. He had never seen a more timid or innocent woman. She was inhibited, and painfully shy. He couldn't imagine her entertaining any man when even to be seen in public with her husband was difficult for her to do.

When the rumour persisted, Boon Haw became angry. But he had to keep his rage in check. It would be beneath his dignity to deny the lies. There were many who would be delighted to see the arrogant Hakka millionaire taken down a peg or two.

Boon Haw discussed the matter with his brother.

"This nonsense has gone far enough," Boon Haw said as he

fidgeted impatiently round the room. "Something must be done to put a stop to all the malicious talk."

"What will you do?" asked Boon Par.

"What would you do?" a frustrated Boon Haw retorted.

"I don't really know. What is important is to find out where and how the gossip originated. Or if there's any basis for it. What do you think?"

"I don't know. I haven't seen Geik Cheah yet."

"Then do what you have to do. You know best, as always."

"Thanks for your support. I am sure Peh Ka Chua is innocent. Why, up to today, she's even shy with me. I shall bring the poor woman to Singapore. That would show the rumour mongers how much I despise their base thoughts, and put an end to all the gossiping."

"Wouldn't that cause more trouble?"

"Peh Ka Chua and her mother will live in a separate house. Please get some workers to clean up the Cantonment Road house, and clear out the staff living there. Furnish the house as comfortably as possible. That is going to be Peh Ka Chua's house."

The new residence of Mrs Aw Boon Haw of Penang in Cantonment Road was situated at the junction of Neil and Cantonment Road, within sight of the Tiger's head office, Eng Aun Tong, a hundred metres away.

Geik Cheah, heavy with child, left Penang and moved into her new home in Singapore with her mother and a servant. Geik Cheah's father had died two years earlier. He had been spared the anguish of the malicious gossip about his daughter. Geik Cheah was still miserable. There had been no indication from Boon Haw whether he believed or disbelieved the nasty rumours. The suspense was compounded by the proximity of the Tiger's headquarters.

She complained to her mother. "It seems to me he brought us here so that he can keep an eye on me. Why has he not come to see us since we arrived? Perhaps he believes the wicked gossip and is avoiding us."

Boon Haw had other pressing matters to attend to. Two months earlier, on 29 October 1929, the Wall Street stock market had crashed and triggered an American slump and world depression. Global economies collapsed. Millions of workers were thrown out of employment when companies, big and small, collapsed and went bankrupt.

The two brothers were locked in their office engaged in a deep discussion over the possible effects on their business consequent to the crash. Boon Haw, ever the optimist, was confident that the depression was an opportunity to make another fortune.

"Remember the last war?" the Tiger said.

"What about it? Many people got killed for nothing."

"Not the dead. The living. The survivors. Remember how we cornered all the raw materials and produced even more medicines through the war when others just went out of business? How much money we made?"

"But if the whole world is going poor, where are the people to buy our medicines?"

"Rich or poor, people get sick and sick people need medicine. The poor cannot afford to see a doctor or even a *sinseh*. But they can afford a few cents to buy our medicines. We will keep our prices low. Our suppliers need money. They will sell cheap, even cheaper than previously. So you see, my brother, we can afford to maintain low prices and sell to make bigger profit."

Putting his words into action, Boon Haw immediately despatched orders to his suppliers in the four corners of the globe to ship without delay the quantities he ordered. And in view of the world situation, he demanded, and was given, a generous discount.

He thrived on the misfortune of others. It was all part of business. To the far-sighted the gains. Misfortunes were not of his doing. He regarded his acumen as a gift to the poor: cheap medicines to relieve them of their suffering.

Boon Haw then turned his attention to domestic affairs. Piah Hong had asked to meet the newcomers from Penang, but her husband had put her off for the time being. Kyi Kyi put on a detached, distant air to signify her displeasure but the Tiger had become used to her constant displays.

Ah Po, the servant Boon Haw employed when he married his third wife, was a great help and comfort to Geik Cheah and her mother. She cooked and cleaned and did all the household chores. In between, she would slip into her mistress's room to ask if she needed anything.

The good woman prepared special dishes to tempt the expectant mother's flagging appetite, and cajoled her into eating. "You must think of the little one inside you, if not yourself. Try to eat, *towkay lung* (big boss lady), I beg you."

The servant dipped into her meagre savings to buy herbal preparations which she double-boiled with spring chicken from dawn to dusk to produce the most strengthening soups to fortify her heartsick mistress. Ah Po, hovering like a second mother, made life easier for Geik Cheah.

Bibi Ooi spent her days and half her nights worrying. What would become of the baby if its father rejected it? What would become of her in her old age if financial support ceased? A string of "what ifs" increased her gloom.

"I think I'm going to visit Peh Ka Chua this morning," Boon Haw told his brother after a final look at the previous month's returns just submitted by the accountant. The report was written in Chinese calligraphy, the characters fancifully drawn with the elegant strokes of a brush. It was translated into English for Boon Par's benefit.

"It was a very good month," Boon Haw commented. "It should get better for us as the months get worse. Pity the doctors. I hope Tsai Kuen will not lose many patients."

"You said you were visiting sister Geik Cheah. The morning is nearly over. Why don't you go now and leave me to study the accounts more closely?" Boon Par had been a little puzzled by his brother's attitude towards his youngest wife. He didn't think he had tired of her after only five years of marriage. If anything, he should feel closer now that his wife was about to present him with a child.

Bibi Ooi was, as usual, staring at the Hall of Everlasting Peace, and wishing her son-in-law would come. Then she saw the Tiger the instant he stepped out of the building, and brushing Singaram, the driver, aside, he started walking up the street.

Bibi Ooi watched every step. Was he heading elsewhere or was he finally on his way to pay the long overdue visit? Yes, he was heading her way, carrying a small parcel. It was only a short distance, but Bibi Ooi felt it was the longest walk she had witnessed. She was glad, and fearful at the same time. Glad to have the opportunity to clear the air, but dreading the meeting for fear he was going to question her daughter's fidelity.

"Mother-in-law, have you eaten?" he greeted the old lady after climbing the three steps to the verandah.

"Not yet. Have you eaten?"

"No, it's still early."

"Then you must eat with us. Come in, come in. Ah Po is cooking lunch."

"Did you bring Ah Po with you? I am glad."

"She looks after us very well."

"Then you must pay her well. Good servants are hard to find. Here, I brought some ginseng for Peh Ka Chua, I mean, Geik Cheah. Where is she?"

"Upstairs." She was about to add "crying" but instead called, "Ah Po, your *towkay* is here. Quickly, bring a cup of tea."

Bibi Ooi went upstairs to fetch her daughter. Boon Haw looked over the house, and frowned his disapproval at the modest furnishing. He made a mental note to instruct his manager to refurbish the house.

Geik Cheah followed her mother down the stairs. Her eyes were swollen but her face was calm. "Jee Ko, you have come," she said by way of greeting. "Have you eaten?"

"No, don't bother," he said. Boon Haw looked hard at his wife whom he had not seen for some time. She looked sad, her eyes red, and he guessed that all the gossip about her had taken its toll. But there was still the bloom of impending motherhood. She was very pregnant.

"You have been crying?" he asked, slightly annoyed that she had.

"Any woman would cry her eyes out if wicked lies were told about her. Do you believe all those lies?"

"Ai yah! You silly woman. Would I come to see you if I believed?"

"Then why did you not come to see us for a long time? Why did you take me away from Penang?"

"Why can't I take you away? Why can't a man send for his wife?"

"To prevent me from seeing the men gossipers said were my lovers. To keep an eye on me."

"You talk like a child. You allow gossip to cloud your good sense. You should lead a serene life when you are pregnant. If you don't think of yourself, think of my baby," he scolded.

"What have I done to make people say such awful things about me? As heaven is my witness, the child I carry is yours and nobody else's."

Bibi Ooi interrupted. "Come, Boon Haw. Come, Nya. The food is on the table." She had heard enough. Her son-in-law had said he did not believe the rumours. To belabour the point might only render the situation irredeemable.

Mother, daughter and son-in-law sat down to share their first meal in Singapore. Boon Haw, as usual, was the first to finish. He was in a hurry to return to the office.

Excusing himself even before he could eat the follow-up fruit, he said, "Geik Cheah, you must remember to ask Ah Po to boil the ginseng with chicken. You must fortify your health for an easy birth."

Her mind set at ease by her husband's words, and after making some adjustments to her new life in a society where she had no friends and where none spoke her brand of Hokkien, Geik Cheah began to add bloom to her matronly proportions.

True to his resolve, Boon Haw made extensive refurbishing on the house. But unlike his own house where every piece of furniture was custom-made, creature comforts at the Cantonment Road residence were purchased from Robinsons.

Boon Haw did not show up again for many days after the first visit. Geik Cheah began to fret. Her apprehension re-surfaced. She imagined fresh gossip circulating. Her mother tried to reassure her. "You know how ambitious he is: always trying to become even richer, always very busy."

But Geik Cheah was not completely convinced. Until Ah Hin, one of the fetch-and-carry boys in the family, came one mid-morning with a cut of roast pork, a pot of duck stewed with salted cabbage, a whole roast duck, Chinese sausages, sharksfin soup, and a basket of assorted fruits.

"*Towkay* asked me to order the food. He will come for lunch at twelve o'clock," Ah Hin told Mrs Ooi.

The old lady allowed herself a smile. How could anyone interpret the gesture in any other way but that Boon Haw had buried the rumours and the gossip for good.

"Nya, Boon Haw is coming here to eat. He has ordered food enough for ten people. Quickly, go put on your new *sarong kebaya* and get ready," Bibi Ooi called out to her daughter.

Piah Hong visited one week later at Boon Haw's request. She had not dared to broach the subject, not knowing how her husband felt about the rumours. It was traditional for a younger wife to make the first approach, but discretion cautioned her against hurting Kyi Kyi's feelings further. Piah Hong was bursting with curiosity about the third wife young enough to be her daughter. She had reached forty-four, and Geik Cheah was only twenty-one.

The eldest wife came with gifts for all. Bibi Ooi received an expensive *batik sarong*. Geik Cheah was given a beautifully decorated ceramic jar of ginseng wine. "Drink a small cup of this before each evening meal," she advised the younger woman. "I prepared this specially for you so that you will have an easy delivery. I hope it is a boy."

Piah Hong then produced a parcel wrapped in brown paper. She handed it to Geik Cheah.

"Open it," she urged. "It's for the baby."

The contents of the parcel were absolutely adorable. But completely impractical. They were woollen knits for a baby's christening. Impractical because the baby was not likely to be baptised a Christian. And the heavy knit wool might be just the thing in a chilly English church, but certainly out of place in the sweltering tropics.

Geik Cheah was puzzled as she held up the bonnet, robe and booties.

"I saw them in Robinsons and I thought they would make baby look nice," Piah Hong said. "They were the most expensive, too, among all the baby clothes. Do you like them?"

"Yes, they are very beautiful. Thank you, eldest sister." Geik Cheah had already decided that her baby was not to be cocooned in those heavy clothes. But it would be extremely discourteous to speak her mind, especially as this was their first meeting.

Out of courtesy, Geik Cheah enquired about second sister's health. "Very good appetite," Piah Hong replied. "I asked Kyi Kyi to come but she said she was not feeling well."

Geik Cheah sensed the second wife was resentful.

Their common origin, that of being born in the same town, Penang, was a bond that made for instant rapport between a principal and secondary wife. Geik Cheah was thankful that Piah Hong, who was married to Boon Haw for twenty-four years, accepted her so readily. They even spoke the same dialect, Baba Hokkien.

Their relationship established, Piah Hong came to visit again and again, each time showing more interest in the unborn baby. And each time expressing the hope it would be a boy.

For the moment another project with sentimental ties distracted Boon Haw's attention. The Chief Abbot of Kek Loh Si temple in Ayer Itam, Penang, had sought a donation from the millionaire to expand the forty-six-year-old place of worship. The meeting concluded with a gift far beyond the Abbot's expectations.

"I will build you a pagoda that will be the most magnificent of its kind in Malaya," Boon Haw told the delighted monk. "You may not be aware of it, but it was on the grounds of Kek Loh Si that I met my third wife."

"My ten thousand blessings fall on you and your descendants," intoned the holy man. "Truly, your generosity has no equal. We shall call it the Aw Boon Haw Pagoda in your honour, and your name shall live on long after you are gone."

"No, the honour must not be mine alone. My brother is equally responsible for making the donation. We built our fortune together and everything we own we share equally."

"Then what shall we call it? It must have a name as grand as the structure you have in mind."

"Call it the Pagoda of Ten Thousand Buddhas. A Buddha for every blessing you offer." And thus the most famous pagoda in Malaya was conceived, and stands to this day.

One day in February 1930, an employee assigned to look after the welfare of the occupants of the Cantonment Road residence, hurried to his boss with good news. Boon Haw looked up in annoyance when the man entered, without his usual timid knock. Manners had taken a back seat as the man had great tidings to deliver.

"Big boss," he began breathlessly. "Third boss lady has given birth."

Boon Haw had been expecting the event and, therefore, did not show any unusual excitement. "When?" he asked in a matter-of-fact manner.

"An hour ago."

"Boy or girl?"

"Boy. Big and strong."

Boon Haw looked at the man and nodded his pleasure. "You may go," he dismissed the messenger.

Boon Par came congratulating his brother. "I am so glad for you, Jee Ko. We now have each a son of our blood. Cheng Chye by Daw Saw, and – by the way, what are you calling your son?"

"After me, of course."

"Fathers don't name sons after them. Only the family name," Boon Par said.

"Not my full name – part of it. I shall call him Aw It Haw." (It Haw means first tiger in Hokkien dialect).

"Quite unique. Another tiger in your family."

Boon Haw had given considerable thought to a name for his son. If his business empire were to last a thousand years, the name of its founder should last as long. An Aw Boon Haw dynasty, no less.

The Tiger recalled the abbot's blessings. Now that another had been realised, it would be fitting to visit the temple again. He was also anxious to see that the pagoda was built according to his specifications.

"I am going to Penang soon," he told his brother, "to see if they built the pagoda to my instructions. Seven tiers, no more, no less. Otherwise I shall have it pulled down and rebuilt."

The Leopard was used to the Tiger's impulsive decisions which had occasionally led to difficulties. The trip to Penang appeared harmless enough. "Yes, it's a good idea," he agreed. "Go and give thanks for It Haw."

Exactly seven tiers. He counted them and was satisfied. The Pagoda of Ten Thousand Buddhas was indeed a splendid structure. It stood on the uppermost level of the hillside on which Keh Loh Si was built, and commanded a panoramic view of the tree-clad terrain below.

Geik Cheah's son was fair, and resembled his mother to a remarkable degree. Like any grandmother, Bibi Ooi was full of joy and pride, but she could not help wishing the boy looked more like his father. Piah Hong too was happy for Geik Cheah. She continued her visits, and the more she saw of the baby, the more she wished he was her own. Each time Piah Hong came to the house, and she came often, she would pick It Haw from his cot and rock him in her stout arms.

He was a plump mite, all pink and cuddly. He cried only when he was hungry, and promptly went back to sleep after his bottle of Cow and Gate was finished. He loved being carried, and everybody loved to carry him, Piah Hong most of all.

Boon Haw was leaving for Hongkong the next morning. All day long Piah Hong had been rehearsing an approach to her husband on a matter very close to her heart. She wanted It Haw for herself. Geik Cheah would surely object. Only their husband could persuade the mother to part with her baby. She must speak up now or it would be too late. The natural mother's love for the baby would grow deeper with each passing day.

"Jee Ko," Piah Hong began tentatively when they had a moment to themselves, "I have seldom asked you for anything because you have given me everything I could ever want. But now there is something I would like to have more than anything. Only you can make it happen."

"What is it this time? Another diamond? You never wear them. They must be turning mouldy in the safe."

"No. I don't want any diamonds. I was thinking how happy it would make me to raise a baby once again."

Boon Haw was astonished. Had his wife gone dotty even before old age could set in? She was forty-five, too young to be senile, and perhaps too old to conceive. He stared at his wife. She had shared his ups and downs for nearly a quarter century. He asked, "What do you mean?"

"Do you agree that the eldest wife is entitled to claim the first born male of a secondary wife?"

"It has happened." It dawned on him then what Piah Hong was driving at. "Are you talking about Peh Ka Chua's baby?"

"He is so adorable. He takes to me like I was his natural mother."

Just then, Kyi Kyi walked in. She had caught the exchange in another room, and could not resist intruding. "Who does the baby look like?" she asked.

"Just like the mother. Fair and beautiful."

"A son should look like his father," Kyi Kyi commented and walked away.

"What makes you think Peh Ka Chua will part with her baby?"

"She is not giving him up to an outsider. Whether I raise him or Peh Ka Chua does, he will still be in the family. He is still your son."

"Would you give up your baby?"

"There is no comparison. I am the eldest wife."

Boon Haw agitated an ear lobe as was his unconscious habit when debating a decision. She had been a good mother to Aw Swan whom she regarded as almost her flesh and blood. She had treated Aw Kow like a real son even though he was already six when he came into the family. She had been a good and loyal wife all these years, and had believed in him completely. She deserved whatever he could give her to make her life even more fulfilling.

He would also like his son to live in the big house, close to him, instead of the humble abode in town.

The Tiger made his decision. "If you think you can really care for the baby the way my son deserves, I shall see what I can do. I can't promise. Peh Ka Chua might misunderstand."

Geik Cheah did not misunderstand. Not after her mother had explained to her the implication of the request.

"It's an honour when the eldest wife asks to raise the son of a junior wife. It means you are accepted. I think it is best for the boy. Your refusal will only cause bad blood. The baby takes his proper place in the family without question."

It Haw was taken away when he was one month old, which corresponded with the end of the Chinese confinement. Piah Hong, the new mother, as was customary, gave Geik Cheah a token. This was one hundred dollars wrapped in red paper.

"Please do not worry about It Haw," she consoled the mother who was close to tears. "I shall look after him as if he came from my own womb. He is also still your son as his father is also your husband. The house is always open to you whenever you wish to see It Haw."

One year into the depression, and the world was in a sorry state. There were no signs of better times ahead. More factories went out of business because consumers had no money to spend. Tin mines in Malaya ceased operations. Rubber estates stopped tapping. The tin barons survived on the fortunes they had made during the boom.

Planters were recalled to England where they joined the ranks of the unemployed. Better to be beggar at home than to be destitute in the colonies. Singapore's entrepot trade slowed down. Hard times descended on everybody except Boon Haw.

He kept prices low and created more customers. The poor resorted to self-medication on Tiger brand products. A dollar saved at the doctor's meant a dollar's worth of extra food for the family.

Eng Aun Tong prospered as never before. Boon Haw's donations to charity increased as more people joined the throngs of the hungry each day. He donated countless bags of rice to the public kitchens where no one who came to seek a bowl of rice was turned away. He gave freely and his beneficiaries blessed him just as freely.

The monsoons were blowing their worst and dark clouds intensified the gloom of the depression. But to Boon Haw, that wet December day was one of his brightest. His dynasty was taking firmer root.

Ooi Geik Cheah was delighted her dutiful act had been amply rewarded. The gods had acknowledged her noble deed and sent another son to replace the one taken away from her.

Bibi Ooi was the happiest grandmother alive. Geik Cheah's future was of paramount importance to her, and her place in the family was now doubly secure. She had given the proud Hakka two sons. The grandmother's worries were over. She could now die in peace when the time came.

Piah Hong was glad for Peh Ka Chua's sake. She had felt guilty and was a little sorry when she took away the secondary wife's first born. She would understand another woman's sorrow for her sacrifice. With another son to lavish her love on, the younger woman would recover the joy of living once again. The pain of the malicious gossip would be banished forever.

Kyi Kyi was sullen if not furious. Married eleven years and denied the joys of motherhood, she nursed a feeling of inadequacy, and was resentful of the younger woman who had borne her husband two sons in ten months. She did not have it in her to share Boon Haw's joy when he came home with a happy expression and unwittingly rubbed salt into her wound by declaring, "Peh Ka Chua is a good wife. She is capable of bearing many sons."

"Who does the baby look like?" Kyi Kyi asked.

Aw Boon Haw's grin widened. "Like me! Another tiger. I have named him Jee Haw (Second Tiger)."

It Haw was the apple of his foster mother's eye. He filled her otherwise idle days with delight. His every little action was a wonder. When he turned on his stomach at three months, she boasted that he was the cleverest baby alive. When he sat up at six, she went into raptures. He was now attempting to stand up on his chubby legs after having mastered the crawl. She doted on him and gave him a name of her own. She called him Aw Wan. Boon Haw raised no objection to humour his wife, but continued to call his son It Haw.

Bibi Ooi was surprised and a little flustered when her son-in-law came in on the day Jee Haw was born. She had not been expecting him as he had taken his time to call when It Haw made his appearance. The visit made her day. Geik Cheah was nursing the baby who was showing his temper when the milk flowed too slowly. "Wah! You little one, fierce like a tiger," the father smiled indulgently. "I'm going to call you Jee Haw." The mother nodded her approval, and added, "He's only a day old, and already showing such a temper. A real *haw kia* (tiger cub) he is."

From then on, the baby became known as Haw Kia. Even his father called him that. He was proud of his replica.

Three months were to elapse before Geik Cheah set foot in the Tiger's mansion for the first time. It was Piah Hong who suggested it. Boon Haw did not want to antagonise his second wife. "Peh Ka Chua has given you two sons, and yet she has not yet been invited to the house," Piah Hong complained. "It is very awkward for me each time I visit them. She must think that we regard them as lepers."

Boon Haw had often thought of inviting Geik Cheah and her mother. Many a secondary wife with the gifts of two sons would not only be the equal of her elders but would most likely elect herself first among her equals.

Now that Piah Hong had brought up the subject, he thought it as good a time as any for his three wives to get together.

"If you like, why not bring Peh Ka Chua back with you when you visit her next? Introduce her to Kyi Kyi. And bring Haw Kia."

It was neat. He wouldn't be there should there be any confrontation. Piah Hong was capable of putting the younger women in their places. Kyi Kyi retained a lot of respect for her eldest sister's muscle.

"I'll go today. Will you be home as usual?"

"You know it's Thursday today, my club day. Do not wait for me." Boon Haw seldom visited the Ee Ho Hean Club after the quarrel with Tan Kah Kee. Together with a few prominent Chinese who found the Bukit Pasoh atmosphere stifling, he had found another watering place, the Weekly Club situated in Club

Street. A regular partner in leisure, fun and games at the club was a wealthy merchant named Ong Peng Hock, who was later to open an amusement park known as the New World.

Piah Hong called out to Kyi Kyi as soon as she entered the house, "Peh Ka Chua is here. Come and meet her."

Kyi Kyi approached out of curiosity to see the mother of her two stepsons.

"Jee Chi (second sister), are you well?" Geik Cheah greeted her rival a little nervously.

"I am well."

"I have brought Haw Kia to show his second mother."

Kyi Kyi looked closely at the child cradled in her mother's arms. Her heart ached to cradle one of her own. The longer she looked, the more the baby's resemblance to his father struck her. She softened and asked, "Is he a good baby?"

"Yes. Would second sister like to carry him?"

Kyi Kyi reached out for the baby. She could not help remarking, "He looks so much like Jee Ko, his eyes, his nose, and especially his big ears." The strange voice made the baby look up. Seeing a strange face, he howled and struggled to be free. Kyi Kyi quickly handed him back to Geik Cheah.

"So fierce, like a tiger," she laughed. "Now I know why you call him Haw Kia."

Ah Weng, the servant, brought in a tray of tea. Geik Cheah immediately reached out for a cup. "Second sister, this is the first opportunity I have to serve you tea. Please drink."

Surprised but pleased, Kyi Kyi accepted. Piah Hong looked on with approval. "You must give Peh Ka Chua an *ang pow* in return. This is the custom," she said.

Kyi Kyi hurried to her room and returned with her handbag. She took from it a little red packet. "Just a small token," she said as she made her first gesture of friendliness since Geik Cheah was married to Boon Haw. She dug into her bag again, and produced another *ang pow* for Haw Kia. "May he grow big and strong," she said, and pressed the packet into his little fists.

The most junior wife had made her peace offering. The haughty second wife had reciprocated. Their husband would be very happy, Piah Hong thought. "And now, let's have some snacks," she said happily.

Piah Hong carried Aw Wan on her hip. Geik Cheah held Haw Kia to her breast. Kyi Kyi walked alone. She gave the two a wistful look.

Boon Haw would have reason to boast to his friend, the fruit seller, of the harmonious relationship among his three wives.

Dim sim and soya bean milk were served. Piah Hong and Geik Cheah chatted while they ate. Kyi Kyi could not take her eyes off Haw Kia. The baby kicked and nearly fell off his mother's lap. Kyi Kyi made an instinctive grab for him, and the baby was tugging at her clothes the next instant. He did not cry this time. He cooed and gave a frothy smile. This aroused Kyi Kyi's maternal feelings.

"How would you like to come and live with second mother?" she whispered to the baby, holding him close.

That evening she said to her husband, "Jee Ko, Aw Hoe is nine years old now, and I feel lonely when he is away at school, and you are away on business." The Tiger, as usual, was seated on a bench among his fabricated deer and storks. He was relaxing after dinner. The cool air cleared his head and fortified his mind for the next day's problems. He did not like intrusion when he was meditating, one slippered foot on the grass and the other on the bench, while a limp hand rested on a raised knee.

"What's on your mind now?" he asked, sounding a little surly. "I've told you I'll take you the next time I travel."

"Peh Ka Chua's baby is so cute. He looks so very much like you. He smiled at me when I carried him."

"Did you and Peh Ka Chua get along?"

"Oh yes. She served me tea and I gave her an *ang pow*."

"It's the right thing to do. For both of you."

"I was thinking ..." Kyi Kyi searched for the right words. "Elder sister is so happy with It Haw. He is so happy and well looked after here. He would be happier still if his little brother is with him. They can grow up together and be as close as brothers should be. Like you and Boon Par."

"What are you getting at? Do you want Peh Ka Chua to come and live here?"

It was not what she wanted. She ignored his question.

"I have a lot of time to look after a baby. I would like to be a mother to Haw Kia."

"What you like may not be what Peh Ka Chua likes. She has parted with one son, and she's not going to part with another."

"If she could give her first-born to the first wife, it is only fair she gives her second baby to the second wife. Other families have done this before. Anyway, like It Haw, he will still be in the family. I want Haw Kia."

"You want many things. Even another woman's child."

"I don't want another woman's child if I could have one of my own. And I don't think I am to be blamed for that."

The implied blame pricked Boon Haw's conscience. It was Kyi Kyi's trump card and he had no desire for her to play it any more than he could help it.

"All right," he snapped, "I shall speak to Peh Ka Chua. But I don't promise anything."

"When will you speak to her?"

"When I see her again."

"When will you see her again?"

"When I am not so busy."

"See her tomorrow."

"Oh that woman! I should have known she was scheming to take Haw Kia away from me," Geik Cheah complained to her mother. "Why was she so kind to me the first time we met? Why did she want to carry Haw Kia when she never bothered to visit us? Now I know!"

Geik Cheah seethed with indignation after Boon Haw left. He had visited her the next day as he had promised Kyi Kyi.

"Peh Ka Chua," Boon Haw began as he sipped tea, "It Haw is alone in Tanglin. It would be good for him to have a playmate. I think the best playmate for him would be his own brother."

"You mean Haw Kia?"

"Yes, our second son."

"But Haw Kia is too young to play. Why he's only a baby and needs looking after all the time."

"I know. I'm thinking of one or two years' time."

"But there is no room for us in the big house. I prefer to live here with my mother."

"I'm not asking you to live there, only Haw Kia."

"Who's to look after him?"

"Kyi Kyi has asked me to ask you if you would let her take care of Haw Kia. It Haw is doing very well with Piah Hong. Haw Kia will do just as well with Kyi Kyi to love and care for him. And I shall be very happy to have both my sons with me."

"What about me? Does nobody care for my feelings? First I had to give It Haw to eldest sister. Now second sister wants to take Haw Kia away from me. Does a mother have no rights at all?"

"They are still your sons no matter who looks after them. You can visit them any time you want."

"I would like both my sons to be with me if I could. I was prepared to part with It Haw because it was expected. But Haw Kia stays with me. I want to look after him myself. To see him grow day by day. To hold him and to feed him. To nurse him if he should fall ill, and to laugh with him when he is happy. I love my baby."

"All mothers do. You have borne two healthy boys. You can have many more to compensate. After all, you are only twenty-three years old. Many women bear children until they are past forty."

"I don't want to bear children for other women. I am sorry if I make you angry. But I want to keep Haw Kia."

"Kyi Kyi will be very disappointed." Boon Haw did not press his second wife's case. His heart was not in it.

The second wife was more than disappointed. She was furious, and accused her husband of not trying hard enough.

"You disappoint me in the things most important to me," she scolded her husband. "Peh Ka Chua has no respect for the wishes of her elders."

The truce established only recently appeared shattered.

Twenty-five

The owner would be only too pleased to sell his land at any price. Consequently, his estimation of the Tiger Balm King slipped a few notches when the reputedly shrewd millionaire made an offer very much in excess of what he was prepared to accept.

The property possessed few advantages. It occupied a steep hillside strewn with boulders and was not very accessible. Tai Hang Road which fronted the plot was anything but fashionable. Vegetable patches patterned the neighbouring slopes haphazardly. The rest was clothed in weeds and shrubs. "How could a man so successful in business be so ignorant in buying land," the vendor wondered as he pocketed the money.

Boon Haw, however, could see no flaws but only possibilities. There were no houses nearby and this ensured the privacy he sought. The view was magnificent. The property overlooked the dreary outskirts of the city below and stretched unobstructed to the harbour and beyond towards Kowloon across the water. What was foolish to others was good sense to him.

This was just the site he had sought since he established his branch office in Hongkong. "I shall build my house on solid foundation," he told himself. "What could be more permanent than rock? My house shall last for generations to come."

The Japanese occupied Mukden in 1931. Japan eyed China as a vast hinterland and sought Chinese territory to relocate its industries from its overcrowded islands.

Japan staged an attack on the South Manchurian railway and blamed it on Chinese warlord Chang Hsueh Liang's troops. Japanese forces attacked Chang's army outside Mukden and occupied the area. It was the beginning of their drive to annex the whole of Manchuria, which they eventually did.

Henry Pu Yi, who would come to be known as the Last Emperor, was proclaimed provisional president and later became the puppet emperor of Manchukuo.

Nineteen thirty one also saw the Communists setting up a Chinese Soviet Republic in Juichi, Kiangsi, with Mao Tze Tung as chairman.

Neither the Japanese incursions nor Mao's rivalry with Chiang Kai Shek caused Boon Haw much alarm. He laid more plans to accelerate his expansion into China. More schools were built and more financial support was given to the Kuomintang. Meanwhile, anti-Japanese sentiments mounted. The Chinese in Shanghai organised a full-scale boycott of Japanese goods in 1932. In retaliation, the Japanese staged the murder of some of their own priests and used this as a pretext to attack a centre of anti-Japanese plotters.

The Japanese navy landed marines to reinforce their troops. The Chinese 19th Route Army battled the invaders to a standstill. An army division was hurriedly despatched to bail out the marines. The 19th Army kept up its stubborn resistance and the Japanese sent in two more divisions. The Chinese defenders finally withdrew against overwhelming odds.

Anti-Japanese riots which broke out in Shanghai gave the Japanese the excuse to send still more troops to China. Widespread fighting broke out and the conflict was to escalate across China and lead to full scale war in 1937.

Meanwhile, the Shanghai fighting put paid to the Tiger Balm business there. It had become the most profitable China branch next to Hongkong. Li Shai Htone, the Shanghai manager, fled the troubled city for the safety of Singapore.

Li was like family to the Aw brothers. He was a bachelor and had no marriage intentions. "No woman can look after me like my sister does," was his standard reply whenever the subject of a wife was mentioned. True enough, Ah Chee, his younger sister who was also a confirmed spinster, served him hand and foot. She was beside him wherever he went and no brother and sister could be more loving or show more concern for each other. Boon Haw sent the brother and sister to live in the little bungalow behind his mansion in Tanglin. They were treated like members of the family, eating with them and sharing the services of the many servants.

Li was appointed manager of Eng Aun Tong. The position made him the third ranking member of the Tiger Balm organisation. He enjoyed Aw Boon Haw's confidence as no other had, so much so that the Tiger gave him his power of attorney.

Li, a trained accountant, could not help noticing how loosely the business was run. Boon Haw made all the decisions, sometimes after consultation with his brother, other times deciding on the spur of the moment. It was a marvel the undertaking had progressed so phenomenally in spite of indifferent accounting and inadequate records of the most important transactions.

Li employed whatever expertise he possessed to tidy up the mass of tangled schemes constantly cooked up. The sheer volume baffled belief. Boon Par had a hard time keeping up with his brother. Li was himself flabbergasted. Such methods ran the risk of falling into irretrievable situations.

Obviously, the business ought to be reorganised. Eng Aun Tong had outgrown its role. A partnership between the two brothers was all right for a small scale business but definitely outdated for an enterprise as big as Tiger Balm. The brothers should form themselves into a limited company.

Boon Haw was deservedly proud of his achievements without the aid of any of the Western methods of management. He did not understand them and had no desire to adopt them. Li was aware of this. But because of his genuine affection for the Aws, he took it upon himself to persuade the proud entrepreneur to put his affairs in a more businesslike order.

He had consulted a solicitor who had come from England with a good law degree and who had fallen in love with the tropics. John Laycock had built up a successful law practice in the Straits Settlements and was glad to have such an important man as Boon Haw as one of his growing number of clients.

"I'll be glad to incorporate a company according to the laws of the colony for Mr Aw Boon Haw if he so desires," Laycock readily agreed.

"But I have done very well as it is," Boon Haw protested when Li mentioned the proposed business revamp as delicately as he could. "Tell me, how many companies with modern ideas and high salaried staff have done as well as I have? It's the government's pretext to control people's business, wanting to know everything and prying into offices which are none of their business. I know their tricks. I know my business more than anybody can ever teach me. You can't teach business. You learn by doing it. You succeed if you work hard. And, of course, you must be clever. Give a fool a sack of rice, and he will soon turn it into sand."

"It is true, Jee Ko, what you said, most of it, anyway. But your business is too large for one person to attend to all the details. You have more important things to occupy your time. And as important, you want some system by which you can get information easily without having to ask many people for it, or search for days to find a document. It is time wasting, and your time is precious."

The Tiger listened impatiently, but found some substance in what Li said. Many a time had he searched in vain for a document to substantiate a deal or raked his brain to recall an agreement made. He loathed making notes and committed undertakings to memory. His word was his bond, and he expected his associates to be similarly honourable.

Boon Par lent his support. He had some appreciation of the

advantage of forming a limited company. Foremost was the fact that the company and not the proprietors would face litigation in case things turned sour. He hated tangling with the law and he knew his brother shared his sentiment.

"What Shai Htone said made sense, Jee Ko. We do not want to run Eng Aun Tong like shopkeepers. We are too big for that and our reputation is second to none."

"This would be a most auspicious year to write another glorious chapter in your family business," Li declared. "You have just turned fifty and it is fitting that we mark the occasion of your half century on this earth by an event that will continue to bear fruit for generations to come."

This pleased the Tiger. Any act to perpetuate the Aw name was a thing very much to his liking. But he still had many doubts to clear.

"Will the kind of company you have in mind deny me my privilege to do what I please and how I please?"

"Not at all. As long as you are the main shareholder. And you are, whether the firm is a partnership as at present, or a company limited by shares."

"I am not the sole proprietor. Whatever we have is shared equally by Boon Par and me. And even if we form the new company, it will still be half his and half mine."

"There is no problem there. The lawyer can easily make it legal for whoever to own shares and state the amount without question," Li assured him.

Something still bugged the Tiger. It has to do with his charity, the one interest which gave him as much pleasure and satisfaction as making one fortune after another. After some thought he asked, "Will it restrict the amount I give to charity, to feed the poor and house them, to cure the sick and bring them comfort, to support any cause and to give to whoever I please and however I choose?"

"That can be written into the objectives of the company," Li answered.

"If you two are sure that what you have in mind is best for the business and for us, I shall consider it seriously. Now, Shai Htone, tell me, is my new tiger car ready?"

"Yes, ready and waiting in the garage. And something else that I'm sure will please you even more."

"What's that? I don't like surprises."

"You'll like this one. The new tiger has a very good number 8989."

"Why is the number so special?"

"Well, *paat* (eight) sounds like *faat* (prosper) in Cantonese. There are two eights, so the car will bring double prosperity."

The Tiger smiled and shook his head. "The superstitious Cantonese, they have an interpretation for everything."

The interpretation of the number 7257 on the superseded car was not at all flattering. In fact, it was downright vulgar. The seven sounded exactly like a part of the anatomy seldom mentioned in polite company. It was never uttered in the owner's presence.

Boon Haw, with Li close on his heels, marched to the garage situated just across the old railway line which ran beside the Tiger Balm factory. He was like a boy with his face all lit up in anticipation of a new toy. The old tiger car which had thrilled and terrified so many since it made its appearance five years ago had developed a wheeze in its throat and a splutter in its innards. The roar had turned into a feeble cry and the once purring engine sounded like a rattling pile of metal. It had served its master honourably but it did not receive an honourable demise. Its final resting place was some junkyard on the island.

The new tiger car was even more of a monster. It was fabricated around what was once a shiny black Humber. The original tiger head was cannibalised from the discarded NSU and given some drastic cosmetic surgery. It looked more like what the fearsome beast should look with its distinctive colours faithfully reproduced. The whole car was striped black on a gold background to simulate the tiger's appearance.

"What a beautiful tiger," Boon Haw acclaimed at first sight. "Does it roar?" Without waiting for a reply, he pressed the electric horn on the steering wheel and the metal beast erupted into a two-note protest, one note following the other. There was no roar but the new sound was even more weird, if that was possible. Apparently, it met with the Tiger's approval. He smiled and laughed in delight, and said, "Let's go for a ride."

Li followed him into the car. Singaram backed the car out and drove to the office to pick up Boon Par. His brother must share the pleasure of that first ride in what cynics were to call Aw Boon Haw's alter ego. He needed the ride to soothe his rumpled feelings. He had had to eat humble pie not once but twice during the past year.

The *Sin Chew Jit Poh* had celebrated its second anniversary the previous year in grand style. It had been a tremendous success in that short space of time and had built up a wide and faithful readership. The editorial pages were hard hitting and often biased against a certain section of the community. It was not difficult even for the most obtuse reader to detect an anti-Tan Kah Kee flavour. The rivalry had not subsided. If anything, it was more acrimonious than ever.

Tan Kah Kee was not averse to hitting back at Boon Haw. Readers bought both papers to read what these two great rivals had to say. The kettle claimed the right to reply to the pot. It was not only a case of two popular newspapers competing for a greater following but of the two most prominent Chinese employing the press to hit at each other.

To commemorate the occasion of the second anniversary, the *Sin Chew Jit Poh* produced a supplementary publication. The contents were of a general nature, dealing with politics, economics, social affairs and, at some length, on the Japanese incursions into China. But the Hokkien community took exception to one article which made some uncomplimentary comments on affairs in Fukien Province.

This was an indirect attack on the local Hokkien leaders as they, especially their leader Tan Kah Kee, had contributed much to the welfare of their province. The Hokkiens were incensed. The accusing finger was pointed at Aw Boon Haw.

The affair soon developed into a slanging match via the columns of the pro-Hakka *Sin Chew* and the pro-Hokkien *Nanyang*. The Hokkien Huay Kuan, the most powerful association of the Hokkien community, joined in the battle. The dispute threatened to develop into an irreconcilable split in the Chinese community, Hokkien against Hakka, though it had started only as a tit for tat between two personalities.

The escalated dispute alarmed the authorities. It was the last thing they wanted to have – a civil unrest on their hands. The world depression was biting deep into the economy and widespread unemployment was sowing increasing discontent. The Chinese Protectorate summoned leaders of the contending factions to a meeting. The face-to-face confrontation only led to more acrimony.

The colonials persevered in the best traditions of British tact and diplomacy. Reason refused to prevail. Thinly veiled threats to close down both newspapers and curb certain individual rights drew some encouraging response.

The bone of contention was the offending article. The Hokkien camp demanded an apology. The other side balked. The humiliation to their leader was unacceptable. After months of mediation, the great Chinese dispute was finally settled.

In order to spare Boon Haw the blushes, the blame was placed on the author of the article. A sub-editor of the *Sin Chew* was removed and the newspaper was required to run an apology for one whole month.

Then came the Singapore Chinese High School case against the Tiger, which had the effect of belittling his philanthropic activities. His apologist said the cause was with good intent. The offended maintained the effect was ridiculous.

It all began years ago, in 1920, when on one of his visits to Singapore, Boon Haw donated four thousand dollars towards the school building fund. He was glad for the opportunity to advance Chinese education in Malaya although he was still residing in Burma. Ten years later, when he was firmly established in Singapore, he erected two elaborate gateways leading to the school, which was situated some distance from the road.

An inscription on the gateways proclaimed "Presented by Aw Boon Haw and Aw Boon Par" below another inscription in large letters which said "The Singapore Chinese High School." This gift cost three thousand dollars.

"Now people passing by will know that the imposing building inside is the biggest Chinese school in Malaya," the Tiger said.

But other supporters who had subscribed to the building of the school objected to the smaller inscription. "It would give the impression that the school was presented by the Aw brothers," they protested. A delegation called on Boon Haw to rectify the erroneous impression. The latter refused. "Since the inscriptions are on the gateways, it should give no other impression but that it was the gateways themselves that were presented, not the school," he argued.

A quarrel soon developed. Boon Haw was accused of claiming honour where honour was not due. "Why, even Mr Oei Tiong Ham, the largest contributor with a one hundred thousand dollar donation, only had his name displayed with the others in the school hall," they pointed out. But the man who erected the grand gateway refused to budge.

Two lesser contributors, Messrs Li Leung Ki and Thng Siong Phua, went to court. "Imagine calling a deer a horse," they sneered. Li and Thng sued and won. The judge, a Justice Beckett Terrell, in handing down the judgement, remarked that it was "a petty, contemptible squabble." The inscriptions were obliterated.

The two unhappy episodes were far from his mind on the day he went for his first ride in his new mobile showpiece. Aw Boon Par was happy to see his brother forget the two unhappy events, and enjoy the admiration and wonder of the people they passed. There was another reason he was happy. A bouncing baby boy named Aw Cheng Taik had brought new joy into his life.

"Jee Ko, have you given more thought to what we discussed with Shai Htone?" Boon Par asked. A delegation from a charitable body had just left with the promise of a big donation. The brothers had a few moments to themselves. Boon Haw was unusually pleased with the annual returns which his brother had shown him. The profits surpassed those of the previous year by a good margin. The delegation had called at the right moment.

"About forming a European kind of company? No, I've forgotten. Let's call Shai Htone in again. Between the two of you I might be convinced."

"I've given it much thought myself and I am convinced that it is the right thing to do. We must also think of the future. Anything can happen when we are not here. It is for our own good and for the good of our family."

"I believe you. Do you think Shai Htone could fill me in with more details?"

"Jee Ko," Shai Htone began, accepting a cup of tea from the tea boy, "I hope you have decided to proceed with forming the company we discussed last week. We have to protect the business against what might happen later. Who knows, it may even fall into the hands of outsiders."

"That is unthinkable. This is a family business and I intend to keep it in the family," Boon Haw stated.

"It can be done. A good lawyer will see to it."

"And another thing. Will the new company confine us to do our present business only? You know I have other interests such as land. And even to lend money. I want to be free to do anything that is profitable."

"Of course, you can. That will be another objective of the company."

Boon Haw fired the questions. Li Shai Htone answered them as convincingly as he could. Aw Boon Par supported Li's arguments. The Tiger was finally persuaded.

"Now instruct this English lawyer in whom you have so much confidence to prepare whatever necessary. But do not commit us to anything until you have shown me the papers. Remember what I want. If it cannot be done, then we will carry on as we have done for thirty years. One final thing. Be sure that the company is named after us."

Haw Par Brothers Limited was incorporated on 5 September 1932. John Laycock drew up as tight a constitution as he knew how. The brothers were the original subscribers, each taking up one nominal share to get the company going.

Land, and not Tiger Balm, was among the first objects for which the company was established. The relevant memorandum stated: "to purchase or otherwise acquire for investment or resale and to traffic in lands, houses, buildings, plantations and immovable property of any tenure or any interest therein, and any immovable property of any description, etc."

The trade which had enriched the brothers so immensely was listed eighth: "to carry on the business of chemists, druggists, drysalters, oil and colourmen and importers, exporters and manufacturers of and dealers in all pharmaceutical, medicinal, chemical, industrial and other preparations, articles and compounds, etc."

Thirty-eight following objectives covered every undertaking that could be thought of and which allowed the new company to branch out in any direction. The capital was ten million dollars divided into ten million shares of one dollar each. It was a phenomenal sum for a private company at the time. Each brother owned exactly fifty percent of the shares.

Haw Par Brothers Limited acquired the business of Eng Aun Tong, the stock in trade and all other assets. The valuation of the assets of the Hall of Everlasting Peace was a conservative estimate. It did not take into account the true value of the goodwill built over thirty years. Eng Aun Tong became the trading arm of all the new company's pharmaceutical business.

To ensure that the business remain in the family, Boon Haw restricted ownership of shares and limited the number of members to fifty. Those persons eligible to own a part of the company were confined to:

(a) A son, adopted son or daughter of Aw Boon Haw.

(b) A son, adopted son or daughter of Aw Boon Par.

(c) Lineal descendants through males only of Aw Boon Haw.

(d) Lineal descendants through males only of Aw Boon Par.

The final word and the freedom to act as he pleased with or without consultation with anyone must be Aw Boon Haw's. He accordingly appointed himself the Senior Governing Director for life.

Perhaps one of the most noble aims of the Tiger was his desire to continue his contributions to charity. With this in mind, he had written into the company's constitution this article: "... shall have and shall exercise in his uncontrolled discretion the power to appropriate out of the annual net profit of the company a sum not exceeding fifty percent thereof in each financial year and to pay or contribute in the name of the company or in his own name the whole of the money so appropriated to any local, foreign or other charities or otherwise apply for any charitable and/or benevolent purpose in such proportions and at such time and in such manner as the said Aw Boon Haw shall at the like discretion think fit and deserving."

This so touched John Laycock who was responsible for drawing up the constitution and attending to all the legal requirements, that he volunteered to forego his fee. "My contribution is a mere drop. I like to think that it will join the oceans going to the poor," he told a surprised Li.

"Everything is the same," Boon Haw told some concerned clansmen. "Only a new name is added. Eng Aun Tong is still in existence and shall exist for as long as there is a Haw Par Brothers."

Twenty-six

Taking up residence in his new Tai Hang Road mansion gave Boon Haw great satisfaction. More than anything else, it proved his critics wrong, as usual. They had advised against building a costly house on the much maligned plot and they warned of dire consequences if he went ahead. No builder could do justice to the project he had in mind.

Haw Par mansion had become a reality. There it stood proudly on the hillside basking in all its glory for all to see and to admire. And for his doubters to eat their words. The city lay below, the Fragrant Harbour sparkled in the sunlight, and beyond the water was fast-spreading Kowloon with the distant hills of China in the background. The view was truly magnificent as Boon Haw had expected. The rocky, scrub-infested land had been transformed into a gem.

There was no ceremony or celebration, unlike the occasion in Singapore when priests chanted blessings to the accompaniment of exploding firecrackers and the beat of drums. The family was driven to the house as soon as they disembarked from the s.s. *Canton*. Servants were waiting to receive the master and his ladies.

Kyi Kyi, for whom the house was built, assumed the prerogative of stepping under the piece of red cloth banner strung over the front door even before her husband. She paused and looked about her. It was not what she had expected. The theme was Oriental where the White House in Singapore had been wholly western. One was traditional, the other modern. She was not a student of Chinese culture but the classically Chinese flavour pleased her instantly.

It was totally different and distinctive; from the Chinese style roof of green glazed tiles to the dominant red of the interior. She could boast that her house was an original and not a replica of the one where Piah Hong lived.

"Jee Ko, this is the most beautiful house in the world. I like it," she said quietly. It was the only enthusiasm she showed. A Chinese wife must always maintain a sense of decorum. Not for her a public display of gratitude, no matter how she longed to show her appreciation in a more fitting manner.

The husband gave her an indulgent smile. "Now you cannot say I do not think of you when I am away. A man can show no higher regard for a wife than to build her a house of her own."

Piah Hong, an increasing opulence slowing down her steps, followed the second wife and their husband into the house. "Wah, there's so much red in this house. It makes it feel so hot," she commented.

"Eldest sister, red brings good luck. Red is a harbinger of prosperity. Jee Ko is going to make even more money. You should be glad," Kyi Kyi rebuked the older woman.

"I know. I am only talking about what I see and how I feel. I, too, like Jee Ko to get even richer. Who does not want to be rich?"

Geik Cheah was left behind to mourn the loss of her mother. The old lady had succumbed to an illness which had affected her on and off for the past few years. It was a bad time to die with her son-in-law embroiled in litigation over the Chinese High School affair after the abject month-long apology extracted from the *Sin Chew*. But as expected from a dutiful son-in-law, he gave his mother-in-law more than just a decent funeral with two bands and a host of temple mediums in attendance.

Aw Kow and Aw Swan came over from Canton where they were attending Ling Nam University, to join their parents in the house warming. Aw Hoe was more interested in exploring the landscaped gardens than in admiring the many costly jade carvings in the house. He was fascinated by the many sculptures populating the many terraces carved out of the hillside.

It Haw fretted in the house because *tai mama* (eldest mama) would not allow him to get as grimy and sweaty as *sum ko* (third elder brother).

"You will fall and roll down the hill and break a leg," she told the apple of her eye. "Now be a good boy and I will buy you some toys when we go to town." It Haw loved toys, not so much to play with as to take them apart to see what made them work.

Boon Haw coaxed his eldest wife time and again to see the garden he had built on unwanted land. "It is the only garden of its kind you will ever see," he said. "It is only the beginning. There are many other things I am going to add to it. But it is already quite unique as it is. Come, I'll show you." But Piah Hong begged off each time.

The day was too hot. The climb was too much for her. She was not as young or nimble as she used to be. One excuse after another put the eager guide off, until two days before they were due to return to Singapore.

Piah Hong finally ventured out with It Haw in tow. Aw Hoe jumped from boulder to ledge leading the way. Boon Haw brought up the rear. They came to an imposing pagoda on the highest spot of the property. Piah Hong stood at the foot of the structure and counted the tiers: seven levels. She counted again, this time from top to bottom. Seven levels, no more no less. Frowning, she turned to her husband. "Jee Ko, do you know how many tiers there are on your pagoda?"

"Seven, why?"

"Do you know that it brings bad luck to build a seven-tier pagoda?"

"There you go again. Why are you so superstitious?"

"This was what I was told. We can believe it or we don't."

"If I believe in all the superstitions I hear, we won't be where we are today. I would be too timid to do all the things I have done and all the many more things I shall do. I don't see the Pagoda of Ten Thousand Buddhas bringing us any bad luck. The opposite is true. We are richer than ever before. And I have been blessed with It Haw and Haw Kia. Bad luck indeed!"

Piah Hong said no more. She dutifully and laboriously followed her husband to admire the rest of his garden. But the seven tiers of the pagoda preyed on her mind.

The shipping clerk came up for the third time to ask the manager, Aun Ee Han, if *tai si tow* was busy. "You know the boss is always busy, especially now when he is about to leave for Singapore. Why do you want to see him?"

"I've just taken delivery of two crates which I was told to handle with care. They are supposed to hold some valuable articles meant for the boss."

"Why didn't you say so earlier? I'll see what the boss wants to do with them."

The boss wanted the cases brought up to his office. He had been expecting them. If the contents were what he thought they were, he intended to take them with him to Singapore.

The Tiger personally supervised the opening of the cases. He cautioned care over the handling and scolded the storehand when the latter wielded his crow bar a little less gently. Boon Haw scattered the shavings and brought out a heavy object wrapped in hessian. He removed the covering with tender hands to reveal an exquisite piece of green jade carved in the shape of a rooster. His expectation confirmed, he returned the carver's masterpiece to the crate and ordered the lid resealed. He was satisfied that both crates contained the gifts he had been promised.

The city officials of Swatow and Amoy had conferred long and hard as to what would be the most suitable gifts to present to the philanthropist for his generous contribution of a hospital each to their cities.

They had learned from a member of their benefactor's staff that the millionaire collected rare jade and other similar ornaments. He was also about to complete his Hongkong mansion for which art objects were being purchased to grace the house. The officials therefore had little hesitation in deciding on the gifts.

In due course letters couched in flattering language were despatched to Aw Boon Haw requesting him to accept their humble token in gratitude for his beneficence. The delighted recipient graciously accepted the gifts in letters of equal refinement crafted by the brush of a professional letter writer.

What started off as a gesture of esteem and gratitude became a tradition. The two cases of jade ornaments were added to the magnificent collection the Tiger had acquired on his own.

Word soon spread of the millionaire's hobby and those beneficiaries who sought to return favours did so in the form of carved jade and the like, in a myriad of shapes, colours and sizes.

As the millionaire's philanthropy in China increased, so did his collection. It was said that for every school he built in China, a crate of jade was presented in return. The millionaire became more discriminating in his own purchases. Only the rarest won his fancy. Quantity had become a reality. Now only quality counted.

Jade in the 1930s, other than the rarest, was still comparatively inexpensive. Many refugees from the north of China fleeing the Japanese invaders gathered their most treasured and easily convertible possessions when they abandoned their homes for the south. Among these possessions were pieces of jade, many of them precious family heirlooms passed down from one generation to another.

The bulky and less-easy-to-hide items were the first to be turned into cash. Desperation cancelled the natural desire to obtain the highest price. The market was flooded and bidders had the choice and advantage.

In many cases, a whole collection of the best as well as the mediocre went to one bidder for a ridiculously low price. Better to shed the temptation for others to rob, and get something in return instead of carrying the burden of fear. It was also difficult to find buyers. Many were in similar circumstances and money was hard to come by.

Aw Swan, twenty years old and newly graduated from Ling Nam University, was in Hongkong to learn the business. His learning process was mainly devoted to drinking coffee and chatting with the staff.

"You can learn just by observing," his father had told him. He was idle because there was no one to show him the ropes. Observing was just a fruitless exercise. Fraternising with the lowly staff earned him popularity.

The rickshaw pulled to a stop at the entrance to Eng Aun Tong, and a tall gentleman stepped off. Another rickshaw followed and the panting puller deposited two bulging sacks at the doorway.

"Is Mr Aw Boon Haw in?" the tall man asked the watching Aw Swan.

"Yes, what do you want with my father?"

"Oh, you're his son. My apologies, Master Aw. May I see your father, please?"

"He is very busy. I don't think he wants to see anyone."

"I am Shen Shi Yen from Shanghai. I hear your father collects valuable jade objects. I have two bags of good jade which I think Mr Aw Boon Haw will be interested to buy. Please tell him."

Aw Swan was well aware of his father's interest in jade. Often he was a one-man captive audience while his father expounded on the beauty of each acquired piece. The green stone would certainly arouse his father's interest. "Wait here. I shall see if my father will see you."

Boon Haw himself came out to meet the Shanghainese. The visitor knew at once it was the Tiger.

"Mr Aw Boon Haw, I am honoured to meet you. My name is Shen Shi Yen. Your former Shanghai manager, Li Shai Htone, is my good friend. He told me before he left Shanghai to see you if

I happened to be in Hongkong. I am here, and I hope you can help me."

"How can I help you?" The Tiger was wary. There had been far too many coming to see him for a handout. But this tall man before him was well spoken and appeared to be a man of substance.

As if reading the Tiger's mind, the man said, "I have not come to ask you for a loan or anything like that. I have something to offer which I think you will like."

Boon Haw glanced at the two sacks lying in the doorway. If they contained what the man had come to offer, whatever in those ugly sacks could not be valuable or pleasing to him. The man is only wasting my time, he said to himself.

Shen continued, to forestall a dismissal, "Yes, all my valuables are in these two sacks. It is a safe way to keep them. No one would suspect these humble gunny sacks contained anything of value. My family collection of jade ornaments is in them."

"May I see them?" Without waiting for a reply, he turned to Aw Swan and asked the young man to help carry the sacks into his office.

Shen untied one sack, and brought out an object untidily, but adequately, wrapped in more gunny sack. He untied the strings and peeled off the wrapping to reveal a fine piece of dark green jade carved in the shape of a phoenix. With tender care, he held it up for the wealthy connoisseur.

"One of the better pieces in our now abandoned family home," Shen said sadly. "My grandmother's favourite."

Shen produced more items from the sack, each equally beautiful. Birds, dragons, bowls, incense burners, vases and others. Each was placed on the Tiger's desk. The last item was an exquisite six-panel miniature screen, folded into a small rectangle. Shen unfolded it, and the translucent green jade glowed, each panel framed in lacquered rosewood and all six linked by golden hinges. On the extreme right panel was a delicately carved inscription identifying the screen as a Ching dynasty piece, about two hundred years old.

"Mr Aw, this piece alone is worth more than all the others combined," Shen said. "It has been in my family for generations." He folded the screen, and placed it beside the others. He went to the other sack.

"Enough. No need to look." Boon Haw was convinced all the man had in the sacks were genuine and valuable. "Ah Tai, bring tea," he shouted to the fetch-and-carry boy hovering near the door.

"Now, Mr Shen," he sounded happy, "tell me, why do you want to sell these beautiful pieces? I can see you are a man who appreciates artistic objects."

"We lost everything when the Japanese took Shanghai. They confiscated my factory which produced enough garments to clothe half of Shanghai. I am now a refugee. All my family are here in Hongkong. I want to buy and set up another garment factory here. It's the only business I know. I need cash very quickly, or the owner will sell the factory to another buyer. Li Shai Htone told me you were the only man who always had a lot of ready cash. So here I am, hoping you will give me a good price for my jade."

"How much do you want?"

"I know I can never get its true value from anyone. You are a collector. You know the value of good jade. Please make me an offer."

The Tiger knew he could hold the man to ransom. The man was desperate for quick money, to build a new life. The market was already flooded with refugee jade. Too many pieces, both priceless and near duds. Too many sellers chasing the few buyers with the cash and the inclination. But the millionaire would not take advantage of this refugee who was forced into misfortune.

"It's your property. It's proper for you to name your price."

"I'll accept ten thousand dollars for the lot. The jade screen alone is worth that. But it'll be enough for me to start afresh, and build another fortune. Perhaps even enough to buy back the screen from you at twice what you paid."

The man might be down but he was by no means out. He had pride, and he had determination: virtues the Tiger recognised and respected. The contents of the two sacks were worth many times what the man wanted. Boon Haw was nobody's fool. Neither was he as unscrupulous as he was often made out to be.

"I'll give you the ten thousand dollars you asked," Boon Haw told the man.

Relief spread all over his face, the Shanghainese replied, "Thank you, thank you. One day, with your permission, I would like to visit your mansion, and perhaps, to renew acquaintances with all the friends which I am entrusting to you."

Obviously, the parting from long cherished family possessions, inanimate though they were, was painful. The Shanghainese did not linger. He accepted the money from Boon Haw with both hands, took a last look at the jade pieces on the desk and walked away.

He had taken less than ten steps when he heard the Tiger call him back. He held out the precious jade screen.

"Mr Shen, in life one must retain at least one old and valued friend. I want you to keep this screen," he told the surprised seller. "You don't have to buy it back, now or ever. Here, take it."

Shen was too overcome with emotion to do more than murmur his thanks as he accepted the gift. He boarded the waiting rickshaw and left without looking back.

Aw Swan, a silent witness all along, was bewildered by what he had seen and heard. "Papa, why did you return the best piece to the man after you had paid for it?"

"My son, I did not return the screen to the man. I was buying his goodwill."

One sack of the unexpected treasures went to the Haw Par mansion. Another accompanied the Tiger to Singapore to join his collection of priceless ornaments finished in jade, topaz, aventurine, jasper, rose quartz, agate, crystal, lapis lazula and other minerals.

Jade, of course, was dominant.

Twenty-seven

"I was thinking, Boon Par, what an inconsiderate brother I have been. You have contributed so much to our success. I should have shown more gratitude to you for obtaining the Tiger Balm formula which started us off on our road to fame and fortune."

"What are you talking about, Jee Ko?"

The brothers found time to relax and gloat over the past years' trading. In spite of serious dislocations in North China due to the Japanese invasion, business in the rest of the country was better than ever. Ten more sales outlets had been established. Singapore had quadrupled its production. Swatow was hard pressed to meet demand even with additional supplies from Singapore and Hongkong.

Rangoon, where their business originated and now a little neglected and run by squabbling relations, was healthier than it had ever been. The cash rolled in, Boon Par struggled to keep tabs on the receipts but Boon Haw could not be less concerned with the bottom line as long as his fortune escalated.

"I was thinking, and feeling ashamed of myself, for building two mansions for myself, while you are still living in an old house."

"It is not old. You have spent so much money on improving it. Any millionaire would certainly be pleased to live in it. I know I am."

"That's your trouble, my brother. You are so careful about spending money."

"The English, you know, have a saying: A fool and his money

are soon parted."

"And I have my own saying: 'A fool is he who hoards money and lives in misery.' I am not saying you are a fool, or that you are miserly. But I believe you must live up to your position in life. A man is judged by his home."

Aw Boon Par's residence was on the west coast, about seven miles away from the city. It was a solid two-storey building with spacious grounds and a beautiful garden tended full time by a gardener. Canna, dahlia, chrysanthemum and bougainvillea bloomed and vied for admiration with their brilliant colours. A big bedroom was specially fitted out on the ground floor for Boon Par in deference to his physical impediment. It was beyond his capability to climb up the polished staircase. The deciding factor in the acquisition was the location by the sea. A cool, invigorating breeze blew all day, and the ozone was thought to be a tonic Boon Par needed to put more zest in his life.

"There's nothing wrong with my home. I am very happy in it."

"You need to live in a grander house. One we build ourselves. Not one others built."

"I get worried when you talk like that, Jee Ko. What do you have in mind?"

"I am going to build you a new home. A mansion, even grander than either one of mine. It is time, my brother, that you live in a house in keeping with your status. I have decided for you. Don't try to make me change my mind."

The Tiger summoned the chief clerk and asked him to compile a list of all the properties they owned: land, built-on and vacant, houses in the city and on the outskirts, rows of shop houses and private dwellings scattered on the island.

The buildings brought in a sizeable combined revenue in rental; some close to the factory housed expatriate staff from Rangoon, others were left vacant for future development.

Many of the properties had been pledged for loans from Boon Haw and acquired when the owner did not have the means to redeem them. Many were bought without seeing the property as long as the title was clean.

"You can't go wrong with land and houses," the Tiger would reply when asked why he seldom turned down an offer. "They are better than keeping the money in the bank."

The list, however, yielded no property to match the vision Boon Haw had conjured. "Loh Si, call the land brokers and find out what they have," he commanded the chief clerk. The intimidated clerk immediately scrambled to do the Tiger's bidding. Brokers came and sang praises of the land they offered. None satisfied the Tiger, though he did make a few purchases despite Boon Par's objections, for his land bank.

"We have to make room in our safes," he excused his action. "The money will start falling out if we attempt to stuff more into them." But the plot where Boon Haw intended to build a dream house for his brother could not be found and the brokers, one after the other, finally gave up.

On his way home one evening after visiting his brother, Boon Haw was startled by a loud report. His metal tiger wobbled. The human tiger swore. Singaram brought the car to a halt as he applied the brakes. "Sorry, boss, we have a puncture," he apologised.

While the millionaire fidgeted in the back seat, the driver struggled to replace the offending wheel. Boon Haw looked around. To his right was the sea. A steamer belched smoke as it sailed towards Tanjong Pagar wharves. To the left was hilly ground, the highest point about twenty metres above the road level. It was overgrown with *lallang* and *belukar*. A few coconut trees swayed gracefully in the evening breeze.

Two squatter huts built from salvaged packing crates and rusty corrugated iron sheets occupied a narrow ledge half-way up the hill. A grunting pig foraged in a pile of garbage.

It was a squalid scene in a rugged terrain which could draw no more than a fleeting glance from anyone else. But not the Tiger.

His heart beat faster. Memories of the Tai Hang Road lot surfaced in his mind. He got out of his car and walked towards where the sloping land met the drain beside the road. His eyes scanned the hillock from top to bottom, and then right to left. He slapped his left palm with his right, and gave a triumphant grunt. Boon Haw had found the spot to build his brother's villa.

Within a month, the land on the hill changed hands. Haw Par Brothers became the new owners of the neglected eight acres.

Boon Par did not have the heart to dampen his brother's enthusiasm. The latter brought him to the site to see the plot.

"If you could turn ugly Tai Hang Road into the beauty that it is, I am sure you can also make the Pasir Panjang Road property a place for all to admire," he said.

An architect was quickly found. The Tiger had a brainwave, and he was impatient to translate it into reality. "Many have derived pleasure from our jade collection," he told his brother. "What I have in mind will draw a hundred times more people. It will be an unforgettable mix of East and West. It will be unique, like nothing anybody has seen. We shall call it after us: Haw Par Villa, and you shall be the master of all around you. We will be remembered for generations to come."

An architect from the West was out of the question, although he did not doubt western ability. For the latest project, the Tiger required a man who was also familiar with Chinese culture, and well versed in Chinese myths and legends. The new project, he envisioned, would be a Chinese garden, ancient in its theme, and a place for all to visit and enjoy.

The residence, in contrast, would be modern and classical, completely western in style, and borrowing the best attributes of old European architecture. Boon Par appreciated things western, and it was fitting that his residence should match his taste.

Ho Kwong Yew, one of the better known local architects, was chosen for the job. Ho listened as Boon Haw expounded on his ideas to make the villa truly unique. It was difficult to absorb all he heard, but he was confident he could do justice to the residence Boon Haw had in mind. But the part involving the creation of sculptures, figures and tableaux to depict scenes of Chinese mythology and legends was something neither he nor any architect he knew had ever attempted.

The architect was evidently puzzled. The Tiger asked him, "Do you understand what I am telling you? Tell me so if you don't or can't do it. I do not want to waste time."

At thirty-one, Ho was the youngest Singaporean to own his own architectural firm. His father managed a tailoring business but the boy's talent for drawing earmarked him for a more august profession. When he left school at age nineteen his principal had recommended him for a job with the Public Works Department.

The government architect, H.A. Stallwood, saw the young man's potential and took him under his wing. Ho was soon promoted to assistant draughtsman in the Municipal Architect's office where he won two first prizes in a competition. The budding architect was involved in many public projects and gained valuable experience.

Ho left government service in 1926 to take up a partnership in a local architectural firm, Messrs Chung & Wong even before he qualified. This he did the following year on passing an examination set by the Board of Architects, a government-recognised body.

Ho then spent a year studying designs of buildings in Hongkong and Canton. He was particularly impressed by the skill and craftsmanship that went into the construction of the old Chinese temples and spent long hours studying them.

Shortly after his return to Singapore, Ho started his own practice and his reputation earned him many commissions. Boon Haw was impressed by the young architect's credentials.

Unfortunately, Ho Kwong Yew was among the thousands of Chinese rounded up by the Japanese one week after the fall of Singapore in February 1942. He was never seen alive again.

No architect worth his salt would admit a job was beyond him. He was not about to give up. This would be his most lucrative undertaking. Even if he could not carry out the project on his own, there were others who would be more than willing to be associated with such a prestigious undertaking. Without hesitation, Ho replied, "Of course, I can do it. No problem."

Among Ho's first priorities was to seek a contractor who not only had the credentials acceptable to his employer but one who also possessed a working knowledge of ancient Chinese culture. He found him in Sze-to Tuck of Chok Soon and Co. Sze-to was by no means a culture buff but he brushed that aside as of little consequence.

"There are many in Swatow who are very good artisans," he told Ho. "I even have relatives there who specialise in building temples and creating deities of every description. Do not worry. If Aw Boon Haw wants statues, I will give him statues."

He assured the architect, "I can import as many artisans as you require. They will be only too glad to come to Singapore. It is very hard to earn a living in China."

Boon Haw was pleased with the architect's enterprise. "Now you must proceed without delay," he said as he studied the plans with Boon Par in their comfortable office. There had been many modifications, deletions and additions. Boon Par directed his interest towards the mansion, and fully approved of Ho's concept. Boon Haw laboured over the proposed garden and its theme. Finally, he said, "This is not the complete picture I have in my head. But carry on. Don't waste time. We will improve on it as we build."

The improvements were to be a continuous labour of love until the day he died.

Friends and relatives could not help remarking how much he resembled his father. The resemblance became more obvious with each passing year. Now three and a half years old, Haw Kia also had a temper to match his father's. And the determination to be a leader.

It Haw, the elder by ten months, was just an inch or so taller and perhaps a kilogramme heavier. He was gentle while the other was brash; guileless where his brother was artful. It Haw recoiled while Haw Kia squashed an offending cockroach at his father's behest. It Haw would simply ask for a toy he liked while Haw Kia would say, "Papa, do you like that toy?" Which father's heart would not melt when his offspring sought approval with such diplomacy? The salesgirls in attendance would be instructed to wrap up the article the next instant. Haw Kia didn't have to ask.

Three-and-a-half years, and the boy had already learnt the art of tugging at the Tiger's heartstrings. The formidable Tiger was like putty in his child's hands. He loved the boy as he had never loved any child before.

A day did not pass without a few private moments with his cub, whenever he was in Singapore. To overcome the constraints of visiting his third wife daily – constraints imposed partly by Kyi Kyi's displeasure and partly through pressure of work – the Tiger instructed the nanny to bring the boy to his office every morning after his nap. And the child never went home without another toy, a box of sweets or other goodies after each visit.

The Tiger decided he must spend more time with this son who showed every promise of growing up to be his chosen heir. As such, his son was too precious to be left entirely in the care of his mother and the servants.

Boon Par had earlier moved out of the Tanglin Road mansion to the west coast house. How convenient now for Boon Haw to put his heir apparent into the vacant house, next to where he lived. It Haw would have his brother next door and the two sons would grow up together.

He gave instructions for Peh Ka Chua to move with Haw Kia into the vacant house. Within a week, Geik Cheah took up new residence.

Twenty-eight

Boon Haw's father left Chung Kan to seek his fortune in Rangoon. Aw Ah Tee's father left the village to make a better living in the southern regions. He made it as far as Malaya and eventually settled down in Bukit Mertajam to run a small medicine shop.

Chu Kin's sons prospered after his death while Ah Tee was content to carry on his father's business. It produced a modest living, enough to raise his family. It was Ah Tee's disinterest in claiming kinship which won Boon Haw's respect when they first met years ago. All that Ah Tee asked was an assurance that Eng Aun Tong would keep him supplied with Tiger medicines. From that day on, Boon Haw never failed to call on Ah Tee whenever he made his dealership tour.

Kyi Kyi accompanied Boon Haw on this particular visit. It was mainly social; Kyi Kyi had come to like Ah Tee's family on a previous visit. A dainty little girl in a cute *samfoo* outfit ran out as soon as she saw the visitors. "Uncle, aunty, you have come," she greeted them with girlish delight. She took Kyi Kyi's hand and looking up at the equally delighted woman asked, "Did you bring me another present, aunty?"

Indeed she did. The child tore open the parcel with feverish little hands and squealed with pleasure when she beheld the English doll in a pretty frock. She turned her adoring eyes on Kyi Kyi who immediately wished the child was hers.

A woman in her thirties, wearing sarong and blouse, walked out. They called her Siam Moi which means "Siamese Miss" because she was born in Siam. She had been cooking and was wiping her hands on a stained apron. She flashed a broad grin which displayed gold teeth. "Ah Ko, Ah So (elder brother, sister-in-law) I'm glad to see you again. Please sit, I shall bring some tea."

Kyi Kyi felt at home in Ah Tee's house. It reminded her of the shelter and care her aunt provided when she was orphaned. Here, she could be her natural self, among the kind of people she had known from birth – humble, honest and hardworking. They sat on straight-backed chairs with sagging bottoms and sipped Oolong tea.

Ah Tee knew his guests had arrived even before he dismounted from his bicycle. That hoarse voice and guttural speech could belong to none other than the richest man the clan had produced. "Brother Boon Haw, Sister Kyi Kyi, this is a happy day for us." He placed his well-worn medicine bag on a shelf and sat on a stool to chat. "I've just come from visiting a patient. He's old, his time has come."

They chatted while the little girl, whose name was Seh Moi, vied for Kyi Kyi's attention to play dolly with her. "Seh Moi," Ah Tee patted his daughter's head, "why don't you help Ah Ma in the kitchen and let aunty talk with us."

"No, no, don't go. I like little girls, Seh Moi especially. She's so cute." She was indeed. Nearly five, Seh Moi was slim and fair. Her limbs could be more rounded, but they were long and straight. Her dark hair was cut in a short bob and every now and then she squinted slightly to better observe an object.

"You spoil her, Sister Kyi Kyi. She's always asking about you, waiting for you to bring her another present."

"I have another gift for her," Kyi Kyi smiled and Seh Moi stared in anticipation. The child was too delighted with the gift to remember her "thank you." She ran into the kitchen to show her mother the shiny gold chain and the locket around her neck.

The Tiger and his wife beamed. The little girl's joy was their joy. "Gold makes the best gift for a child," he said. "A child with gold from young will soon learn of its great value."

Seh Moi insisted on sitting next to Kyi Kyi at the table. She was too excited to eat and kept looking at the elegant aunty with adoring eyes. Siam Moi teased, "Seh Moi, since you like aunty so much, would you like to go home with her and live in Singapore?"

The child, taking her mother's words in all seriousness, turned to Kyi Kyi and in a tone more plea than question, asked, "Can I come and live with you, aunty?"

Kyi Kyi replied without hesitation, "I would like that; I would like that very much."

"Aunty has no time to look after you," Siam Moi interrupted.

The little girl was unconvinced, "Can I come home with you?"

Boon Haw's mind raced as the child pleaded. Why not? he thought. Everyone can see that the child takes to Kyi Kyi, and she to the girl. Moreover, the child was born an Aw, sharing a common ancestor. She would make Kyi Kyi forget her disappointment with Geik Cheah's refusal to part with Haw Kia. The most persuasive argument of all perhaps, was that he himself was very much taken with the little girl's winning ways.

True to form, the Tiger made another instant decision. What had begun as a tease was now a serious matter. "Ah Tee, Siam Moi, I shall be very pleased to have Seh Moi come live with us. She will be well-looked after, I promise you.

The parents hesitated. The child had never left home since the day she was born. Singapore was so far away.

The Tiger pressed his case. He was not used to being turned down. "Ah Tee, Siam Moi, I am serious. We are very fond of Seh Moi. I would like to have her with us." The parents were at a loss for words. "I would like to adopt the child if you will agree. I mean no disrespect to you, I know you have done well for her as for your other children. I have no daughter and I would very much like Seh Moi to be my daughter."

Surprised into silence when her husband made the unexpected request, Kyi Kyi's face glowed with gladness when the full import of his words sank in. It was replaced by extreme anxiety the next.

She had never wanted anything more in all her life. "I shall be the happiest mother if Seh Moi becomes my daughter," she declared.

Ah Tee had no fitting reply. Siam Moi was flabbergasted with the turn of events. How could this wealthy relative of her husband take her teasing remark so seriously? How could he decide on a matter that involved a child's future in so short a time? She just couldn't understand the Hakkas, she concluded. Not even after being married to one for so many years. "Strange people," she softly commented in her native Teochew dialect.

The country physician and his wife excused themselves and conferred long and earnestly in their kitchen. They were reluctant and agreeable at the same time. Their realisation that a backwoods town like Bukit Mertajam had little to offer their daughter decided the issue. They, too, would like their child to grow up clever and respected. And perhaps, one day, even as famous and illustrious as the Tiger Balm King.

"Give us more time to think it over," Ah Tee requested. "And also give yourselves a second thought. If you still decide to take my child after a month, I shall take Seh Moi to Singapore."

Boon Haw sent an emmisary to escort Seh Moi and her parents to Singapore exactly one month later. She was adopted within a week. Her new father named her Aw Sian.

Kyi Kyi fell ill again. Her husband suggested she move to the seaside residence he had bought earlier. The mansion, called Hawpar Lodge, was near to Boon Par's house. Its sprawling grounds grew stately pines which whistled in the wind blowing in from the sea. The building was a substantial structure with a basement. It was quiet, comfortable and altogether a desirable place in which to recuperate.

Kyi Kyi took up temporary residence with a full household staff. Two handmaidens took turns attending to her every need. One was a slim girl from Burma named Soh Hla. She was English educated and occasionally functioned as secretary to Kyi Kyi. The other was an attractive woman with flashing eyes and a ready smile. She was twenty-two, born in Penang of poor parents, and had taken up service in the Aw household some years earlier. Her name was Khoo Siew Eng. She was a good worker and always ready to oblige. It was her accommodating nature that prompted Kyi Kyi to make her a personal attendant. That and her strong and yet gentle hands that had the knack of massaging away her mistress's weariness.

Occasionally, but only with Kyi Kyi's consent, were Siew Eng's soothing fingers employed to ease the Tiger's aches after a hard day at the office. This was done only in the wife's presence. But an indisposed Kyi Kyi could not always exercise her supervision if there were other massage sessions.

Siew Eng became pregnant. Those who professed to enjoy the Tiger's confidence said he urged the girl to abort the baby. But she would have no part in it.

An unwell Kyi Kyi was not aware of her handmaiden's condition until the signs were too obvious to conceal. She went to Hongkong to seek a speedier recuperation and to enjoy her husband's undivided attention away from the other two wives in Singapore.

The climate in Hongkong was more conducive to a quick recovery. But the sight of her handmaiden's condition raised her gall. What brazen behaviour. How dare she carry on with whoever he was? She was quite sure it must be one of her husband's employees. A new problem presented itself. What to do with the woman.

Boon Haw, meantime, was considering the options he had. One option was to buy her off. But it was not as easy as it sounded.

"I'll give you any amount within reason if you would just go away and say nothing," he had offered. Siew Eng shook her head and would neither accept the money nor take herself away. The months passed. Siew Eng's proportions expanded. The Tiger lost sleep. Kyi Kyi no longer allowed the girl with the soothing hands near her.

Boon Haw offered a handsome sum to one of his employees to marry Siew Eng and give her baby his name. No one dared accept for none dared incur the wrath of Kyi Kyi.

The fateful day arrived. A baby girl was born in September. No one visited the mother in the maternity hospital. Siew Eng could not care less. She was happy to have her baby. And she was determined that the father would recognise the girl as his own sooner or later. She expected no more than what she deserved. And what her baby deserved.

The midwife came into the confinement room with a printed form and asked the happy yet anxious mother, "May I know the father's name, please?"

"Aw Boon Haw," Siew Eng replied without a moment's hesitation. The midwife thought she had heard wrongly and repeated the question. Everybody knew Aw Boon Haw, the Tiger Balm King, the great benefactor of the poor. Surely his munificence could not extend to giving his name to every waif who needed a father?

"Are you deaf?" Siew Eng asked. "I said Aw Boon Haw is the father. You know, the man who makes Tiger Balm."

Boon Haw eventually resigned himself to accepting the baby. He sent Siew Eng and the baby back to Singapore. He instructed the manager to rent a house in Bedok, a suburb on the eastern side of the island, for the mother and child to live with a servant.

He entertained a sneaking admiration for her, for having the courage to stand up to him. Normally docile and of a pleasant nature, she had exasperated her mistress and placed him in a very awkward position.

As for Siew Eng, she had gained what she wanted and readily agreed to return to Singapore to face whatever the future might hold. She did not fear that Boon Haw would abandon her and the baby. The baby was of his flesh and blood, and seldom was a Hakka found to be unprotective of his own. Kyi Kyi's wrath would one day descend upon her, of that she was sure. But for now, her love for the baby was a shield against pain. She took a certain consolation in having the last laugh at those who sniggered and whispered when she had to fight her own battle. The smirks turned to admiration for her courage in standing up to the dominating figure who so recently regarded her as just one of the many who were at the family's beck and call. The baby was named Aw Seng.

Boon Haw returned to Singapore when Kyi Kyi's health had improved sufficiently for her to accompany him. She was glad to see Singapore again after a long absence. The Tiger was looking forward to seeing his baby daughter but not the inevitable confrontation with Kyi Kyi when the secret was revealed.

The baby was thriving. The mother was radiant. She was overcome when he walked into the house. "Jee Ko," she greeted him. The words sounded strange to her. Hitherto, like all the other girls in the household, she had always addressed him as "Uncle."

The Tiger acknowledged her greeting and enquired about the baby. She needed no further assurance that Boon Haw had accepted both mother and child. "She is well and growing fast," Siew Eng answered.

The Tiger did not remain long in the humble house. He left without finishing his tea and told her to get in touch with the office whenever she needed anything.

But he did call again. And again he was taken up with the bright-eyed baby who smiled at him every time he carried her. He showed more appreciation for the gentle nature and pleasant disposition of the mother of his child each time they met.

Several evenings a week after dinner, Singaram the driver would be waiting to drive him to Bedok. The Indian had received prior instructions. He could keep a secret and he was the only one to chauffeur the boss around whenever he was in town.

To Kyi Kyi's offhand question as to where he was going, he just as casually replied, "Oh, just going for an airing."

Kyi Kyi believed her husband. A man needed to clear his head after facing the problems his business generated. She had not fully recovered from her illness and there was no point risking a chill in the damp evening air. She stayed home while her husband made his secret visits.

The airings continued with monotonous regularity. A spark of suspicion flared. What was the old man up to? Age was not a reflection of a man's debility. The Tiger looked anything but old at fifty-six.

Kyi Kyi decided to go for an airing with her husband despite his protests.

"I shall put on warm clothes and you will put the hood up," she said. "I am tired of waiting for you each evening."

Boon Haw had no choice but to go for a proper airing. Siew Eng sat at home and wondered why the old man had not called in a week and more. Three consecutive airings together got the Tiger fuming. Time to declare my secret, he decided. She will know sooner or later. A blunt man at most times, he said, "The baby Siew Eng carried was mine." He looked sideways at his wife and saw how rigid she had become. But not a word from her.

"She's nearly six months old now and I intend to keep her," he continued. "I know you are angry but what is done cannot be undone."

Kyi Kyi was hurt to the core. She wanted to lash out but could not think of any words to inflict equal pain. The airing dragged on for endless minutes, vibrant with tension. Finally, she asked in a voice so calm she surprised herself, "Were your airings actually an excuse to visit Siew Eng and the baby?"

"I didn't want to distress you as you had been ill."

"I am touched," she said without conviction.

"A man is only a man. Even the king of England cannot remain a saint all the time."

He was referring to Edward VIII who abdicated to marry the twice-divorced American Wallis Simpson.

"I don't want to hear any more. But I ask you this: Do not bring

Siew Eng into the house, ever."

Kyi Kyi ordered Singaram to turn the car around. Her fury burned throughout the drive home.

The Tiger's emotions were a mixture of remorse and gladness. He, too, said not another word, being thankful for the explosion which did not occur. He could even draw humour from the exchange. History repeating itself, he chuckled inwardly. Piah Hong forbade me to bring Kyi Kyi into the house so many years ago. And now Siew Eng is having a dose of Piah Hong's medicine dispensed to my once-unrecognised bride, he said to himself.

The path to the undetermined peak might be strewn with obstacles both political and domestic, but the Tiger stable of medicines never paused in garnering more converts to their healing properties. For every outlet put out of business by the Japanese invasion, another two sprang up to take its place. It was a constant pressure to meet demands for Tiger Balm, Headache Cure, Balashin Sai and Chinkawhite in the China market.

A new manufacturing-cum-distributing facility became a priority. The Bonham Strand East premises had become sadly inadequate long ago. But the time involved in building a new factory would tax the owner's patience. Boon Haw bought an old biscuit factory in Wanchai Road and converted it into a Tiger Balm operation. He sold the biscuit making machinery to a Malayan businessman for a good profit and installed new equipment to produce his medicines. Production was greatly increased.

The completion of the new and vastly bigger factory fitted in nicely with Aw Boon Haw's calculations. A succession of conflicts from 1931 led to full-scale war with the Japanese in 1937. He had recently completed the construction of a sixteen-storey building in Canton, the tallest in the city, where he intended to house his biggest factory in China. Swatow had not been able to cope for some time. A newspaper to be called the *Sing Yuet* (Star of Canton) was also to be published here. The war put paid to his advanced plans. The machinery already in place in the proposed twin-facility was shipped to the converted building in Wanchai.

The declaration of war and the rape of Nanking in December 1937 had shocked the world. It was estimated that more than three hundred thousand had died. The victors embarked on an orgy of looting in any form they saw fit. The defenders had inflicted heavy casualties on them and it was now their turn to seek revenge. Chiang moved his capital to Chungking.

Haw Par Villa made its debut in March 1937. Many guests were invited. Public curiosity had been stirred to fever pitch during its two-year construction, involving scores of workmen at its peak.

Boon Par, the lord-designate of the manor, performed the function of host with a grace that belied his physical condition. Boon Haw, who had conceived of the extraordinary garden, deferred as much as possible to his brother. But it was mostly to him that the guests heaped their praises and offered their congratulations. For everybody knew that it was Boon Haw who built the pride of the Aw empire.

The villa was a blend of classical West and whimsical East. Centrepiece was the mansion situated on the highest point of the hill. The theme was one of spheres and curves. If the White House in Nassim Road might be described as quietly impressive, the structure in Pasir Panjang projected an air of magnificence.

The building was conspicuous by its seven saucer domes. The view from the reception hall provided a spectacular experience. It overlooked the sea and stretched towards the Riau Islands and beyond. Steamers big and small sailed in and out through the deep channels, shimmering in the sunlight. It was inspiring.

There were also a central hall, drawing room, bedrooms with separate dressing areas and a large dining area. Halls and rooms were crowned by domed ceilings finished in gold. Clusters of orbed lights were suspended on chandeliers imported from Austria. Walls of highly polished marble shone in various colours and mother-of-pearl shells added glitter to the ambience.

Sunlight streamed into the circular central hall through a specially designed panel at the centre of the dome. Doorways and strategic spaces were decorated with bronze panels of tigers in postures fierce or benign. The stamp of the tiger was evident in the home of the leopard. It lead one VIP guest to remark that perhaps Mr Haw intended Mr Par to be only the caretaker of his brainchild.

The splendour of the central dome was enhanced at night by clever floodlighting. A mixture of coloured lights hidden in built-in troughs around the top of the circular wall provided a psychedelic effect. It was original and never failed to impress guests.

Furniture, fittings and furnishings throughout reflected the best money could buy. It was here that Boon Haw displayed some of the best pieces from his collection of art objects. Exquisite marble sculptures bought in Italy in the course of a world trip the previous year graced the house as well as the terraces.

A considerable area surrounding the house was terraced and transformed into lush lawns of fine carpet grass. The beauty of each level was further enhanced by pure white globular walls and globed lights. Domed as well as pagoda-styled pavilions provided welcome shelters to pause and admire the panorama.

There were two fish ponds. One, circular in shape, held an island on which rested life-size storks in frozen postures. Gold and mottled carps swam their lazy way round and round the island.

The other pool was a delight to the eye and a fine example of the work of craftsmen from China. The captive carps here were merely incidentals. What gave pleasure were the weaving canals, hump-backed bridges and little pavilions striding the water. Every item was rendered in authentic detail.

The rest of the villa seemed a world apart; a world which has seen innumerable ages. The caves and grottos, the ancient trees with gnarled roots and knobbly trunks were a startling contrast to the modern curves and proportions of the modern mansion. It was a contrast in cultures, a clashing of the old and the new.

Tableaux depicting scenes from Chinese folklore and myths were variously described as grotesque, crude, fascinating, horrible or revealing, depending on how one perceived them. But these were the objects that made the garden so unique and an attraction that would draw thousands to gape and marvel. An archway of polished imitation marble stood at the entrance to the driveway. A marble elephant stood on each side of the entrance.

A wide concrete drive wound up to the mansion. It was flanked on one side by miniature caves and grottos and on the other by a long balustrade made up of hundreds of globules. The cost of the garden and the mansion with its art works was estimated at over one million dollars. The most delighted man was certainly Aw Boon Haw.

"His Imperial and Royal Majesty George VI of the United Kingdom and Ireland, King, Emperor of India and Defender of the Faith confer on you the Title of Officer of the Most Excellent Order of the British Empire for your endeavours in the realms of Commerce and Philanthropy."

The royal notification was despatched through the office of the Colonial Secretary and translated to Boon Haw by an aide. It might not have appeared as high sounding in Chinese as in its original language but it lost none of the imperial tone. This single honour bestowed on the fifty-six-year-old philanthropist by the forty-three-year-old king in 1938 was most gratifying to the recipient. This recognition was long overdue, he reflected.

The cynics said the honour was no more than a bribe to blunt the Tiger's barbs. A peace-offering intended to nudge Boon Haw into muzzling his newspapers.

His many beneficiaries, individual as well as institutions of varied inclinations, lauded the honour. It was overdue to a man who devoted so much of his time and wealth to the less fortunate and unendowed. Whatever the true reason, the millionaire wore his OBE with just pride. His largesse swelled. His name became even more synonymous with benevolence.

Undaunted by his aborted plans to publish a newspaper in Canton, Boon Haw began again in Hongkong. He enlisted the help of Chiang Kang Hu, a sixty-year-old politician who had close connections with the Kuomintang. The association lasted two months. Chiang did not see eye to eye with Boon Haw.

A well-known Shanghai journalist by the name of Fung Lea Shan was called in to organise the publication. Fung, too, lasted two months. Another Shanghainese, Ching Hung Hwa, succeeded Fung. Ching, himself a publisher in his native Shanghai, had definite ideas which did not match the Tiger's. Once again, Boon Haw was left high and dry. But not for long.

A journalist from the mainland was recruited. Chung Chang Poh, a no-nonsense man of forty-two, set about the job to meet the boss's deadline. He demanded, and was given, more leeway than his employer intended.

The *Sing Tao Jih Pao* finally saw the light of day on 1 August 1938. Aw Hoe, then only seventeen years old, was appointed manager. He had no desire to finish his studies in Ling Nam University. His heart was in business and his father, on the urging of Kyi Kyi, agreed to allow the quick witted boy to prove himself.

Hitler's army invaded Poland on 1 September 1939. Britain and France declared war on Germany. History repeated itself. The Second World War had just begun.

Was history to repeat itself for Aw Boon Haw's benefit? The First World War had enriched the Aw empire beyond expectations. His enterprises at the outbreak of the Second World War were much more widespread. He had an abundance of materials stored in his many godowns. His manufacturing facilities were greatly expanded. His market covered half the world and more despite Japanese conquests in China.

Fruitful days followed the outbreak of war in Europe. He became a father-in-law a third time when his eldest son, Aw Kow, married Tan Kah Joo, a pastor's daughter, in 1940.

His second son, Aw Swan, married Lim Saw Swee, who was born in Penang, in 1938. The third son, Aw Hoe, and Chan Sau Yong were married in Hongkong the following year.

To nobody's surprise, Eng Aun Tong's business accelerated. Dealers, anticipating shortages, stocked up on supplies. The hard-pressed workers were put on extra shifts. Factories churned out additional millions of jars and packets to meet demand.

A son was born to Siew Eng in 1941. Boon Haw was in Hongkong. The baby was named Aw Sar Haw (Third Tiger). The senior Tiger had chosen the name before he left for Hongkong, so confident was he that the child would be another male heir.

However, the father was not destined to set eyes on the new heir.

Twenty-nine

The world of the Tiger Balm King came tumbling down when Japan entered the war on the side of the Axis. Hitler had subdued France and driven Britain out of the Continent. Mussolini lent whatever support he could to his fellow dictator. Churchill had replaced the ineffectual Chamberlain with the pledge that, "I have nothing to offer but blood, toil, tears and sweat ..."

Boon Haw fretted and cursed as a prisoner of Tojo. His empire was disintegrating and his family scattered. Boon Par fled Singapore for Burma. His entourage included his wife Hong Yin and son Cheng Taik; his brother's eldest wife Piah Hong and favourite wife Kyi Kyi; son, It Haw; and daughter, Aw Sian. Geik Cheah chose to stay put and insisted Haw Kia remain with her. Siew Eng, for obvious reasons, was not among the evacuees to Burma. Her children remained with her in an increasingly chaotic Singapore.

The Leopard left Singapore with a heavy heart. He had refused to leave until the Tiger joined him. But when Hongkong fell on 25 December and Boon Haw was presumed to have been captured by the Japanese, he was finally persuaded to depart. He had no desire to be taken by the Japanese who had also captured Ipoh the day Hongkong fell. The enemy had overrun half of Malaya and were racing down the peninsula to Johore across the narrow straits separating the island from the mainland.

His plea for his brother to avoid going to Hongkong had been in vain. Was his fear that they would never meet again about to be fulfilled? Boon Par remained in his cabin throughout the voyage to Rangoon.

He brooded day after day like a man in a trance. His food was barely touched, and tears continually welled in his eyes. He refused to be comforted. Neither his wife nor Piah Hong, the sister-in-law whom he respected most of all, could bring an iota of cheer to the lonely figure in the darkened cabin. He was like a man without hope.

On 31 January 1942, the last British troops left the Malayan mainland and marched across the Johore causeway. They were the remnants of the Argyll and Sutherland Highlanders regiment who had a few days earlier fought so heroically against an army superior in men and armament. Pipers Stewart and McLean led the brave warriors into Singapore to the stirring strains of two famous Scottish melodies *Blue Bonnets* and *Jeannie's Black 'ee'*. The causeway was dynamited by army engineers after the last trooper had crossed.

The next day, General Yamashita, soon to be known as the Tiger of Malaya and Conqueror of Singapore, ordered his guns to be lined up along the coast facing Singapore. He occupied the Sultan's palace on top of Bukit Serene and mounted artillery pieces on the tower. The bombardment by land and air of the beleaguered "impregnable" fortress began. At the same time, his men commandeered whatever craft was available and crossed the narrow straits to establish a foothold on the northern shores of the island. The battle for Singapore commenced.

On 14 February, Haw Kia and a cousin were playing in the grounds of the White House in Nassim Road. A Japanese shell landed in their midst and killed both boys. More shells rained on the Tanglin area where the HQ Far East Land Forces was located. The Tiger cub was hastily buried in the bomb crater; his cousin in another. The Tiger's favourite son and heir had died. Blissfully ignorant, Boon Haw thought he was safe and sound with the rest of the family in Burma.

General Percival's command capitulated on 15 February. He surrendered the colony to Yamashita in the Ford Motor factory in

Bukit Timah. The Japanese renamed Singapore "Syonan," meaning Light of the South. Tens of thousands of British, Australian and Indian troops were taken prisoner.

The *jaga* at the gate saluted and said, "*Salaam* master, the *tuan* is not in Singapore."

The young lieutenant barked an order and the private elbowed the Sikh aside and threw open the gates. Six other soldiers followed the officer as he marched towards the house. Leather heels clip-clopped up the granite steps. The lieutenant had come to claim the priceless jade collection, but all he found were empty showcases.

Face contorted with rage, he strode towards the group of frightened servants huddled in a corner and demanded, "Where is the collection? It is now the property of the Imperial Japanese Army. All enemy goods are hereby confiscated."

His demand was met by a stony silence. The group was too frightened to answer or too cautious about giving away the Tiger's secret. Lieutenant Kimuira drew his samurai sword and approached an employee of Eng Aun Tong who had come to help guard the mansion. "Do you want your head chopped off?" he thundered. He raised the glistening blade and the man blabbered, "No, no master. Come, follow me. I will show you."

The treasure was hidden in the basement underneath the house. The booty hunters found twenty crates of assorted sizes in the dark, dank hiding place accessible only through a small opening hidden under the staircase leading to the dining room. The collection was taken away in two army trucks the same evening.

Geik Cheah watched the departing vehicles without emotion. No treasure could match the son she had lost the day before. She prayed that her other boy had survived the flight to Burma. Together with every occupant of both residences, she was ordered to vacate the premises in two days' time. A house in Tanjong Pagar was rented for her temporary shelter.

Boon Haw was given a conditional release from his hotel jail on 25 January, one month after the fall of Hongkong. It was also his sixtieth birthday and he wryly joked that his release was the only birthday present worth receiving. They had brainwashed him off and on during his confinement to induce him to embrace the Japanese cause. The suave Colonel Ito coaxed and subtly threatened in turns, but the Tiger held his ground.

"You will do us great honour to work with us," the colonel persuaded. "We respect you and the people of Hongkong respect you. I have been given the pleasure of offering you the appointment as a member of the Hongkong Governing Council. Only very special people are considered. You are most special to us."

The Tiger was pleased that he should be selected for such singular honour. But he had never worked for any government – not even the British or the Chinese. He did not take orders, he issued them. His way of benefiting the people was through his purse and not from an official position, however senior that might be.

"I am deeply honoured. Please convey my thanks and my regard to your general," Boon Haw replied. "As you know, I am a businessman. I know nothing about government. I don't like politics. My newspapers speak for me. Thank you again. And my thanks to your government."

The colonel was determined to obtain a commitment. It would not serve his cause to return and tell his superiors that he had failed to enlist the millionaire's cooperation. Assuming a sterner tone, he said, "My superiors might misinterpret your intentions. They depend on you and other important people in Hongkong to help make this a better place. You should thank us for driving the foreigners away. You must show some appreciation for the great sacrifice we have made."

Yet another veiled threat did not go undetected. The Tiger eventually agreed to start a company to import rice and other foodstuffs for the Imperial Army, and to supply whatever surplus there was to the public.

He was confident the rice was obtainable due to his contacts and influence in the rice-producing countries of China, Burma, Siam and Indo-China. In due course, a trading concern styled under the name of Kok Sui Kai was formed with a few local businessmen under similar pressure. Some members of the family were also made shareholders.

Boon Haw made only token imports as his intention was to appease the conquerors and not to make money. In return for this cooperation, he was allowed to continue his Tiger Balm business and to publish his newspaper whose name he changed from *Sing Tao Jih Pao* to *Hong Tao Jih Poh*. He had no desire to sully the name of *Sing Tao* with enemy propaganda for some instinct told him that Japan would not triumph over the Americans and the British in the long run. The Tiger was allowed to continue living in his mansion but was not permitted to sleep elsewhere without the Kempeitai's knowledge. The dreaded military police were also the intelligence arm of the occupying power. They were a law unto themselves. Both the military and the civilians came under their scrutiny.

In March 1942, when civil communications were restored between Hongkong and Singapore, Boon Haw received news of Haw Kia's death. It was a great blow to him. He spent three days brooding in the mansion and refused to receive any visitors. Another letter arrived from Rangoon shortly to say that the rest of the family were safe and sound. He derived some comfort from this but worried over the welfare of the new son he had not seen. But the war was to claim another heir. Sar Haw contracted cholera and died not quite one year old.

Life under the Japanese went on and followed an uncertain course. The Singapore factory was taken over by the Japanese, and the Tiger Balm empire was reduced to a single unit under the Aw family control in Hongkong. Geik Cheah was taken away from her temporary home in Singapore and locked up in a cell in the YMCA which was turned into the headquarters of the Kempeitai.

She was tortured for information about a hidden Aw treasure. She had no knowledge of any treasure and suffered beatings and the water treatment in which water was forced down the victim's throat through a hose. She was released after three nights and spent three months recovering from her ordeal.

Piah Hong was distressed over the news of Haw Kia's death. She was very fond of the boy and she grieved also for her husband. She knew he had placed great store by this son. When more tragic news of Sar Haw's death reached her, Piah Hong recalled what someone had once told her, that a seven-tier pagoda brought tragedy to be repeated thrice.

There had been two untimely deaths in the family. Was there to be a third? She prayed for the end of the curse. The family had suffered enough, in wealth as well as lives.

Boon Haw himself was treated with some courtesy by the Japanese. He was not subjected to any personal harshness nor deprived of the luxuries he had come to regard as his due. A chauffeur drove him to and from office, and he could have anything he wanted within reason. But he missed his family, and he missed Kyi Kyi whose support he had come to value.

Shortly after his release from the Peninsula Hotel, Boon Haw was flown to Japan on a bomber for a familiarisation tour of Japan. He was accorded VIP treatment. The Japanese were determined to win him over. After three weeks in the Land of the Rising Sun, he returned to Hongkong with his views intact. "A Chinese must always give his allegiance to his mother country no matter under whose rule he lives," he told his son, Aw Swan, who was with him throughout the Occupation.

He had not lost his arrogance in spite of the unpredictable Japanese. A group of important Japanese paid him a courtesy call in his mansion and to see his jade collection. Tea and cakes were served and courtesies exchanged. A visitor noticed a picture of Chiang Kai Shek hanging on the wall and asked, "Why do you display a picture of our enemy, Aw-san?"

The Tiger looked his visitor straight in the eye and replied, "I am Chinese. He is my leader. If you want to talk peace with China, he and his government are the people to talk to, not Wang Ching Wei." Wang was the puppet head of the government set up by the Japanese in occupied China. The Japanese understood what patriotism was. They themselves had pledged their lives and unquestioning obedience to their emperor.

The glorious victories in the early part of the Pacific War turned into ignominious defeats by 1944. The Japanese forces were hopelessly overstretched. Supply routes were constantly cut off. A rearmed America had built up a navy and air force far superior in quantity and quality to those of pre-Pearl Harbor. Marines came in their hundreds of thousands. Slowly but steadily, the Japanese were overcome on one island after another, and pushed back towards Japan. General Douglas MacArthur was to make good his promise "I shall return" to the Philippines.

Mussolini was overthrown and hanged by the partisans. Hitler had his hands full on both fronts – the Russians to the east and the British and Americans to the west. In June 1944, General Eisenhower began his liberation of Europe with a combined force of Americans, British and Australian troops. Hero of the North African campaign, General Montgomery commanded the assault. US bombers continued their raids on Tokyo with the "Flying Fortress." The B-29s were the biggest bombers yet to take to the skies. The war had come to Japan itself.

Japanese forces were on the retreat. The British had retaken Burma. Boon Par and his family were then in Rangoon. The liberation brought little comfort to the Leopard who was seriously ill. Deprivations, especially of proper medical care, further deteriorated his health. On 7 September 1944, he succumbed. His fear had come true. It was almost three years ago when he had uttered the fateful words, "I fear we may never meet again, Jee Ko."

Even on his deathbed, his last thoughts were of his brother. So were his final words when he solemnly pronounced to the sorrowing relatives gathered around him, "My dear brother will survive me by ten years." These words of doom shocked Piah Hong and Kyi Kyi out of their grief for the brother-in-law they had loved, each in her own fashion. The elder wife regarded him almost as a real brother, having known him almost forty years. Kyi Kyi's affection was an extension of the intense love between the brothers. She sometimes felt that Boon Haw loved Boon Par more than he loved her. She respected that bond which was now irrevocably severed.

Both women were greatly troubled by Boon Par's last words. They wished he had not uttered them. Two sons and a brother were lost to the patriarch in three years. And if his brother's words were to prove fateful, the very head of the family himself would be taken away from them in ten years. He would die at seventy-two. Surely too soon considering his lifelong enjoyment of great health and the means he possessed to obtain the best medicine money could buy.

The seven-tier pagoda in Hongkong kept nagging at Piah Hong's thoughts. She was convinced one moment and refused to be convinced the next that the magnificent structure was a curse to the family. Demolish the curse and live the rest of their lives with peace of mind would be her choice, if she had her way.

But she knew her husband too well to hope for this to happen. He would be the last person to admit that his treasured pagoda was the cause of the family tragedies. What he had built let none dare to tear down.

Boon Haw bore the news of his brother's death with great pain. A courier had hitched a ride on a USAF transport across the Hump into Chungking and then worked his way overland through Japanese lines to Macau from where he took a junk to Hongkong.

Boon Haw grieved as he never had before, and he grieved alone, for he wished none to see or to share the greatest sorrow of his life. His inestimable loss in things material was nothing compared with his brother's death. Riches could be regained where there was life. A life once gone was final. But life must go on. There was much to be rebuilt and regained. He owed it to his brother whose words he had not heeded and who died without even the satisfaction of a last farewell. He would devote the rest of his life to restore the fortune lost and the labour ahead would be in memory of the one he loved most.

American soldiers landed on Japanese soil in early 1945. Kamikaze pilots in their hundreds could not stop the allied advance. The battle for Iwo Jima raged with considerable casualties on both sides. Hongkong was bombed with increasing frequency. Boon Haw had no desire to be a victim. He had ahead of him a mission to fulfill for his dead brother. He decided to evacuate the island with or without Japanese blessings. But where and how was he to seek asylum?

The free world was shocked when Roosevelt died of cerebral haemorrhage on 12 April 1945. He was sixty-three and had served twelve momentous years in his presidency. Vice-President Truman was sworn in three hours later. The little man from Missouri turned out to be one of the most decisive presidents. He cracked whips and bruised egos. The war effort lost none of its irresistible momentum which had begun with the Normandy landing.

On 3 May 1945, the Russians captured Berlin. Hitler was trapped in his underground bunker with his longtime mistress Eva Braun. There was no escape. The German High Command had disintegrated. The thought of being taken alive by vengeful Russians was beyond consideration. Hitler married Eva. Suicide for both followed. Better death than humiliation. Stalin bristled in frustration.

Four days later, Germany surrendered unconditionally after five years, eight months and six days of unparalleled bloodshed and destruction. The Allied powers now had only a stubborn Japan to subdue. The end was near.

Boon Haw could not wait for the end. Escape was on his mind. The raids on Hongkong had became unbearable. With the help of some Japanese officials whom he had bribed, two junks were secured. The obvious refuge for runaways was the Portuguese enclave of Macau. Portugal was a neutral country and, like Lisbon, Macau was a nest of spies serving their respective masters.

The Japanese were driven to using junks to transport troops and materials between Hongkong and the mainland. Every vessel leaving the harbour faced attacks from American planes. Many were sunk. Boon Haw realised the hazards he faced but judged the crossing was a lesser evil. He expected American soldiers to land in Hongkong and was not prepared to find himself in the midst of a battle that would surely result in great loss of life. He did not want to die.

Dawn was breaking when the near derelict junks set sail on a choppy sea. The Canton coast to their right was engulfed in a shroudlike mist. "Good," the Tiger thought, "the mist will prevent the American planes from taking off. Macau is not far and we should be in Portuguese waters soon."

But the sun was neutral and as it rose higher in the sky, the sheltering mist cleared to reveal a blue sky over the distant mountains. The sea had calmed but danger lurked. The drone of a plane grew louder and everyone on board the two ships turned his face skywards. An unseen bomb whizzed through the air and Boon Haw watched in horror as the leading junk disintegrated into floating debris on the emerald sea.

He gave a silent thanks that no member of his family was on board the ill-fated ship. He was to be spared another attack. The Aw family landed in Macau without further incident.

Costs were exorbitant but many luxury items were available on the black market. Boon Haw was not lacking in funds to live well in his temporary haven.

The Americans prepared to invade the Japanese mainland. Truman was surrounded by his top generals for a final briefing.

"Unacceptable!" he pronounced when told of the projected casualty figures. "I do not want to sacrifice more American lives unnecessarily."

There was a way out, however. And it was to alter the course of history.

The *Enola Gay* took off from an airbase near Guam and flew high over Japan. It carried one single load. An atomic bomb. Hiroshima was the target. As the bomb fell on the doomed city, a huge mushroom cloud rose miles into the sky. Hundreds of thousands died and countless others were injured, many to suffer slow lingering death through radiation. The city was obliterated. All Japan was numbed by the horror.

Still no surrender.

The only other atomic bomb in existence was dropped on Nagasaki four days later. Stalin decided it was time to share the spoils of war in the East. He declared war on Japan the day Nagasaki was wiped out and ordered one million troops to launch an all-out attack across the Manchurian border.

Japan surrendered unconditionally on 14 August. The world was at peace again, but it was also in ruins. Loss of life and property was incalculable. It was a world of misery. The task of rebuilding began.

Boon Haw returned to Singapore to commence fulfilling his promise to the brother he had not ceased to mourn. He had his own empire to reclaim and to rebuild, and he set about the task with little waste of time. The British extended the courtesy of flying him to Rangoon first in a transport plane for the long-awaited reunion with the family.

Tears of joy flowed with tears of sorrow. Joy for his survival and sorrow over Boon Par's death.

"Where is Boon Par buried? Take me to his grave now." The others stood at a distance while the Tiger made his peace beside the grave.

The RAF could not accommodate the family for the return to Singapore. He flew alone after an assurance from the British that his kin would be evacuated as soon as a plane was available.

No one was aware of his arrival. There was no reception committee at Tengah Airbase to meet him. The base commandant provided a staff car for the drive to his Nassim Road home.

It was another sad home coming. Only third wife Geik Cheah was there to receive him. He had heard of her torture and expressed his regrets in a voice tinged with sadness.

"Show me where Haw Kia is buried," he said even before he drank his tea. Geik Cheah sobbed as she led the way to the spot beside the mansion. It was the first time she viewed the mound of earth under which her son was buried. The pain had anchored her feet every time the thought occurred.

Haw Kia was reburied in the Hakka cemetery in Lim Chu Kang. Sar Haw had been buried in the same cemetery by his mother. The father had never seen the baby, and therefore, there was no image to recall but a lot to regret. Boon Haw visited the grave with a weeping mother and derived some peace of mind from it.

His three acts of love to brother and sons performed, Boon Haw was determined to put the past behind him and concentrate on rebuilding his fortune. The house was bare and forlorn. The job of refurbishing took one month and soon, the White House was restored to almost its former grandeur, but the costly display cabinets remained empty. It would take the rest of his life to replace the treasures looted by the Japanese.

It was not until early 1946 that the house welcomed the return of its residents from Burma. Geik Cheah, who had been living in the Nassim Road residence, returned to her house next door. Ah Boon, the cook, and his brother, Ah Heng, survived the war and were delighted to be once again cooking in the huge kitchen.

Boon Haw had never felt more dejected in his life than on the first day he returned to his office. There was no brother to share the intimacy of their inner sanctum. He wore a woebegone expression and stared unseeing at the wall. He could weep with yearning for the company of his beloved brother. He blamed himself and remained despondent all day.

A knock on the door startled him out of his reverie. Tan Cheng Chuan, the acting manager, came in. "Boss, there are visitors to see you," he said. "Do you want to meet them?"

"Who are they?"

"Some British officers. They say they have some good news for you."

"What good news?"

"They won't tell me. They only say it is very important."

"All right. Show them in. You will also stay to interpret."

Major Anthony Dumont of the British Military Administration was a tall man in his thirties, thinning at the top and wearing a perpetual smile. Dumont was also a ranking officer in the War Crimes Commission which later tried and hanged General Yamashita and other war criminals.

Dumont introduced himself. The Tiger shook hands and looked at the officer in anticipation.

"We've found your jade collection," the major said without preliminaries. He looked at the greying man seated opposite him, but the face did not beam with delight as he had expected. Tan repeated the information in Burmese. Boon Haw was sceptical. He believed his treasure had been shipped to Japan long ago and distributed all over the country.

"We found twenty crates under a pile of empty packing cases in a warehouse in Tanjong Pagar," Dumont said. "They bore the words 'Eng Aun Tong' and there was no difficulty establishing the right owner. We knew Eng Aun Tong were the manufacturers of Tiger Balm. The jade must therefore be the property of the Tiger Balm King."

Tan interpreted and added, "I remember counting twenty boxes when we hid them under the house. They must all still be here." He almost shouted in triumph.

The Tiger was as much delighted by the imminent recovery of his lost treasure as by the fact that mere soldiers from thousands of miles away had heard of his famous nickname.

"*Hau, hau*," he said as Dumont grinned wide to see the beam finally lighting up an impassive face. He stood up and surprised himself as he put an arm around the equally surprised officer.

"It's my pleasure, Mr Aw. It's all part of my job."

Dumont became a friend of the family. He was often a welcome visitor to the White House on important anniversaries and occasions.

The Japanese intention of sending their loot to Japan had been delayed due to lack of ships. All available vessels were diverted to the Philippines after the fall of Singapore. Yamashita had subdued Percival. MacArthur was next on his list. The few ships which sailed for Japan carried mostly tin and rubber seized from Malaya. They went to feed the factories which produced the armaments to fight the Americans. Jade could not be turned into guns and, therefore, could wait.

Thirty

Boon Haw surveyed the destruction around him with growing anger. The handsome balustrade was now an unsightly row of broken or missing globules. There were holes in the once immaculate lawns, and garbage strewn in the fish ponds. The beautiful statues imported from Italy were either missing a head or a limb, or both. Grottos were defaced with obscenity and the stagnant water in the swimming pool was a breeding ground for mosquitoes. His heart nearly broke when he saw the beautiful home he had built for his beloved brother vandalised beyond repair.

He could weep in frustration. But he composed his anger and made a resolve. He would demolish the mansion. It was Aw Boon Par's home but now that he was gone, it was never to shelter others. But he would keep on improving the gardens and grottos for as long as he lived and visit the place as often as he could. Where else but here, where his brother had once lived, could their spirits communicate?

He dedicated this labour of love to the memory of his brother. Boon Par would be pleased to see the wonder and delight on the faces of the many who would surely flock to visit the villa once it was restored. And he was sure many of the future visitors would remember or be told that the brother of the Tiger Balm King once lived here. Boon Haw assumed a more placid demeanour as Singaram drove him home.

The bumpy seat of the dilapidated Ford Prefect felt less uncomfortable. New cars were not yet available. His stable of shiny limousines had been confiscated by Japanese officers and eventually junked for lack of spares. The tiger car was mutilated beyond repair during the Occupation and ended up in some scrap heap. There was not to be another replacement. The war had robbed the Tiger of much of his flamboyance.

The task of rehabilitating his business empire during the postwar years was a challenge Boon Haw tackled with feverish fervour. There was now no brother to caution and to counsel, to cool tempers and to support.

The two main factories in Singapore and Hongkong were producing at near capacity by 1948. Most of the China branches had also resumed business. The Swatow factory was destroyed by the war and its manager killed. Production was moved to the multi-storey Canton building. The cash flowed like in the prewar days. But more trouble was brewing.

That year saw the beginning of the collapse of the Kuomintang. Stalin was determined to turn the Middle Kingdom red – in ideology as well as in blood. There were a billion potential comrades who would turn the balance of power in his favour. He poured arms and advisers into China to support the People's Liberation Army. Chiang suffered one defeat after another. Quarrelling commanders and corruption in high places disenchanted the masses who gave their support to the Communist Party of China.

The Chinese communists, in turn, sponsored insurgencies in Southeast Asia. In Malaya, guerillas who had fought alongside the British during the Japanese Occupation, now fought their ex-comrades-in-arms. The Malayan People's Anti-Japanese Army embarked on a campaign of murder and terror to drive the British out and turn the country into a communist state. The authorities declared a state of emergency on 12 July 1948. Rewards were offered for the heads of leading members of the Communist Party of Malaya. The secretary general was worth sixty thousand dollars. Each member of the Party Politburo would fetch fifty thousand dollars while a Central Committee member had forty thousand dollars on his head.

The terrorists stepped up their insurgency in defiance of the Emergency. More planters were murdered, police stations burned and plundered of their arms, and civilians, mainly Chinese, intimidated into supplying food and medicines to the guerillas. Those who dared to report terrorist movements were executed. The authorities were quite helpless to deal with the situation without information.

Collective punishment was ordered. Any area where a crime was not reported suffered the consequence of having its shops closed. Heavy fines were levied to help cover costs of additional troops to police the area. Those who did not pay up had their properties seized.

With few exceptions, shopkeepers were Chinese. And being a Chinese himself, Boon Haw picked up their cause. He thundered his wrath in the editorial columns of the *Sin Chew Jit Poh*. The British were puzzled.

He was a foe of the communists but he behaved like a sympathiser. Agitating against steps to contain the terrorists was tantamount to aiding the enemy. He bore watching, and the *Sin Chew* too. Meanwhile, Aw Hoe was causing problems of his own. Now a very self-assured twenty-seven-year-old, the favourite son roamed the mainland wheeling and dealing with whoever and whatever he considered would turn in a fast and fat profit.

Aw Hoe enjoyed the most freedom among the Tiger's three grown-up sons. The eldest, Aw Kow, was given the job of looking after the *Sin Chew Jit Poh*. Aw Swan was in charge of the *Union Times*, a second-string Chinese newspaper. Both stayed put in Singapore while their younger brother travelled wherever his interests took him.

Aw Hoe had fallen out with Sau Yong, but she remained a daughter-in-law and lived with the family. He married Hoi Lai Yin, a vivacious socialite, in 1947, and set up another home for her away from the family. A desire to prove he was the ablest among the brothers drove him into business undertakings where risks were great but gains were greater.

One venture nearly landed Aw Hoe in jail. He was alleged to have been involved in unlawful currency and black market deals in Shanghai. Major General Chiang Ching Kuo, son of the Generalissimo, ordered his arrest. Aw Hoe escaped by the skin of his teeth to join his anxious wife, Lai, in Hongkong.

Boon Haw grounded his ambitious son and ordered him to devote his energy to running the *Sing Tao*. He had other problems to tackle. The Kuomintang was in full retreat on all fronts. Mao adopted guerilla tactics. Chiang only knew how to conduct conventional warfare.

Another unorthodox war in Malaya was going badly for the British. Chinese suspected of being communist sympathisers were detained in large numbers. Many innocents languished with the guilty behind barbed wire. The Emergency Regulations permitted detention without trial. Boon Haw was incensed by the treatment of his compatriots. His newspapers conveyed his displeasure with even greater force.

Enough was enough, the authorities decided. It would cause an uproar and lose the goodwill among the majority of pro-British Chinese if such a great philanthropist was detained. Upholding the tradition of freedom of the press spared his meddlesome newspaper from closure, but the Tiger's ill-considered roars must be muzzled somehow. The authorities decided to ban Boon Haw from entering Malaya.

The British authorities in Hongkong were thrown into a flap when the ban was imposed. They were about to convey to one of the colony's great benefactors the news of another honour by George VI.

"Utterly ridiculous," commented an aide in the Governor's residence. "The Colonial Office won't be amused. Imagine, one hand not knowing what the other is doing."

A furious round of consultations between Hongkong, Singapore and Kuala Lumpur followed. A solution was soon found. The ban was lifted. Boon Haw was made an Associated Knight of the Venerable Order of St John of Jerusalem.

Though the Tiger had the last laugh, his satisfaction was short-lived. That same year, 1949, the Kuomintang was driven out of China and Chiang Kai Shek and his government evacuated to Formosa (Taiwan). The fate of Boon Haw's business in China hung in the balance.

He had intended to publish English-language newspapers shortly after receiving his OBE in 1938. "The English never bother about any language other than their own," he told Boon Par when the latter admired the medal hanging from his neck on a ribbon bearing the colours of the Union Jack.

"I am sure much of what I said in our newspapers was distorted so that my views cannot be more accurately conveyed to readers." But the outbreak of war the next year required him to shelve his plans. The idea lived through the vicissitudes of war and immediate postwar years.

He resurrected his plans in 1948, and by spring the following year, his long-awaited English daily was organised. The *Hongkong Standard* was launched on 9 May 1949. *The South China Morning Post*, an entrenched newspaper, had a worthy rival to contend with.

Aw Hoe, the apple of his mother's eye, and whom many expected to succeed the "Old Man," was concurrently General Manager of the *Standard* and *Sing Tao*. Both newspapers shared the Tiger Balm premises in Wanchai Road and were printed on the same machine.

The new paper's readers were mainly English-educated Chinese. Though it faced a daunting task catching up with the *Post*, Boon Haw was prepared to give it all his backing to ensure success. So confident was he that he immediately laid plans to publish another English newspaper in Singapore. It would serve both the colony and the Federation of Malaya.

The publication of the *Hongkong Standard* lessened the pain of another humiliation the Tiger had suffered two months earlier. He had commissioned an architect named Wong Pek Shun to prepare plans for a luxury hotel. The Elite Hotel was to cost three million dollars and would stand on a commanding site in Tanjong Pagar.

The architect carried out his instructions and the Tiger was pleased with the sheaves of detailed drawings submitted. He had a picture of the proposed hotel published in his newspaper together with a glowing write-up.

The prospective innkeeper suddenly decided to abort the hotel venture. "Running a hotel is not compatible with my image," he said. "I shall employ my money in something more dignified. A bank for instance."

Architect Wong was not about to sweat for nothing. He sued. Boon Haw was not prepared to expose himself to ridicule in court. He paid.

"Sixty thousand dollars is a piffling amount," he sneered. "I've given more to other charities." But the rancour lingered.

The more he thought about being a banker, the more the notion pleased him. He had the money. A successful industrialist and the envy of his peers. An eminent newspaper baron. Why not a prestigious banker as well?

Being a man ever impatient to translate words into deeds, Boon Haw began to put his idea into reality. He confided in some intimates. They were not only enthusiastic, but were eager to lend financial support. Lim Soo Ban, a wealthy merchant and close associate, was prepared to participate as much as Boon Haw would let him. All who were approached wanted to ride on the wagon of the man with the Midas touch. "Who can we trust to manage so much of our money?" Lim wanted to know.

"Trust me. I know who will make our money work for us," the Tiger replied. "He's a member of the family."

This information drew no enthusiasm. They could only presume one of the three sons would be put in charge. They knew the Aw siblings well, and they did not think any was made of good banker's material. But to withdraw at this stage would only alienate Boon Haw's patronage, something they valued highly. Better to swim or sink with him. After all, he would be contributing the lion's share of the capital. It would be his bank and failure would reflect badly on his integrity.

However, none of his sons figured in the Tiger's calculations. About the only one who merited consideration was Aw Hoe. But the third son was prone to take unacceptable risks. And bankers were supposed to be ultra cautious people.

Lee Chee Shan was general manager of Eng Aun Tong. He was second in command, but not a replacement for the late Boon Par. No one could replace him as far as the Tiger was concerned. Lee was also the son-in-law of the late Boon Par, and a cousin on his mother's side. He was a son of the younger brother of Lee Kim Peck, wife of Aw Chu Kin, father of Boon Haw and Boon Par.

Lee, forty-one and balding, was a tall and well-built man who wore a constant smile. He married Boon Par's daughter, Cheng Hu, in 1932.

Lee did replace another very senior member of the Haw Par organisation. Li Shai Htone was ousted as general manager in 1935. Lee took over. No one knew the real reason for the falling out but everyone was sorry to see such an able and likeable person go. It was indeed a great surprise to many as Li was a close confidante, counsellor, friend and almost brother to Boon Haw.

He was the person the Tiger trusted most of all next to his brother. Those who claimed to be privy to the family intrigues attributed the separation to Kyi Kyi's disapproval of Shai Htone's influence. Others tendered various causes, but whatever the truth was, it remained untold as Shai Htone refused to be drawn. Chee Shan's banking experience was acquired through circumstances rather than through choice. He had remained in Singapore after seeing the family off to Burma when war broke out. He waited for Boon Haw to return from Hongkong so that they could evacuate together. But events turned awry. Hongkong fell and the Tiger was caught. The last boat for Rangoon had sailed, and Chee Shan was lucky to board a ship heading south. He eventually found himself in Australia where he spent the war years and obtained a job in a bank. He was a diligent worker and acquired a good knowledge of the banking business as a refugee.

The Tiger therefore had to look no further than his office door to find the man for his bank. The Chung Khiaw Bank opened for business on 4 February 1950. It occupied the building in Robinson Road where the *Union Times* was published. This second-string newspaper had ceased business the previous year. It had lost money. It was superfluous, being an echo of the *Sin Chew's* editorial policy, and it was badly edited. Aw Swan became a none-too-reluctant pensioner.

The bank was a success. Chee Shan was a prudent but shrewd banker. Chinese merchants came to deposit their substantial profits and the bank profited by lending their money to others seeking other profits.

The conflict between the North and South Koreans threatened to develop into World War III. Traders scoured the Indonesian archipelago to stockpile on rubber and tin, two of the most essential materials of war. They needed capital to obtain the goods needed. Chung Khiaw Bank was there to provide. It could not have opened at a more opportune time.

The joy was short-lived. Mao wiped the smiles away. The Tiger was asked to contribute three hundred and fifty thousand dollars to the communist victory bonds. Boon Haw balked. His loyalty was to Chiang and not the usurper. It cost him dearly. The new masters of China confiscated all the Tiger Balm properties and factories on the Chinese mainland.

Tan Kah Kee returned to China for good at about the time Boon Haw's properties were being confiscated. It did not make him feel any happier when the new communist government received his rival with open arms. Tan was a patriot who believed that Mao was the only man who could unite China.

He had written off the Kuomintang long before the outbreak of the Pacific War.

"Ideology is not important," he said. "Whether communist or nationalist, the really important thing is who can save the mother country from the follies of her rulers. Who can bring unity and who can restore the greatness that was China's. I have faith in Mao," Tan had said.

There was an attempt to reconcile the two overseas Chinese leaders after the war. Their supporters arranged a grand Lunar New Year dinner after the war to patch up their quarrel. There had been too much bitterness for too long between the two factions. China was now free of foreign domination and the destiny of the nation was in the hands of its people.

It was time for all Chinese to bury the hatchet and start anew. But the differences between Tan and Aw were too wide to bridge. Each stuck to his principles. Neither would shift or compromise. The dinner was a flop. The gathering dispersed amidst recriminations.

The chance to show his father that he was capable of more than merely overseeing the running of a newspaper finally presented itself to Aw Kow. All along it had been Aw Hoe who was given the important jobs to do. He enjoyed a disproportionate measure of authority denied the other brothers. He was always in the limelight and, perhaps more galling than any other consideration, Aw Hoe was known as the "Crown Prince of Tiger Balm" in Hongkong. The third son was indeed the favoured boy thanks to a doting mother who was unstinting in her backing. As it was, there were many who had already assumed Aw Hoe to be the chosen one.

Aw Kow now had the opportunity to display his true mettle. But he had always felt uneasy in his father's presence. As he now was. In answer to a telephone call from Aw Cheng Chye that morning, he had excused himself from a staff meeting and hurried to his father's office in Neil Road. Cheng Chye, the son of Boon Par, had spent a few years in America studying business administration, and had assumed Chee Shan's chair when the latter was appointed Managing Director of Chung Khiaw Bank. Aw Kow sat facing his father across the desk. "Aw Hoe is doing very well with the *Hongkong Standard* and I want to start another English newspaper in Singapore," the Tiger said. "Can you organise an English newspaper?"

What the Tiger meant was: Can you match your younger brother? If not, Aw Hoe will do it.

Aw Kow sensed what his father really meant. His father thought it was kinder to ask Aw Kow first, and had sincerely wanted him to succeed.

"Yes, Papa, it is not difficult," Aw Kow accepted the challenge. "I have been looking after the *Sin Chew* for many years and am very familiar with all aspects of producing a newspaper. I can do it."

"Where are you going to get the staff? I want good men to produce a good paper. Perhaps I shall ask Aw Hoe to look out for some experienced journalists in Hongkong."

"No, Papa. No need. I can get the best men here. I know many people. We pay good salary and they will come."

"You're sure you can do it?"

"I promise." Aw Kow would promise almost anything. Whatever Aw Hoe could do, he was out to prove he could do as well. Even better. The new paper was to be his baby. Nobody was going to share the praises when it was successfully launched.

The Tiger was encouraged by Aw Kow's confidence. Perhaps he had not given this son sufficient leeway to show his talent.

"All right. Go ahead. How soon will it be?" The Tiger expected instant result once he had made a decision .

"As soon as possible. I'll start today. Can I go now, Papa?"

"Go. But remember, this newspaper is very important to me. Work hard and don't spend too much time on your night life." There were many who made it their business to report on his son's doings. He was familiar with a young man's urge, and tolerated a certain amount of sexual licentiousness.

The *Singapore Standard* made its appearance on 3 July 1950, but

Aw Kow was not there to witness its birth. It was his brother, Aw Hoe, who reaped the rewards of his early efforts. But unfortunately, Aw Hoe was to pay for it with his life.

The old man was seething with anger. "These people talked my son into all sorts of wild schemes and they now have the audacity to come to me to collect his debts," he thundered as his staff trembled. "What about the profits they enjoyed? Did they give me a share? What do they take me to be: a philanthropist to swindlers?"

Calling his son's creditors swindlers was perhaps harsh. And to imply the son was reckless was not doing Aw Hoe justice. He was as shrewd as the next man and as calculated as any in taking risks. But as so often happens in business, the best calculations could sometimes turn sour. Aw Hoe had more than his fair share of vinegar, which had completely drained his cash flow.

The first seeds of doubt were planted when one high yield, but high risk, venture failed. The seeds took root and sprouted when companies elsewhere incurred sudden heavy losses where profits once flowed. When one faithless associate demanded a return of his capital, other partners panicked. They rushed to stake their claims before the well ran dry. Aw Hoe found himself strapped and avoided his once fawning partners.

But there was an inexhaustible well which would redeem the offspring; the king would surely bail out his crown prince. No price was too great to pay in order to avoid blemishing the family name. Or so they thought.

The Tiger refused to be held to ransom. He showed his son's claimants the door. They persisted. Some threatened court action. It was too much for the father to be so humiliated. He threatened to disown his son.

"They cannot bother me any more if Aw Hoe is no longer my son," he said.

"But he is my son too," Kyi Kyi protested. Her faith in Aw Hoe never faltered . "Just because his luck deserted him does not mean his father should desert him too. You know he is the smartest among your sons. Who better able than Aw Hoe to look after your business in time to come?"

"He has failed and I have lost faith in him."

"Everyone fails at one time or another. But not everyone fails forever. Aw Hoe is not just anyone. He is the son of Aw Boon Haw. He will make good again. And it's up to you. Besides, how can we live down the disgrace of your disowning your son? How can you turn your heart into a piece of iron?"

Kyi Kyi did all she could to help her son. She reasoned and pleaded; she cried and she threatened. "If you can disown Aw Hoe, you can also disown his mother. I beg you to spare him and save his mother's face."

If tears and eloquence did not sway the Tiger, perhaps it was his lifetime affection for his distressed wife which won the day for Aw Hoe. The notice to disown, all set and ready for publication in the *Sing Tao* and the *Hongkong Standard*, was withdrawn.

It was the patriarch's prerogative to have the last say. "Aw Hoe must leave Hongkong," he pronounced. "He has caused me enough trouble here."

"But where can he go?" Kyi Kyi asked. "This is his home and he will have nothing to do if you send him away."

Fate stepped in. Aw Hoe had done a good job launching the *Hongkong Standard*. There was now the *Singapore Standard* to launch. What better vehicle was there than the new paper for this ambitious son to get out of harm's way for a while? In spite of Aw Hoe's recent complications, the Tiger still valued his talent more than that of his other sons. He was despatched to Singapore with undue haste.

Aw Kow sadly relinquished complete control of the embryonic *Singapore Standard* to his brother. The charm and friendliness of the new boss soon won over a suspicious staff comprising the cream of local journalists.

The *Singapore Standard* made its debut on 3 July 1950 with great fanfare. Aw Hoe, in spite of his fair weather friends now howling for his blood, managed to retain the partnership of a two-plane outfit called Eastern Charters. Two DC-3 Dakota airplanes were available for charter for whoever required speedy transportation of people or cargo to wherever there was a landing strip. The partner in charge of the operation was Johnny Shoemaker, ex-air force pilot and son of an American missionary in China.

Aw Hoe made one plane available for the exclusive use of the newspaper. He pioneered newspaper airlift in Malaya by flying the *Standard* and *Sin Chew* to reach readers in the northern-most points in the peninsula in time for breakfast where others were lucky to make it by tea-time.

This buccaneering spirit and the romance attached to flying caught the public imagination. Allied to his pioneering venture was the free distribution of a Sunday supplement of all the popular comic strips in full colour. Colour printing in newspapers was in its infancy and thousands bought the *Sunday Standard* for its novelty, if not for the contents.

Circulation grew but revenue was not consistent with high overheads. Aw Hoe was determined to redeem his failure and reinstate himself in his father's graces. There was also Lai Yin, known as Rosina to her socialite friends, to consider. Rosina had been unhappy since the day she joined her husband in exile. Compared to her beloved Hongkong, Singapore was utterly provincial to her.

She found the people naive, their speech peculiar and their many customs strange. The place was hot and inhospitable whereas Hongkong was vibrant with life and fun. Singaporeans were staid and didn't seem to know how to live. Their food was atrocious and so unlike the fine Cantonese cuisine served even in the humblest restaurant in her home town.

Worst of all, she had no friends of her own in this island of unsophisticated people. Just as bad was the fact that her presence was barely tolerated by her in-laws. Her freedom was restricted.

Rosina was homesick and she pined for Hongkong where society accorded her the deference befitting the daughter-in-law of the most famous man in the Orient.

Aw Hoe loved Rosina dearly. His heart ached to see Rosina pining away and he longed to restore her to the life where she was queen among her peers. But he was yet to regain full favour with his father. This was vital to his plans. A complete pardon would embolden him to ask for his return to Hongkong where so many unfulfilled schemes awaited him. He would show the faithless how deeply they had erred in abandoning him during his time of need. With his reinstatement, Rosina would then be able to resume the life to which she was accustomed.

The Old Man would surely forgive him completely once the *Standard* showed profits. Aw Hoe was determined to explore every avenue in this direction. One such avenue was to exploit the possibilities of the Malayan hinterland. The newspaper plane returned each day with its hold empty. Why not fill it up with commodities sought after in Singapore? The prices obtainable in the colony would be at least twice or three times the cost. His staff agreed it would be a venture well worth trying.

On 13 January 1951, six months after the *Standard's* debut, Aw Hoe flew away on a journey of no return. With him were nine others, including a crew of three, and associate editor Paul Feng.

Captain Paul Epperson, a retired colonel of the US Air Force who had seen service against the Japanese in the Pacific, was at the controls. *Easy Peter*, the sobriquet for the Dakota, was headed for Kota Bharu, a town on the northeastern side of Malaya. It was the monsoon season and flying conditions were poor. Rain clouds blanked the skies and heavy downpours caused rivers to overflow and flood the inhabitants out of their homes.

Easy Peter shuddered against banks of clouds heavy with moisture and tumbled into air pockets whilst the passengers imagined they were on a roller-coaster ride. Epperson fought the elements and wrestled with the controls. He was perhaps the only one who realised the danger. He was flying blind. The plane was enveloped in unending cloud.

The control tower in Kota Bharu airport lost touch with the plane shortly before it was due to land. It was not until twenty-seven days later that *Easy Peter* was seen again. It was a mass of wreckage strewn over a wide area on a mountain top a few miles inside the Thai border. The search party, after three attempts to locate the wreck, accounted for all ten bodies, Aw Hoe among them.

Boon Haw was stunned. Perhaps he blamed himself for sending the boy to his death. Kyi Kyi was devastated. The son she had prepared all her life to take over from the father was dead. There were other heirs-in-waiting. Whether they would be considered was a matter for speculation. Aw Kow and Aw Swan had not distinguished themselves in their father's eyes. It Haw, nearly twenty-one, showed neither the aptitude nor the inclination for business. Siew Eng had recently given birth to a son named See Haw (Fourth Tiger). He was too young to be considered.

Kyi Kyi was quick to recover from her shattered hopes. There was her daughter, Aw Sian, whom she would groom to become a worthy successor. The girl, now nineteen, had grown into a gentle and graceful young woman. There was in her a purpose and determination which only the mother could detect. Such qualities deserved all her nursing to bring them into full bloom. All her hopes and expectations which had evaporated in the cold mountain air when Aw Hoe died, were rekindled.

Rosina, in despair, was inconsolable. "I do not deserve to become a widow so young," she cried. "What is to become of my babies?" she wailed as she hugged daughter Mei Sam, two years old, and Toke Loke, her one-year-old baby.

She cursed the day she arrived in Singapore, and prevailed upon her father-in-law to allow her to return to Hongkong with her children. He was generous with his financial support as if to atone for Aw Hoe's death. Sau Yong, Aw Hoe's first wife, was stoical in her sorrow. The gulf between her and Aw Hoe had been a constant hurt, but she mourned the loss as any loyal widow would. Whatever the hard feelings she bore her rival, they were submerged in sympathy for the pain Rosina now suffered.

Piah Hong murmured to Geik Cheah when they were out of their husband's hearing: "Jee Ko didn't believe a seven-storey pagoda is bad luck. What is to be blamed for so much tragedy in our family? Haw Kia, Sar Haw, Boon Par and now Aw Hoe."

Geik Cheah was philosophical. "Everything is decided in heaven," she said. "How long each one of us will live has been determined since the day we were born." She had never been freed from the pain of Haw Kia's death although she had come to be reconciled with it long ago. He would have been twenty had he been alive. And who knows, her thoughts floated, he would probably be his father's undisputed heir today. He was such an intelligent boy, so very much like his father, not only in appearance but also in the many ways that singled out the Tiger as a man apart.

She refused to entertain further thoughts on what might have been, and Geik Cheah went upstairs to agitate her prayer beads before a statue of Buddha.

Thirty-one

I f his life was beset with great personal losses, Boon Haw's commercial empire was thriving as never before. But the staidness of his business could not erase the lingering sadness in the tycoon. He seemed to age ten years in the year leading up to his seventieth birthday, a year after the plane crash. His hair turned white and, where a year ago he had walked with a jauntiness uncharacteristic of a man his age, his steps now seemed leaden.

"He is sad because Aw Hoe is dead," thought Kyi Kyi.

"He wouldn't have turned so old so suddenly if Haw Kia was alive," Geik Cheah said to herself.

"Jee Ko is sad and feels his age because he never stopped missing his brother," Piah Hong believed. And she was probably right. She had been married to the man forty-seven years and knew his strengths and feelings more than anyone else.

Partly to forget and partly to keep the promise he had made to his dead brother, Boon Haw worked harder than ever before. He did not have to. The business was in the capable hands of managers. Sales kept increasing in spite of the China debacle. Demand on the mainland was as great as ever. If Tiger Balm couldn't get in through the front door, there was always someone willing to open the back door for a small sum.

Elsewhere, Tiger brand medicines found even greater favour among the poor and not-so-poor. Profits picked up. More charities benefited. With publicity or without, the Tiger's generosity continued unabated. He became even more renowned. Fading health did not slow him down. Work was a panacea to what really ailed him – the sickness of the spirit.

Concerned clansmen brought the dearest ginseng roots and one or the other of his wives dutifully double-boiled the precious herbs to restore the absent bounce. The once unfailing tonic now failed to revive.

"There is nothing wrong with my health," he insisted. "I am fitter than any man my age. You cannot expect a man of seventy to bounce like a boy of twenty, can you?"

"At least see a doctor," Piah Hong urged. "Perhaps some western medicine will do you good."

"I have seen doctors. They have done me no good."

Indeed he had. Dr Hu was his constant physician, with or without summons. He was alarmed by his kinsman's failing health and made it a point to visit Eng Aun Tong regularly. The Tiger submitted to his tappings and probings, and took great delight in seeing the bafflement on the good doctor's face when the latter failed to pinpoint the cause.

"See, I told you. Nothing wrong. Let's go to the club for dinner." Club life was now an irregular affair. Gone were the days of merriment; feasting and drinking without care. The chase was a thing of a more distant past.

Headstrong and stubborn as ever, the Tiger ignored advice to discontinue his frequent commuting between Singapore and Hongkong.

"I like flying," he said. "I feel so close to heaven. My spirits are free of all the worldly cares when I am up above. Nothing to see but the blue sky. So clean, and so serene."

Every time he flew, part of his family flew with him. His party consisted almost always of Kyi Kyi, Aw Sian and Sau Yong.

Cheng Chye, Boon Par's son, assumed greater authority, and the day-to-day running of the business fell on him. The Tiger was pleased to see his nephew turning out to be an able manager. He could, of course, never replace his father but it was most gratifying to have his brother's son work alongside him.

He could rest assured that the family business would be in safe hands if the boy kept up his diligence. Hope was for Cheng Chye to continue in the tradition of the Aw family. If none of his sons could live up to the standards he had set, to nourish and take the family concern to even greater heights and most of all, to uphold the proud name of Aw, then his last hope lay with his brother's son. He had to admit to himself, if not to others, that he was tired.

He was sick and he knew it. The pain inside him recurred with increasing frequency. He would like to live at least another ten years. But one must be prepared, at his age. Had he not offered condolences to so many widows of close friends and associates whose husbands were in seemingly vigorous health one day, and an object of mourning the next? Boon Par's deathbed prophecy came to his mind. "My brother will survive me by ten years," he had breathed to Piah Hong the day he died in Rangoon in 1944.

Was Boon Par allowing him ten years to put right all his worldly affairs so that the two inseparable brothers in life could be together again in the after-life?

Boon Haw was not an overly superstitious man, neither did he entertain a death wish. But the pragmatic man in him counselled preparedness. He began to teach Cheng Chye as much as his nephew could absorb, all there was to know about the business – to seize opportunities, to sift the grain from the chaff and to be decisive.

"A wrong decision is better than none," he lectured. "A mistake realised early is easier to correct. Never allow a problem to fester like a boil. You may have to cut off a limb," he told his nephew as he had told others.

"Above all, Cheng Chye, you must have compassion for the underprivileged," he repeated. "Remember, what we have is what we profit from society. And we must give back to society what we have taken from it. As much as we can afford."

Kyi Kyi decided that Aw Sian should get involved in the business when the latter turned twenty-one in 1952. She saw no reason why a girl should not do as well as a boy in business. She had every confidence that her daughter would outperform every member of the family if given the chance. But she knew her Tiger.

He was a chauvinist in this respect. There had been no female employee in his organisation holding a senior post.

"Women are not equipped to fight the battles of the business world," he would say whenever Kyi Kyi broached the subject. "It can be dirty. They will get hurt. They are not strong enough to take the hard knocks. Men are offensive when they lose. I do not wish to expose my daughter to all this."

Kyi Kyi would persist. "But I know Aw Sian will prove worthy. As you can see, she spends so much time in the office watching how things are done and asking so many questions. I know she has been sheltered all her life and you are fearful that others will take advantage of her. But how do we expect her to show her talent if we continue to treat her like a child. She wants to help her father. And I want to encourage her. I think it is better for your own daughter to work for you than to take in so many of your clansmen who do not always prove honest."

"Men feel uncomfortable dealing with women bosses. They resent them."

"How do you know? Have you dealt with any yourself?"

"No, but ..."

"There you are. You don't know yourself, but believe what others say. You will be proud of Aw Sian in time to come."

And, as so often happened, Kyi Kyi's wishes prevailed. But it was an easy victory. The Tiger had been aware of his daughter's interest in business for some time, and only needed convincing. There had to be a precedent. Why not commence with their daughter who possessed a nature which elicited trust and confidence?

Aw Sian was assigned a desk of her own in the office of the *Hongkong Standard* and the *Sing Tao*. She had been interested in the publishing business and secretly hoped to be a publisher in her own right some day.

Aw Kow had been reinstated as managing director of both the *Sin Chew Jit Poh* and the *Singapore Standard* after Aw Hoe's death. It was a just return to the post he had filled so well, yet been deprived of just before the birth of the *Standard*. With Cheng Chye comfortably in the seat vacated by Chee Shan, and Aw Sian fitting in so well at her job in Hongkong, the Tiger decided to inject more young blood into his organisation.

Consequently, Cheng Chye's younger brother, Cheng Taik, was appointed to take charge of the *Singapore Standard*. He was only twenty, and fresh from school. Once again, the eldest son in the Haw Par family was ousted by a younger member. Aw Kow was thirty-eight. But this time, he was allowed to remain in charge of the *Sin Chew Jit Poh*.

The Tiger, pleased with his game of musical chairs, smiled in satisfaction. Who of the two youngsters would turn out to be the better manager? he wondered. Aw Sian had set a family precedent and there was another daughter waiting in the wings. Aw Seng, Siew Eng's girl, was already fifteen and attended school in Singapore.

The constant concern over improvements and additions to Haw Par Villa became almost an obsession. The Tiger set himself a daily routine which he seldom missed. Up with the lark, he would change into trousers and a short-sleeved shirt and walk down the granite steps of his White House. Singaram awaited in the blue Buick Roadmaster. Pal Singh, the *jaga*, saluted and opened the door. The six-mile drive to the villa took a leisurely twenty minutes. Pia Hooi, the contractor, greeted him on the plateau where Boon Par's mansion once stood. The sun cleared the horizon and bathed the morning with a soft, post-dawn light. Silhouetted against the eastern glow, the Tiger surveyed the panorama below and around him.

"*Towkay*, I'll wait near the fish pond for you," Pia Hooi excused himself and walked down the curved steps. This was repeated each time they met. The contractor had no wish to intrude for he sensed that this was a moment when the boss communed with his dead brother.

Was there another man whose love for a brother was greater than this? Pia Hooi glanced back and observed the Tiger staring into the distance. Could any man so rich and powerful appear so lonely? The Tiger's reverie lasted but a few moments and he was soon walking down with careful steps to give Pia Hooi his instructions for the day. Labour for gain to the contractor was a labour of love for Boon Haw.

The city had come alive on the drive to Albert Street. Trishaws jostled bicycles, car horns tooted as pedestrians jay walked, and overloaded buses belched smoke as they groaned their intermittent way from stop to stop. The fruit shop was as it had been the past thirty years. The only addition to it was a refrigerator to pamper young customers who favoured cut pieces of chilled fruit.

"*Towkay*, good morning. I have the durians. The best from Johore. How many do you want?" Ah Lek had grown old and gaunt. One solitary tooth clung stubbornly to his gum and a pair of horn-rimmed spectacles kept slipping down his nose.

"Ten big ones," the Tiger replied. "And fill a basket with the usual fruits."

Ah Lek shouted instructions to a son and turned to engage his millionaire friend in conversation. "You don't look too well today," he said. "Perhaps you should not eat durians. It is heaty and too rich for old blood such as ours."

Boon Haw laughed. They were worlds apart in wealth and in stature, as different as cheese is to chalk, but Ah Lek was genuine. He liked the man's frankness and his honesty. He made a humble living but asked no favours. He owed no man and he was his own master. He made good use of whatever little money he earned but never allowed money to make use of him. His frankness was refreshing after the hollow praises of the deceitful.

"Yes, Ah Lek, you are right. My body does not seem able to keep up with my mind. Ginseng does no good. Perhaps durian is what I need." He had steadfastly refused to admit to being unwell. Ah Lek was the first person to hear it. They were old friends. Ah Lek was special. A poor man's sympathy was genuine.

The third stop in the morning routine was the Orchard Road market. There was no need for him to buy any food. It was the cook's responsibility. But the Tiger needed a variation from the task of presiding daily over a multi-million dollar concern. Buying ten cents worth of bean curd or twenty cents worth of vegetables was an edifying contrast to handling thousands as a matter of course.

The stallholders were confounded, bemused and delighted that a great man such as he should perform such a menial task when there were servants to attend to his every wish. They talked freely and each one seldom failed to praise his Tiger Balm and to tell him how much the family depended on it. He opened up just as easily. The Tiger, often arrogant to the pretentious, was uncharacteristically sociable among these common folks.

The communion in the villa, the verbal jostles with Ah Lek and the banter with stallholders lightened his sagging spirits. The fruits, the vegetables and the meats he bought were superfluous to the day's needs but they had a therapeutic effect on him.

"There's little incentive left in life once you've reached the peak and there are no more challenges to meet." He brooded over the thought.

The grind he had set on himself was beginning to take its toll. He fell ill. Medication, both eastern and western, failed to cure him. He complained of a constant pain in his stomach. The pain grew worse. A very alarmed Kyi Kyi and other members of the family urged him to seek specialist attention in Europe. He gave in and left with Dr Hu.

The doctors suspected an abscess in the bowel and recommended surgery. On extracting an assurance that his condition was not critical, he opted for medication and returned to Hongkong.

In spite of his many disappointments with Aw Swan over the latter's disinclination to distinguish himself on the job, the Tiger had always nurtured a great affection for this son. Due perhaps to some premonition, Boon Haw had called his son into his office prior to his departure for Europe, and confided to him the numbered combination to the safe.

"Don't open it unless necessary," he told his son. He might as well have said, "Here's a sweet, but don't eat it."

Aw Swan reckoned that telling him the secret to the interior of the safe was tantamount to giving him permission to help himself to the contents, whenever he had the need. He had and he did.

An unbridled spending spree left his father blue in the face when he returned.

"How could you go through nine hundred thousand dollars in so short a time?" he thundered.

Aw Swan was unrepentant. He had been kept on a leash for far too long and he was the most generous man alive when he had money.

"I would be silly not to help myself," he said. "What else could my father have intended by telling me how to open the safe if it was not for me to spend some of his money?"

To the great relief of the family, the incident did not cause the Tiger to suffer a relapse. He fought the pain inside him, and he worked as hard as ever in spite of Kyi Kyi's pleas to take a complete rest. It was as if he was determined to make good the money his son had dissipated in as short a time as possible.

"Do not worry about my health," he said. "Work is what I need. I would waste away were I to sit at home and do nothing."

The spirit was willing but the body could not keep up. He tired easily and was forced to cut down his work hours. Kyi Kyi seldom left his side and spent all her time attending to him. So rich and powerful, and yet all the money he had could not buy him the recovery he so badly wanted.

Haw Par Brothers was thriving. Pharmaceuticals, banks, newspapers and landed properties all added up to a wealth which he himself could not determine. The pain of not being able to be at the helm of his empire was perhaps greater than the pain that racked his innards.

While the Tiger fretted, his eldest wife beseeched the favour of the Goddess of Mercy to spare the great philanthropist. Boon Par's prediction kept coming to Piah Hong's mind: "Jee Ko will survive me by ten years."

Boon Haw returned to Singapore in July 1954. The affairs in his head office in Neil Road required his attention. Cheng Chye was now his second in command. Piah Hong was glad to see him again and was shocked at how poorly he looked. "You must rest as much as possible and I shall prepare your favourite brew for you," she said. "And you must stop going to the villa in the morning and then going to buy fruits and vegetables," Kyi Kyi added.

The Tiger missed exchanging small talk with his friend Ah Lek and the market stallholders. It was a pleasure he reluctantly avoided. But he did go to Haw Par Villa. It was a brief visit. Kyi Kyi was with him, and insisted he remained in the car.

The Tiger was unusually silent. His eyes wandered from pond to grotto, fish to stork and other figurines. Every object was a product of his imagination and his desire to leave his mark on earth. There was a lot more work to be done to the villa.

He knew his communion with his beloved brother would be less frequent from this day on. Perhaps even never again. The car glided slowly down the driveway.

"You are in no condition to go to the office," his wives protested when he asked to be helped into his clothes.

"Time is not for wasting at home," he replied.

"When you are old, each day is precious and each year is priceless, if you have a year."

He had his way, ill though he was. But he asked to return home well before the day was done. He sought his bed and tossed in pain throughout the night.

The next morning a thoroughly alarmed Dr Hu told his family, "He is very sick. He must go to America for an operation." Clutching at straws, the family readily agreed. Boon Haw was too ill to resist.

The Tiger flew to the US on 16 July. He was accompanied, among others, by Kyi Kyi, Aw Sian and Dr Hu. Immediately upon arrival, the millionaire was admitted to a clinic in Boston. Back in Singapore, Piah Hong offered more prayers. She had a great fear. Boon Par had died in September 1944. The ten years were nearly up. Was the prediction to come true? Could the doctors in America save her husband?

They had been man and wife for forty-nine years, longer than the lifespan of many. She could never be reconciled to life without him. She counted the days. It would be exactly another fifty-three days from the day Boon Par died to complete the decade. Seventh September would be the fateful day. If her husband could live even one day beyond that, the prediction would prove hollow, and they would have many more good years together. Kwan Yin, now is the time to show your mercy and spare the man who has done so much good on earth, she beseeched the goddess.

The operation was a success. A large portion of his stomach, believed to be cancerous, was removed. The Tiger, weak but in good spirits, was discharged three weeks later on August 20.

"This old tiger is yet too tough for the surgeons to kill," he said with a wan smile to some leaders of the Chinese community who came to offer their good wishes for his health and more prosperity.

There was joy mixed with anxiety when the cable was read to Piah Hong after the discharge. "Heaven has shown mercy to Jee Ko," she breathed in relief. Another eighteen days to go for her husband to live beyond Boon Par's prediction, she anxiously calculated.

The Tiger and his party checked into a hotel in New York for a few days of convalescence before proceeding home. Against his better judgement, he allowed himself to be feted to a grand welcome party by the members of an overseas Chinese group. It was a strain that sorely taxed his stamina.

In San Francisco, more Chinese leaders sought to give him another welcoming reception. He declined, but out of courtesy, agreed to meet a few representatives.

A direct flight home to Hongkong would be foolhardy. The party therefore left for Honolulu on 26 August where they planned a five-day rest. It was not to be so.

News of his arrival had preceded him. The Chinese community in Hawaii was determined to honour one of their most illustrious compatriots. The sick philanthropist could not decline the welcoming reception without giving offence. Fame had its price, and the Tiger's sagging spirits wilted even more.

A sudden attack of acute abdominal pains two days after arrival distressed Kyi Kyi to tears. "He should not have attended those parties," she scolded. "Those people were so inconsiderate." The Tiger was rushed to the Queen's Hospital where his physician, Dr Edmund Lee, diagnosed the illness as a subphrenic abscess – a bowel obstruction. It was critical.

The next day, on 29 August, Boon Haw underwent a major operation. He was reported to have passed the critical stage twenty-four hours later, and his condition improved slowly but not remarkably during the following days.

The heart attack struck suddenly on 4 September, six days after the operation. He was dead by 8.45 pm.

"I am saddened and shocked by the suddenness of the attack," said Dr Lee. "But due to Aw Boon Haw's advanced age, we have been worried it might happen."

Kyi Kyi was stunned. Aw Sian, just turned twenty-three, was more composed. She comforted her mother and was transformed overnight from a carefree girl into a serious woman by her loss.

Piah Hong, waiting and praying at home, knew her prayers had not been answered the instant she saw Cheng Chye walk into the house with a clouded face and moistening eyes.

"Uncle passed away last night," he said. Last night, 4 September in Hawaii, was 5 September in Singapore.

The old lady nodded and sighed in resignation. "I knew there was bad news as soon as you came in. How did he die when the operation was a success?"

Cheng Chye gave her what meagre information the cable conveyed. "Uncle's remains will be brought to Hongkong as soon as arrangements are completed," he said.

"We were married forty-nine years." She choked out the words, "Forty-nine good years," she repeated. "And now he is gone. No more Jee Ko. The head of our family is no longer with us."

"Is there anything I can do for you?" Cheng Chye offered, as much distressed by his aunt's anguish as by his own sorrow.

"No. Bring me more news when you hear anything more. Now I want to be left alone."

She walked into her room to grieve in private. Two more days to the tenth anniversary of Boon Par's death. Three more days – and the prophecy would have been proved hollow.

Kyi Kyi bore her loss with courage even though her heart grieved to breaking point. They had grown even closer after Aw Hoe's death. The initial acrimony was soon forgotten and replaced by a mutual need for consoling. She understood the strains and pressures her husband underwent and gave him all the support and encouragement he needed. He was grateful and reciprocated. He sought her counsel in matters affecting the family and then in others concerning the business. Her judgement was mostly sound and he came to depend a great deal on her advice. They had something wonderful going between them.

Where another might resign herself to brooding over the past, Kyi Kyi pulled herself together to face whatever might be in store. She had her husband's body cremated and the ashes brought to Hongkong. From now on, she would live nowhere else but on the island colony. And her husband's remains would be near her as long as she lived.

Discontent in the family was bound to arise sooner or later, she reflected. The absolute arbiter in disputes was at rest. After the funeral rites were performed and comparative peace descended once again on the house, Kyi Kyi called her nearest and dearest to her and said, "Aw Sian, there are only two of us. From now on we must fight our own battles."

Epilogue

Aw Cheng Chye took over the management of the business after his uncle's death. Like the patriarch before him, he eventually gained near-absolute authority in the conduct of the company's affairs.

In July 1969 he formed a company called the Haw Par Brothers International Limited. It acquired the income-earning assets from Haw Par Brothers (Pte) Limited, the original family concern. The consideration for this acquisition was an allotment of nineteen million shares of one dollar each in the new company and about three million dollars in cash.

The famous "Tiger" trademark and all the goodwill attached to the name became the property of Haw Par International. Other assets taken over included substantial stakes in the Chung Khiaw Bank Ltd; Sin Poh (Starnews) Amalgamated Ltd, the publishing company and owners of the *Sin Chew Jit Poh*; and over three million dollars in shares in the Overseas Chinese Banking Corporation. Haw Par Brothers (Hongkong) Limited, which wholly-owned two subsidiary companies in Taiwan and Thailand, also came under the new company's wing.

The paid-up capital of the company was increased to around twenty-five million dollars in August. In November, approximately eight million new shares were offered to the public. Capitalised at thirty-three million dollars, Haw Par International became one of the biggest locally incorporated companies at the time. Its chairman and managing director was Aw Cheng Chye.

A company brimming with assets and bulging with liquidity such as Haw Par International was an outstanding candidate for a takeover. Slater, Walker Securities Ltd of London was on the hunt for a suitable vehicle to expand its international operations to the Far East. It was therefore a godsend when the chairman of Haw Par "invited" the Londoners to participate in the equity of the company. He had the intention of utilising the British expertise to expand his own company.

Events, however, did not turn out as expected. Slater, Walker employed its much-vaunted expertise to accumulate just sufficient shares to gain control. Five Slater, Walker directors were appointed on 3 June 1971. Of the original six family directors, two resigned from the board, thus giving Slater, Walker the majority.

Aw Cheng Chye yielded authority but remained chairman. D.E. Ogilvy Watson, the mastermind behind the takeover, was appointed executive director responsible for the company's overall management.

Certain laws in Singapore with regard to ownership obliged Haw Par to give up its stakes in Chung Khiaw Bank and Sin Poh. Consequently, Chung Khiaw shares were sold to the United Overseas Bank Ltd for twenty-two million dollars and Sin Poh was reacquired by the private family company for about fourteen million dollars.

Shortly after the takeover, Aw Cheng Chye and some members of his family left for a holiday in South America. While there he suffered a stroke and died in Santiago, Chile, on 22 August 1971.

Slater, Walter was later to lose control of the company. A complex legal action over certain irregularities resulted in the imprisonment of the new chairman, R.C. Tarling, a Slater, Walker appointee.

The best-laid plans of man often go awry through unwilful causes or through events unforeseen. Boon Haw's endeavour to keep his business in the family became unfulfilled seventeen years after his death. But the legend remains alive. The man will be remembered for as long as Tiger Balm continues to bring relief to the sick and Haw Par Villa continues to draw the curious.

The White House, also widely known as the Jade House, was pulled down in early 1990. There were plans to redevelop the property into a commercial complex. The bulk of the famous jade collection was donated to the National Museum by the Tiger's heirs.

The Tiger Mansion in Hongkong, now known as Haw Par Mansion, continues to be the residence of the second Mrs Aw Boon Haw and her daughter, Aw Sian.

The Author

Sam King was born in British Malaya (now part of the Federation of Malaysia) and received his early education in St Michael's Institution, Ipoh. He left for England in the early fifties to further his journalistic experience after a three-year attachment to the now defunct *Singapore Standard*.

Now retired and living in Singapore, Sam's varied career included managerial positions in the automobile and pharmaceutical industries. He travelled extensively but indulges in this passion to a much lesser extent as "this is an occupation more suited to the younger generation."

Sam is also author of a novel, *In Search of Easy Peter*, and is now working on his third book.

The Aw Boon Haw Clan

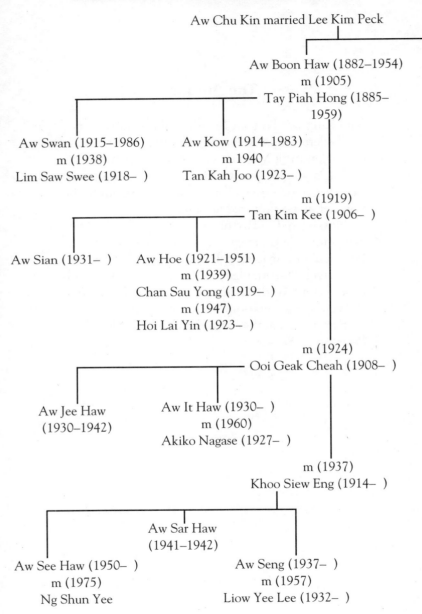

Aw Chu Kin married Lee Kim Peck

Aw Boon Haw (1882–1954)
m (1905)
Tay Piah Hong (1885–1959)

Aw Swan (1915–1986)
m (1938)
Lim Saw Swee (1918–)

Aw Kow (1914–1983)
m 1940
Tan Kah Joo (1923–)

m (1919)
Tan Kim Kee (1906–)

Aw Sian (1931–)

Aw Hoe (1921–1951)
m (1939)
Chan Sau Yong (1919–)
m (1947)
Hoi Lai Yin (1923–)

m (1924)
Ooi Geak Cheah (1908–)

Aw Jee Haw
(1930–1942)

Aw It Haw (1930–)
m (1960)
Akiko Nagase (1927–)

m (1937)
Khoo Siew Eng (1914–)

Aw Sar Haw
(1941–1942)

Aw See Haw (1950–)
m (1975)
Ng Shun Yee

Aw Seng (1937–)
m (1957)
Liow Yee Lee (1932–)

Aw Boon Par (1885–1944)
m (1908)
Tay Piah Lan (1888–1944)

m (1914)
Daw Saw (1898–1985)

Aw Cheng Hu (1915–)
m (1932)
Lee Chee Shan (1909–1986)

Aw Cheng Sim (1921–)
m (1950)
Lee Aik Sim (1925–)

Aw Cheng Chye (1924–1971)
m (1949)
Tay Chwee Sian (1926–)

m (1927)
Teo Hong Yin (1906–1965)

Aw Cheng Taik (1932–)
m (1973)
Lee Siew Chee (1949–)

BY THE SAME AUTHOR
In Search Of Easy Peter

January 13, 1951. A Dakota carrying the heir to the Haw Par empire crashed into a jungle-clad mountain in southern Thailand. Rescuers raced against time to reach the wreck …

Aw Hoe, the brightest and most promising of Aw Boon Haw's sons was earmarked to be the Tiger Balm King's successor. Until he fell out of favour and was banished to Singapore to make amends.

On unfamiliar turf, he started the *Singapore Standard* to rival the *Straits Times*, in the most turbulent era of Singapore/Malayan history. The *enfant terrible* of Malaya blazed new trails for the newspaper industry in the region. Until that fateful day on January 13, 1951.

Against the backdrop of racial riots, communist insurgency and the Korean War, the human drama is played out in a furious pace of passion, fear, high adventure …

Sam King, Aw Hoe's right hand man in Singapore, had the painful task of searching for the wreck of *Easy Peter*, the Dakota that bore the Haw Par heir on a journey of no return.

Eating Salt
An Autobiography

By Ho Rih Hwa

One day in 1928, an eleven-year-old Singapore boy stepped aboard a Dutch freighter bound for Canton. He was embarking on an adventure of a lifetime that would take him through three continents, Asia, America and Europe, during the most turbulent times of social and political change.

This is the autobiography of that boy, Ho Rih Hwa. Child of working class immigrant parents, Ho Rih Hwa left the carefree days of playing with homemade toys for a China torn by political strife and abject poverty after the fall of the old dynastic order, the Qing dynasty. The harsh and chaotic conditions of war-torn China of the 30s and 40s forged the mettle of young Ho Rih Hwa.

In 1943, while the Second World War was still raging, Ho Rih Hwa again set sail, this time from China to that land of opportunity, the United States of America. There, he found love and his life vocation. Starting at the bottom of his father-in-law's company in New York as a despatch boy and typist, he went on to build an empire in Asia.

"Written with dedicated accuracy and telling insight ... he has charted a period of time in a manner that transcends mere historical significance." —Koh Buck Song, *The Straits Times*.

Every Street is Paved with Gold
Success Secrets of a Korean Entrepreneur

By Kim Woo-Choong

Armed with lessons from a harsh and impoverished life in a Korea torn asunder by war, a youth went on to found an international conglomerate that is today the 45th largest corporation in the world with sales of US$22 billion in 1990.

In a series of short, pithy essays that span his childhood and early years, Kim Woo-Choong, chairman of the Daewoo group, shares his life experiences and thoughts, his success secrets with young people.

Kim offers advice on wide ranging subjects from school, choosing jobs, making money, staying ahead to travelling, making friends and being happy. In between, he gives incisive observances, from his travels and business dealings, of people and their behaviour in different situations.

Personal anecdotes reveal the man behind Kim, the man who says, "I can smell money everywhere."

"... 500,000 copies have been sold, and by Christmas should reach 1,000,000."—*Asian Wall Street Journal*

The Shrimp People

By Rex Shelley

As the drinks flowed, the noise and laughter became louder and louder. Female shrieks and uninhibited throaty guffaws. The band sensed the mood and began to play sing-along pieces. Bertha hugged Carl on the dance floor as he sang "I'm in love with two Sweethearts," asking him who the other was, assuming that she was one. They sang "Forever Blowing Bubbles," "Girl of my Dreams" and "Bengawan Solo." Then suddenly it was over. The last dance ...

Singapore 1956. Bertha was from a Portuguese Eurasian family. Pa (Father was what one called the priest) was in "the force" and, together with Ma, Eric and Beryl, her life revolved around Sunday Masses, school, hockey, Christmases, weddings and family gatherings, where one danced, flirted with the boys or simply hung around the bar reminiscing the good old days.

But the cold winds of change were blowing. Political violence and racial riots spilled onto the streets threatening to end forever the peaceful lifestyle of a fragile community.

In this powerful and moving saga, Rex Shelley paints a breathtaking story of life and love from the vast expanse of Malaysia to the crowded streets of Jakarta and strife-torn Singapore, recreating a three dimensional diorama of the Eurasians with vivid brushstrokes and earthy flavoursome prose.

"... a most exceptional novel. It is like a pungent, familiar curry, bringing a Singapore community to three dimensional life." —Dennis Bloodworth

Scorpion Orchid

By Lloyd Fernando

"The days of laughter, of sharing, of blunt comradeship—had they ever been? They had, they had, Tok Said, he cried. We loved each other like brothers …

Like children.

No, it's not true. We believed."

Sabran, Santi, Guan Kheng and Peter—four young men united by the bonds of friendship, brought together in the uniquely mixed society of Singapore. About to graduate from university, they are caught in the political upheavals of the 1950s. These are uncertain times: still recovering from the Japanese Occupation, Singapore is now ready to fight for independence from the British.

As they watch their countrymen confront each other, tearing the country apart, they face up to the reality of their multicultural fabric. Against a backdrop of violence and hatred, each embarks on a journey of self-discovery to reconcile deep-seated cultures and traditions with a new emerging society. In their quest for their true selves, the bonds of their young manhood are sorely tried.

Written in a dynamic and evocative style, *Scorpion Orchid* takes us back to those tumultuous days in the early 50s when a nation was trying to assert its identity.

"Fernando's text energizes [Lord] Jim's story, providing the 'other words' that Jim lacked, and thereby paving the way for a more optimistic prognosis for multicultural contacts." —R. Kurtz in *Conradiana*